❀❀ ONE MAN ❀❀
— AND A —
NARROWBOAT

Slowing down time
on England's
waterways

STEVE
HAYWOOD

summe

D0610287

ONE MAN AND A NARROWBOAT

First published in 2004 as FRUIT FLIES LIKE A BANANA

This edition copyright © Steve Haywood 2009

Summersdale Publishers Ltd
46 West Street
Chichester
West Sussex
PO19 1RP
UK

www.summersdale.com

Printed and bound in Great Britain

ISBN: 978-1-84024-736-7

Substantial discounts on bulk quantities of Summersdale books are available to corporations, professional associations and other organisations. For details telephone Summersdale Publishers on (+44-1243-771107), fax (+44-1243-786300) or email (nicky@summersdale.com).

ONE MAN
—AND A—
NARROWBOAT

For Chris Haynes
1916–2008

Time and tide wait for no man.
– Old English proverb

Time flies like an arrow; fruit flies like a banana.
– Old English joke

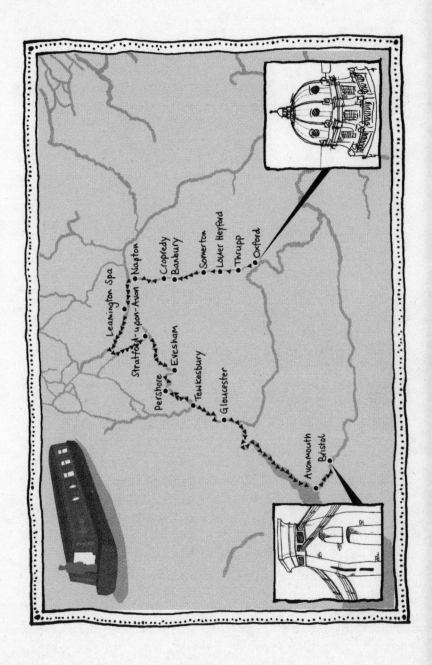

ONE

It was a birthday that finally galvanised me into action.

Well, not so much *a* birthday in the general sense as *one* birthday specifically. One of mine as it happens. It was one of those unsettling birthdays, the sort that have a zero on the end and which come along with alarming regularity every ten years or so.

OK – it's no use being sheepish about it – it was my fiftieth. It happened in November, the same as it's been doing for as long as I can remember, so I can't say it came as a surprise. Actually, my forty-ninth birthday the year before was a bit of a pointer to the way things were going. So one evening over dinner, halfway through a bottle of Cabernet Sauvignon, I began talking to Em about the essential nature of the English soul.

'The essential nature of the English what?' she said. Some of these cheap wines can be high in alcohol; you need to be a bit cautious of them.

'The English soul,' I explained. 'The basis of our being, the core of our identity… I thought, erm, I might take a trip around the waterways of England… to sortta look for it…' My voice trailed off. The truth was that despite what I was saying I hadn't been thinking much about the soul of England at all. I'd actually been thinking about getting out of London for a jolly – all the soul stuff was just an excuse for the trip. And not a particularly good excuse at that. It didn't even convince me. This much was obvious to Em. The more she challenged me on what on earth I was thinking about, the less I was able to justify it.

A search for the soul of England? What planet was I living on? I might just as well have gone on a search for a new design of the wheelie bin. Or the perfect pork pie. Even I could see that getting away from London was the main thing. All this stuff about the English soul was important, yes. But not *that* important.

Even so, Em was surprisingly amenable to the idea, given that it was likely to involve me spending protracted periods of the summer on a boat cruising through some of the most picturesque parts of England while she'd be battling daily on the 7.43 a.m. to Charing Cross on mortgage duty. If you ask me, the real clincher for her was the promise of finally getting shot of me moping about the house grumbling about the sad state of contemporary British television. OK, so I'd been moaning about this on and off for as long as I'd been working in the business, but I think that even Em began to recognise I might have a point after my hard-hitting investigative documentary on the Lockerbie bombing had been beaten for a top industry award by *Who Wants to Be a Millionaire?*

And I'll tell you one other thing: it wasn't a neck-and-neck race to the wire either.

Mind you, there were other incentives for her as well. We've had a canal narrowboat for years, and as any boat owner will tell you, the idyll of getting away for weekends on the water is nowhere near as… well, idyllic, as it sounds. Once you've fought your way out of town through the Friday-night traffic and actually got to your boat; and once you've unlocked it in what's probably by now the dark; and turned on the electricity and the water and the gas; and got the heating going to warm the place through; and made up the bed; and unloaded the shopping (assuming you've had time to do any shopping); and run the engine to charge up the battery and set about those thousand and one other tasks which invariably face you – from clearing out that packet of chicken legs you inadvertently left in the (switched off) fridge, to getting rid of the spiders that have colonised in your absence – well, once you've done all this, it's pretty well time to start packing up to leave for home again.

Perhaps it was the prospect of weekends when she could arrive at the boat like royalty and be taken off cruising that led Em to be so open to my proposal. Or maybe it was because she never believed it would actually amount to much, given my tendency after a few drinks to come up with big ideas that never did amount to much in the sober light of dawn. At that stage I'm not sure I believed it would ever happen myself either.

The fact was, I was totally immersed in my life in London. I might have toyed with the prospect of escaping from the city, but it was more of a fantasy than a reality. Apart from Em, there was the family, friends, the job. And then there was the house which we'd bought a few years before. It was still in such a sad state of repair that, had there been such a thing, we'd have been targeted by the Royal Society for the Prevention of Cruelty to London Victorian End-of-Terraces (This-Room-Hasn't-Even-Been-Touched-Since-You-Moved-In Department).

The house was a constant niggling worry, a sort of agonising mental checklist of things I'd promised myself to do. I hated it and felt responsible for it. But at the same time I loved it too; it was the nicest house we'd ever had. Contemplating the prospect of being away from it for a protracted period, I went all sentimental. Just thinking about the top-floor landing I'd been considering painting for two years made me dewy-eyed; and the idea of redecorating the spare room (and maybe even replacing the carpet, which had become so threadbare that recently even the cat disdained to use it for sharpening its claws) made me come over all soppy.

And the garden! Aaaah, the garden. What wasn't I going to do to the garden? The mere thought of the garden was enough to reduce me to a simpering, tearful jelly.

I thank the washing machine going on the blink for putting paid to all this mawkish nonsense. One day it took it into its head to overflow. This is not a very desirable state of affairs at the best of times, but it's a pretty catastrophic one when it's located as it is in our house in a bathroom at first-floor level. The water went straight through the floor and brought down the living-room ceiling. I was fond of that ceiling. But then again, I was fond of the books and CDs which we kept underneath it and their condition wasn't exactly improved by what happened.

'I suppose we're covered?' Em said anxiously as we surveyed the damage after getting back late from a night out with friends.

'Covered in the sense that at least we have a roof over our heads, if that's what you mean,' I replied grimly.

'I was thinking about insurance.'

'And I was trying not to,' I said. 'I don't know if we have enough of it to put this lot right.'

The collapsed ceiling reignited my desire to get out of London and put the whole day-to-day grind of ordinary life behind me, but it actually delayed my departure. I mean, I couldn't just dump everything on Em, could I? I couldn't just walk out on her without getting things cleared up.

So the next day I rang the claims department and put the whole idea of canals cruising behind me.

TWO

My first-ever trip on a canal boat started one grim, wind-swept day in the early 1970s at an old mill not far from where I was born in the East Midlands. I hadn't used all my holiday that year so after scouring a pile of brochures offering everything from an expensive two weeks in Spain to an exorbitant fortnight in the Seychelles, Em finally suggested that I might care to set my sights a little lower and consider somewhere a bit closer to home.

How about renting a canal boat? She'd taken a canal boat holiday with some university friends one summer a year or two before and she'd had a great time. What was more, holidays on canal boats were cheap. So cheap that if I were able to convince my best friend Dave to split the costs for the first week, she might be able to afford to join me for the second.

So it was that some time afterwards Dave and I found ourselves trudging through mud in a rainstorm, attempting to negotiate a footpath across a field where someone had directed us as a short cut to a boatyard we'd been struggling to find for an hour. From this boatyard we were scheduled to take command of a thirty-foot narrowboat nautically resplendent with the name *Nelson*.

Neither of us, it has to be said, was in the best of humours that morning. The truth was we were both suffering monumental hangovers as a result of a binge the previous night. For this, I take entire responsibility. I'd casually suggested to Dave that we might go for 'a drink', but I knew it was unlikely we'd stop at just *one* drink. Indeed, I'd known we were unlikely to stop drinking until we were totally rat-arsed.

But this was what I'd intended. It was a strategy. And it was a carefully engineered one too.

You see, I've known Dave for a very long time. We were at school together, and over the years I've come to respect him as someone who has his feet firmly planted on the ground. He's a realist, a pragmatist. He recognises things for what they are, not for what he hopes they might be.

He'd been enthusiastic enough about the project at the outset when we'd talked vaguely about lunches at thatched waterside pubs and long languid afternoons cruising. But what seemed like a good idea in mid-August when the sun was shining and there was still some life left in summer seemed not quite such an attractive proposition a few weeks later after our booking had been confirmed, and the weather had broken, and the isobars were in place for what was to become one of the vilest autumns for a decade.

As we'd got closer to our start date, Dave's enthusiasm had waned as every successive day brought another cheerless weather forecast delivered by lugubrious meteorologists who seemed to take personal delight in delivering bad news.

But that's the sort of person Dave is. We all listen to weather forecasts. It's just that he's the sort of guy who takes them seriously. 'It's not as if we'll lose a lot of money,' he tentatively suggested on the eve of our departure. 'If we just didn't turn up, I mean…'

We'd finished the night in predictable fashion with one of those caustic vindaloos made from horse meat marinated in Nitromors which we were so fond of then. By this time the alcohol had well and truly kicked in, and not only had Dave regained his former enthusiasm, but he'd become positively swashbuckling about the whole venture.

'Do you think a man like me's gonna be put off by a drop of rain?' he announced contemptuously to the bemused waiter in the Star of India. 'Do you think I care a monkey's about a bit of bad weather?' he'd asked the Marks and Spencer's mannequins in the High Street as we'd stumbled home. 'I mean, Steve…' he'd appealed to me as I attempted to get him to bed, 'I mean, do you think I'm a soft-centred wuss or something?'

I took some pleasure in reminding him of all this as we were traipsing across the field looking for the boatyard. By this stage the rain was hammering down with the force of a power shower, and I think it had dawned on both of us that starting a holiday with the remnants of two and a half gallons of lager slopping around our insides wasn't exactly guaranteed to launch proceedings on a positive note.

Dave had got his own problems. His curry had begun to repeat on him. He'd already eaten it four times. I'd eaten it three times with him.

'You're making me feel sick,' I said.

'I already feel sick,' he countered. 'I feel like puking, and I want a crap too. Do you think the boat will have a toilet?'

'No,' I replied. 'I think we'll be expected to stand on the roof and evacuate downwind.'

Nelson actually turned out to be a well-appointed, tidy boat; and, for its time, modern enough. It had a steel hull with a fibreglass superstructure, and inside there was a compact lounge with an L-shaped banquette built around a small table set in the floor. Next to it was an open-plan galley with a cooker that had a couple of gas rings; and at the front of the boat – the pointed end – the end we learnt we'd now have to call 'the bow' – there were two single berths.

To Dave's relief there was even a lavatory of sorts, though his delight at discovering its existence was somewhat mitigated by learning that the system worked on a rudimentary 'bucket-and-chuck it' principle in which, rather than wave your waste products goodbye, you bid them a sort of brief au revoir.

'You empty it when it gets full. There are special sanitary points,' said Mr Boatyard Man. 'You'll soon get used to it. Not a problem.' This seemed to be his friendly and all-embracing response to everything to do with boating. Steering this thirty-foot monster by way of a tiller which you had to point in the opposite direction to the way you wanted to go?

Not a problem; we'd get used to it.

Taking the lid off the box in the back and fishing around in the slimy water if anything got wound or trapped around the propeller?

Not a problem; we'd get used to it.

And locks? That extraordinary system whereby water travels up and downhill taking boats with it? That mystery of beams and ratchets and paddles and gates that you had to open and close in exactly the right order at exactly the right time to prevent emptying the canal of water and thus avoid causing such floods and mayhem and disaster that it could threaten the safety of the State and the future of mankind?

'Not a problem,' said Mr Boatyard Man, sheltering under his umbrella as he waved us off from the quay. There wasn't the vaguest notion in his head that he ought to initiate us into some of these mysteries, if only for the welfare of his boat, let alone our safety.

'Not a problem,' he said again. 'You'll get used to it all.'

The extent to which we knew absolutely nothing about canals or boats became apparent at the first lock we encountered. We were suddenly confronted by a man screaming at us in such a tone of voice I was inclined to believe he'd recently been involved in a contretemps involving his testicles and a disgruntled dog.

We couldn't understand it. We thought we were doing well. Dave had steered *Nelson* through the lock and out the other end without any evidence of major damage to either brickwork or boat; and by a combination of pure luck and the application of O Level physics, I'd managed to figure out how the thing worked and had just dropped the metal ratchets that close the paddles that control the water flow.

This, it turned out, was the problem. These paddles were made of cast iron and dropping them in the way I had so that they crashed shut could easily have broken them. Paddles, I learned, had to be treated with care and lowered gently. Like so much else on the canals in that era, they were worn out, and there just wasn't money available to repair them.

It was a steep learning curve all round that day, but Dave and I persevered and we got better as we went along, so that we were able to get a few miles under our belt without further mishap. Then, as a result of some minor inattentiveness, one or the other of us managed to run *Nelson* onto a mudbank where we couldn't get her to move an inch despite heaving and pushing and straining on ropes and bargepoles.

It was exasperating. While she'd been floating, she'd been elegant and graceful, so insubstantial we could move her with our fingertips. Now she was like a beached whale. She'd become ungainly and unyielding, downright cussed. We sat back, breathless after our futile exertions.

'That'll learn you,' said an old bloke who at that moment happened to be passing by with a rodent-like Jack Russell terrier. 'You were going too fast.'

Dave was knackered and not in the mood for criticism. 'We were within the speed limit,' he snapped in a tone of voice that set the dog off yapping.

'Sod the speed limit! You were going too fast,' the old man retorted. 'Bloody wave behind you that you could surf on, washing away the banks! No wonder the canal's so bloody shallow hereabouts.'

Well, there was no denying the truth of that. Even to beginners like us it was apparent that canal depth was more of a concept than a physical reality. In fact, looking back at that trip, it was a wonder we ever got anywhere given that for most of our route there was so little water that strictly speaking we weren't floating at all, but rather floundering through mud. What we laughingly called 'cruising' could be more accurately described as 'ploughing'. I swear it was so bad that in places you could have walked along the cut with no need for a boat at all. But that was the way of things in those days when no one dredged the canals.

The fact was they'd been all but abandoned. That was part of their charm. Cruising them, you found a secret, undiscovered world which was of the present, yet somehow separate from it. The canals were winding, overgrown ribbons of water that took you across aqueducts and over embankments, and through cuttings and bat-filled tunnels to a world that was unchanged for centuries. Or they were black inaccessible ditches tucked away behind factories and leading to the dark, oily recesses of cities unfamiliar even to the people who lived in them.

Where contemporary life touched at all it seemed to turn its back on the canal. Houses faced away from the water, and there were great rusty tracts of corrugated-iron fencing all over the place separating people from it. On a boat you felt like a fugitive in your own land, ignored and spurned, with voles your only company, their tiny noses forming a V-shaped wash in the water as they cut across your course on their way from one bank to another.

Nowadays, in the main, the voles have gone, eradicated partly as a result of mile upon mile of new metal piling, which has been successful in securing crumbling canal banks, but which has prevented the voles getting access to their traditional breeding sites. The corrugated iron fences have been pulled down too, the waste ground behind built over with executive estates or laid with turf and planted out as public gardens or recreation grounds. Canals have become linear parks, and this has had a remarkable effect on the value of any properties which are close to one. Twenty years ago people turned up their noses at houses near canals; today estate agents make a feature of it, and any home that is actually on the canal with its own frontage commands a premium price.

Better than it used to be, yes; who could deny it? But at the same time something has been lost, and lost irretrievably.

It's just that you can't change any environment as totally as canals have changed this last quarter century without fundamentally altering the sort of people who are attracted to them. In the past you had to be a certain type of person to be drawn to canals. You had to be fascinated as much by their mystery as their history. You had to be entranced by their magic.

In those days the waterways were the preserve of hippies who couldn't quite accept that the 1960s had finished, and enthusiasts who were certain that the 1760s hadn't.

The hippies saw canals as offering an alternative lifestyle where they could be left alone to indulge in various solitary pursuits involving illegal substances and psychedelic music. The enthusiasts – 'rivet counters' they were called after their tendency to argue passionately about the details of boat construction – all had old working craft, the equivalent of Victorian lorries, where most of the hold was for cargo and they were jammed for living space into a tiny tea chest of a cabin at the back.

But your average rivet counter welcomed the privation this entailed. He regarded it as part of the enduring pleasure of the canals.

And then there were the cruisers: plastic boats, powered by whining outboard engines which were only the size of food mixers but which generated a sound like an aircraft at take off. Cruisers always seemed to be a gleaming, polished white, despite all the mud and grease that was a feature of the waterways then. And they always seemed to be under the control of middle-aged men wearing captain's caps – the sort of blokes who thought wearing pressed slacks and a cashmere sweater was dressing casually.

Not that it mattered. In that period what boat you cruised was less important than that you cruised at all. Everyone in their own way was a pioneer of the new leisure age; and come the end of the day when the mooring stakes had been driven in for the night, the hippies and the rivet counters and the plastic boaters alike would all repair to the nearest pub where they would chat harmlessly for hours about engines, routes through Birmingham or propeller sizes.

Nowadays it's all very different. Boats, which used to cost nothing, now cost a fortune. And so do the licences for them. Besides this, the dark cloud of bureaucracy has descended on the waterways. Boats today are all required to have number plates, for instance; they all have to be insured. And they all have to pass the equivalent of an MOT in which the heavy hand of the Health and Safety police is evident.

Getting on the water these days, your biggest problem is likely to be whether your door handles comply with regulation 137a, subsection vii (d) of the 1996 Anorak Act, or if your sink taps are in contravention of the 1998 European (Tear Your Hair Out) Directive.

The change came about gradually and insidiously, and even now I'm not quite sure how it happened. All I know is that at some time between Margaret Thatcher becoming Prime Minister in 1979 and Tony Blair taking over in 1997, a new breed of boat began appearing on the waterways. Some had running water. Some – horrifyingly – had pump-out lavatories.

Now this may seem a perfectly modest aspiration for the late twentieth century – but it was just the beginning of it. Today, most boats don't just have pump-out lavatories. They have full lavatory suites. They have showers. They have baths. They even have Jacuzzis and bidets. They also have a huge range of consumer durables: fridges, washing machines, TVs, videos, hi-fis, microwaves, computers… the list goes on.

But there's a paradox which lies at the heart of this, surely. I mean, with all this junk around, why are they bothering to be on a boat at all? Surely if you're on a boat, travelling about like an itinerant eighteenth-century working-class labourer, it implies you reject a little of modern life and what it stands for.

Doesn't it?

★

Dave and I eventually got the boat off the mudbank and we moored up earlier than we'd planned that first night. This wasn't out of choice so much as a result of an unfortunate incident with a rope which one of us had left trailing in the water so that it had got itself caught around the propeller, making it impossible to go on. Whichever of us was responsible, neither of us was admitting it, and we were both feeling testy – a mood not helped by the weather. It hadn't stopped raining all day, and we'd got to the stage where we were just too wet to care. We spent an hour with our arms contorted in the icy water cutting the rope free with a blunt kitchen knife. Afterwards, united in conquered adversity and at least talking again, we dried off as best we could and cracked open a couple of cans of beer we'd brought with us.

By now the rain had finally begun to ease off, and soon afterwards it stopped completely. The wind which had been blowing with it suddenly dropped too, and the dark clouds fell away, allowing us to bask in the surprisingly warm glow of a vivid sunset. I have many times since noticed how, after an appalling day, the English weather can suddenly change for the better in the hour before dark, and I feel sure there must be some meteorological explanation for it associated with the night-time cooling of the earth.

That day we could but gaze in wonder at the metamorphosis. We sat on the deck as a pale mist began to form across the water, watching the fish rise to the surface to feed, while on the bank a couple of nervous coots scratched about scavenging for titbits, their preposterously thin legs scarcely able to bear their weight. Above us the swallows dipped in the air and then dived to the water, skimming the surface until it seemed it must have turned to ice and they must have been skidding along its top. All around us the canal seemed bathed in a sort of magical half light which didn't seem of this world at all.

Before night had fallen I was hooked.

In seven days, Dave and I cruised from Leicestershire into the centre of Nottingham, back up the river towards Burton upon Trent, and from there to Nuneaton and on to Tamworth. Afterwards, when he'd gone, Em joined me for my second week, and we cruised to Coventry and Rugby, into Northamptonshire and back to Leicester to complete a circle of some eighty miles or so.

These are the mundane geographical facts of the trip; but actually, the more essential truth of that journey was that I cruised to Shangri-La. Somehow, by dint of just hiring a boat, I'd gained access to this new and strange world I'd never known existed. It was a world which – strangely – seemed familiar to me, though it was so unfamiliar, like one of those places you've visited in your dreams but can't quite locate. It was my world but it was not my world: it was a world which seemed to exist parallel to the one I knew; an older and quieter and more constant world than mine which was brash and angry and so tiresomely, constantly capricious. It was a world rooted in the soil of the countryside and the changing patterns of the seasons, a world where work was integral to people's lives rather than just imposed upon them to the point of exploitation – which is how it so often seemed to me, observing that great swathe of humanity that dragged itself reluctantly through the rush hour madness at home.

And people were different on the canals – I recognised that straight off. For a start they were less conventional than those who lived entirely on the land, more reluctant to conform to accepted behaviour and more questioning of it. They were more helpful too; less exclusive about their knowledge, and more willing to share it. But the breadth of that knowledge was staggering, derived from shared experiences that linked them together into a community. All around me were men and women who were as comfortable talking about protective anodes as they were about wildlife; people who could tie a rope with a couple of twists of their wrist, or be rolling a cigarette as they steered a twenty-ton boat into a lock with just an inch to spare on either side; people as familiar with the Northern towns as they were with the isolated Fenlands; people who were altogether so much larger and louder and brighter and more alive than the overwhelming majority of people I met in my normal life.

I suppose I'd fallen in love, though I didn't know it at the time, naively believing at that stage in my life that it was only people who could touch your heart and make you ache with yearning, longing for them. I suddenly felt this gnawing, persistent need to be close to the water, and after the holiday was over and Em and I had returned to London, nothing was more certain in my mind than that canals would play an important part in my life.

I think I've hardly been far away from them since for more than a month at a time.

THREE

Plans to find the soul of England were not going well. I was nowhere near to starting the trip. In fact I was further from it than ever. The insurance claim on the ceiling had turned into a nightmare and was taking forever. Then, when it was finally settled and the builders were about to move in, there was a storm over London which loosened our chimney and precipitated another claim. If this wasn't bad enough, there was the whole thing about Debs which held me up even more. I hope after reading this she realises the part she played in this story and is sorry for all the trouble she's caused me. It started when I caught her at work one day gazing at the screen of her computer, the beginnings of a tear glistening almost imperceptibly in the corner of an eye.

Now, I'm not a New Man for nothing. I realise contemporary women are burdened with cares beyond the perception of most of my gender. Ours not to reason why; ours merely to lend what little kind support we can in a world characterised by harsh, unthinking cruelty.

Debs was scheduled to be married soon. For months the office talk had been of little else but dresses and receptions, rings and honeymoons. Had her intended left her in the lurch? Dumped her? Had he posted her a short and bitter email, a twenty-first-century 'Dear Debs' letter, sacrificing her on the altar of new technology?

Actually, when I went over to comfort her I found her gazing at a picture of a car.

'Beautiful, isn't she?' she said.

The image had evidently been downloaded from the internet. I surveyed it critically. I am no car fanatic, and certainly no expert. As far as I could see it was a red car, a convertible, a sportyish number with lots of chrome and rakish American fins. Pretty enough, I thought, but nothing worth crying about. I assumed it was to be her wedding present to her intended. I assumed she'd realised she couldn't afford it.

'Too expensive?' I asked.

'Well, I'm not dropping the bloody price, if that's what you mean!' she snapped at me with a look I recognised all too well. I have worked with Debs for years, you see; I can read her like a book. The look said: *Are you a lunatic or something to think I could afford to buy anyone a car for a present?* Or maybe not. Maybe with the benefit of hindsight this is the look she gives every sucker she sees coming her way when she's selling a car. One way or another, a week or so later, I found myself on a train with her to the nether regions of Surrey, beyond the unexplored badlands of the M25, where in some out-of-the-way barn I took my first look at the 30-year-old Triumph Herald convertible which, although I didn't know it, had already got my name all over it.

There was no denying it: it *was* a pretty car.

For those who, like me, don't know a lot about cars, let me say that the Triumph Herald is not just a rare example of British motor engineering, but an even rarer example of *successful* British motor engineering. Long before 'swinging London' and 'flower power' made the Mini the design icon of the age, British engineers had scored a commercial bullseye by the simple expedient of recognising the disheartening desire of every man on the planet to own a racy sports car.

And realising too that most of them didn't have the money for it.

The answer was the Herald, a low-slung, chassis-built saloon that boasted four seats, the back two so tiny that they weren't much use for anything except kids or those with severe growth problems. This, of course, was actually the sort of inspirational design for which we were once world-famous since it allowed single men to pretend they were buying a sporty two-seater, while a family man looking for a car could persuade himself of exactly the opposite.

The Herald was actually designed by the Italian Giovanni Michelotti who took some of the worst excesses of gas-guzzling American cars of the 1950s and imported them into a Britain still in the grip of post-war austerity. It was all very understated in a way that played well to the puritanical British market. Triumph Heralds, for instance, have rear fins which were made popular on American classics like Cadillacs; but whereas on Cadillacs they're loud and brash and say, 'Look at me, I'm one big f**k-off motor,' on the Herald they're smaller and more discreet, and if they say anything at all they say it with a naughty giggle and the promise of illicit fun, a bit like a Donald McGill seaside postcard.

Actually, for its time, the Herald was really rather a nippy little machine. The later models had 1300 cc engines and generated 60 brake horsepower, which is laughable today, but which in its time was an achievement the designers were proud to flaunt by putting the logo '13/60' on the boot. Between 1959 and 1971 more than half a million of them were sold – which as motor success stories go is OK, but on its own isn't really enough to explain the extraordinarily affectionate place the car seems to occupy in the British psyche.

Part of it, I suppose, is that the Herald was an accessible car. Even if you couldn't afford one, it wasn't so expensive that you couldn't believe that one day you *might*. It was a fun car too, the sort of car which people enjoyed driving, so pretty well everyone you meet of a certain age, men and women alike, seem at one time or another to have owned one, or been associated with one, or had the use of one. And they somehow feel differently about the Herald to other cars they've driven.

With other cars, people remember them as, well… cars. Cars in which they've done the sort of mundane things people do in cars like shopping and ferrying around the kids. But the Herald's the sort of classic driving machine in which a large percentage of the population seems to have undergone some crucial rite of passage: they've taken their driving test in a Herald for instance, or lost their virginity in one.

A rather staid man I met in a pub once in Daventry persisted in telling me at great length one afternoon how he and a friend had been picked up as 17-year-olds by some sixth-form totty from a local posh girls' school who'd borrowed the car off Daddy and used it to give them a fantasy weekend out of the Letters Page of a top-shelf magazine. He was typical. People who've had anything to do with Triumph Heralds are the sort of people who are prone to engage you in random conversation like that, and, once they have, they're the sort to tell you more than they really ought to.

Most of them, I guess, are a little older than me, and brought up at a time when you were expected to display a certain reticence with regard to your personal life. Not that this seems to hamper them where the Triumph Herald is concerned. The mere appearance of one in a suburban street is usually the signal for a horde of sentimentalists to emerge from nowhere, determined to engage you in intimate small talk.

'Let me think about it,' I said to Debs that day in the barn, affecting a certain insouciance which I thought might somehow help me in negotiating a price. Some hope! Once she'd made up her mind about something, Debs was not a woman to be moved. A couple of days later I found myself capitulating to all her demands and signing an enormously large cheque. Mainly to justify the expenditure, I started wondering soon afterwards whether it might be possible to take the car on the canal trip that was still niggling away in the back of my mind. Perhaps by using a bike, and shuttling between the two, I could somehow work it to travel with the Herald and the boat together. This would give me a much greater range for sightseeing as I travelled about.

But an old car isn't a style icon; it's a piece of machinery. And, by today's standards, it's not a particularly sophisticated piece of machinery either. A Herald, for instance, hasn't got what's called 'syncromesh' on its first gear – a term that meant absolutely nothing to me until I attempted to engage first gear just as the car was about to stop at a set of traffic lights. The tumultuous grinding and crashing sound that emanated from the gearbox ensured that though I'd never learn what syncromesh actually *was*, I'd never forget what not having it could actually *do*.

It was the same with the acceleration on the car. It actually wasn't too bad once you got moving, but from a standing start it felt a bit like coaxing a traction engine into life. Of course, I exaggerate; but how can you avoid feeling like a lumbering archaeological relic when every other car around you is so new-century and so damned sophisticated that your mere presence gets up the nose of half the driving population? That is to say it gets up the nose of the male half, or more specifically the young male half who drive cars so powerful they'd take off if only they could only get clearance from flight control at Heathrow.

They tuck in behind you at traffic lights and terrorise you if you don't move on green like a Ferrari off the starting grid. And if you're in front of one on a minor road, you'll be treated to a bizarre 'love you and leave you' ritual in which they'll drive up your exhaust pipe and then, without so much as a post-coital pleasantry, they'll roar past you with only inches to spare, generally on the brow of a hill with a phalanx of articulated lorries bearing down on them just to add a final frisson to the liaison.

Driving back home from Surrey it must have been apparent to every predator on the road that I was a virgin in these matters. The maiden bit of my drive lasted no more than minutes, and within the hour I felt like an addled old courtesan who'd been on the game too long for her own good.

My first plan had been to get home by way of the M25, but I'd soon abandoned that idea. I mean, let's get real here! I may have become a bit slow on the uptake in my dotage, but I'm not totally ga-ga. The M25's bad enough in a modern car; in an old one it's suicidal. A bullet through the temple would be a far more humane way of killing yourself.

However, a glance at the map had revealed that there was an alternative open to me in the form of a road called the A25 which ran almost parallel to the motorway. On my Michelin it was marked in a soft cuddly yellow, the colour of an Easter chick, as opposed to the lurid red, like a flesh wound, which was the colour of its big brother. All in all it seemed a far more attractive proposition for someone in his middle years who was determined to reach his late ones; and indeed, it turned out to be a charming byway which passed through such delightful places as Bletchingly, Oxted and Brasted. I couldn't believe how rural it was. At one point I was held up at traffic lights so close to a village cricket pitch that I watched a wicket fall before they changed to green. Even drivers on this road seemed different. OK, not exactly courteous – that would have been asking too much – but at least they didn't seem totally determined to rip off my testicles through the undercarriage. This was a revelation. So when I got home and retraced the route I'd travelled, it was with a totally different eye that I surveyed the map. It was – if not exactly a life-changing experience – then at least the sort of episode that makes you see the world in a different way.

Extraordinary! I'd travelled on a yellow-chick road, but there were other roads, a whole rainbow spectrum of them. What about these green fronds – B roads – which seemed to be all over the place? The A25 through suburban Surrey was pastoral enough, but these green routes were the very colour of the countryside. What would they be like? What would the insubstantial uncoloured ones be like – the ones which seemed to stretch across every inch of the map like hollow spindly fingers? Or – the ones that intrigued me most of all – the uncategorised roads represented by single black lines, each one as thin as a child's hair. They were all over the place. Being the sceptic I am, I couldn't help doubting that they existed at all; I suspected they were just the figment of some cartographer's imagination, his quiet tribute to an England that had long since gone.

Surely it'd be impossible to use these roads to actually go anywhere. I decided to test it out, and with no real intention of actually doing the journey, I mischievously rang the RAC and requested from them a route to take me from where I was based in south-east London to Leicester, where my family lived, the first two places to come into my head.

The young woman dealing with my request was most helpful and if she was put out by my demand that the route should avoid motorways and A roads, she certainly didn't show it. I heard her hit a few characters on the keyboard of a computer before she rattled off a route that started in the East End and took me to the Midlands by way of a wide swinging arc through Cambridgeshire. It was a journey that involved an intricate series of twists and turns through villages with improbable names like Steeple Morden and Gamlingay, a journey that apparently involved never travelling on the same road for more than a mile at a time.

I was enthusiastic to try it out so the following Saturday I tucked Em into the passenger seat, filled up the Herald with a tank of environmentally unfriendly leaded fuel, and headed for the Blackwall Tunnel. It was one of those rare English summer days when the sky is azure blue for as far as the eye can see, and when what clouds exist are so flimsy it seems their only purpose is to give a depth to the horizon. By 9 a.m. it must have been in the eighties and with every mile we travelled our decision to put down the roof of the Herald seemed less the act of fun that it first had, and more a necessary part of the survival technique we'd need to get us through the day.

We followed the suggested route to the letter and headed for Epping Forest. Soon the busy, blistering roads of London turned into Arcadian country lanes which tunnelled through cool stretches of woodland or wound over tracts of gently undulating farmland which, when we were lucky, caught the slight cooling breath of a breeze. Out of town it was a different world, one where the sun was equally hot and the temperatures equally high, but where it somehow seemed altogether fresher and sharper and brighter and cleaner.

The absence of traffic was almost eerie. Surely England is a country of traffic jams and gridlock? Not in deepest Cambridgeshire it isn't, or the middle of Huntingdonshire either. In each of these counties it sometimes seemed as if we were the only car on the road. Even the villages we passed through appeared deserted.

I remember that near a place called Much Hadham our route took us onto an unclassified road that was so narrow it was as if we'd strayed onto a farm track. There wasn't even a hedge to separate us from the fields through which we were driving, and I was convinced we'd end up in someone's barn. Later, on a similar road, we parked under the damp penumbra of an irrigator, waiting for the water jets to complete their long revolution so that we could enjoy an impromptu shower to cool us in the heat of the scorching sun.

We had lunch in a pub that appeared abruptly and almost miraculously only moments after we'd realised we were hungry. It had a low thatched roof, a long bar with a low-beamed ceiling, and a flagstone floor which made it as cool as a cellar. The place was unspoilt, and so far away from everything and everyone that it didn't seem part of the present. Even the chicken we ordered tasted like chicken used to do; and the bowl of potatoes and salad which came with it were so fresh and flavoursome you felt they'd been growing an hour before.

But that was the way of things that extraordinary afternoon when everything seemed so perfect that we no sooner had to think that it was time for tea than there was a tea shop in a Georgian house around the next bend, with chairs and tables laid out for us on a lawn, and freshly baked home-made carrot cake cut and waiting for us on the plate.

'Do you think this is for real?' I said to Em at one point. 'Do you think we'll wake up soon?'

That's the way it seemed that day, like one of those dreams which you don't ever want to end. I was entranced by it all, by the world I'd discovered and by the Herald which had taken me there. My mind was finally made up now. I had decided the car was coming with me on the cruise.

FOUR

It was a crazy idea, a journey like this; and if I'd really been serious about getting to grips with my mid-life crisis I'd have been better off opting for a course of therapy than going off travelling. Or if I had to travel, I'd have been better choosing somewhere warm with a beach rather than condemning myself to schlepping around England in what was shaping up to be a typical English summer: that is, one that was wet and cold and not summery at all.

Yet I couldn't get the notion of the canal trip out of my head; it was beginning to obsess me. Finally, in the absence of the real thing, I found myself turning once more to Tom Rolt's book *Narrow Boat*. It was the fourth or fifth time I'd read it and it was a solace to me, on the train to work, or climbing into bed at night, to lose myself in his mannered descriptions of the canals as they used to be before I was born.

The book's an account of a honeymoon cruise he and his first wife Angela took through the Midlands in the summer of 1939 on their wooden ex-working boat Cressy. The journey was made at that fateful moment in British history just before war broke out, at a time when the country's 3,000-mile network of canals and rivers was virtually unknown to the general population – a time when it was falling into disrepair, and when the boat people who had worked it for centuries were close to extinction. *Narrow Boat* was published after the war finished and it alerted people to the impending destruction of what Rolt identified as one of our greatest national assets. A direct result of this was the birth of the canals restoration movement which today has grown to such an extent that now we're not just restoring old canals, but building totally new ones.

I've always been fascinated by the book, but I've been equally fascinated by Tom Rolt – a classic car enthusiast himself, as it happens. Old black and white pictures of him make him seem like an army man, with his lean frame, his straight back and pencil moustache. But this aura of old-fashioned respectability is deceptive, and you don't need to learn much about him to realise that though he may have been conservative in his outlook, at heart – paradoxically – his traditionalism was of a radical bent. Or putting it another way, a more contemporary way, he was a bit of a rock-'n'-roller, a man who was always going to beat his own path in the world, unconstrained by society.

Rolt took *Cressy* to Banbury after he'd bought her, and Banbury was where he and Angela adapted her for living, building a roof over her cargo hold and fitting out the space underneath as a houseboat. Banbury was *Cressy*'s home port, the place Rolt returned to whenever *Cressy* needed maintenance. It was also where most of *Narrow Boat* was written.

Maybe my interest in him springs from the fact that Banbury is our home port as well, the place Em and I fitted out our boat *Justice* after she was launched, and where we've moored different boats on and off for almost twenty-five years. It's almost like a second home to us. Indeed, when we first washed up in the town, it was only to find – by one of those strange tendrils of history which bind us to the past – that Bert Tooley, who had worked on *Cressy* and is mentioned in *Narrow Boat*, was still alive and living by the canal in an old caravan. All this made me think Banbury was the ideal place to start a trip of the sort I was planning. The *only* place to start it, you might think. The trouble was though, the boat wasn't actually *in* Banbury. I grant you, it wasn't a million miles away. It was in Oxford where we'd left it one weekend trapped by the Thames that had come up suddenly after nearly a month of incessant rain. But it wasn't where it should be.

I'd considered driving to Banbury in the Herald and giving myself a ceremonial send-off at the famous Banbury Cross, though this hardly seemed in the spirit of the project, especially so early on. Call me a traditionalist, but you can hardly start a boat journey from Banbury in a car from Oxford, can you? It somehow doesn't feel right.

But then I thought, sod it, Steve – you're being too literal about this. The starting gun's already fired on this project, and if that means you're condemned by vile weather to start a journey you're still not certain you want to make from a place you never wanted to be, then just get on with it and be comforted by how much of an analogy for life that is. Besides, I wasn't planning on following Rolt's route slavishly. In fact I wasn't thinking of following it at all – or at least not in that geographical sense of retracing his route. Mine was to be a more spiritual quest for the man, a search to understand him and his world and – yes – to understand the soul of that world, the soul of England.

So I told them at work I wasn't going to be in for a bit, and the next day, I loaded up a few clothes and drove to the boat.

Things were starting at last.

★

There are worse places in the world to be stuck than Oxford. Or maybe not, depending on which way you look at it. Oxford's the sort of place that excites passion in people so that if they don't love it to death, they loathe it intensely. I've found that many Americans fall into this latter category, since along with London and Stratford-upon-Avon, it's one of the few places they come to England specifically to see. They arrive expecting it to be an unspoiled theme park straight out of some costume drama they once watched on PBS, and they become inconsolable when they find out there's been a bit of building work since the 1500s.

Actually, I think there's another reason a lot of Americans don't like Oxford: the fact is the place subliminally affronts their egalitarian principles. They may not know much about the British class system; but what they do know they don't care for; and they certainly don't care for big beefy authority figures with silly names like Bulldog telling them that the college precincts are closed to tourists when they've travelled 3,000 miles on vacation to see them. I have to say that I'm with them every inch of the way. There's no denying that Oxford is a very beautiful city – sometimes breathtakingly so. But it's an exclusive city too, as much for the English as for visitors from overseas. I never totally realised quite *how* exclusive until I once went to the wedding of a friend who, because her father was something big in one of the colleges, was able to commandeer not just the personal use of the fourteenth-century chapel in which to take her vows, but the full college choir to eulogise them, as well as the college dining room to celebrate them afterwards. Tourists were excluded from the place for the whole day.

Mind you, it was a magnificent occasion, and one I wouldn't have missed for the world since it was the first and only time in my life when – with morning suit and champagne glass as my passport – I was allowed to walk legitimately on one of the meticulously manicured bowling greens that pass for lawns in these parts.

There's a pompous story they tell in Oxford about these lawns. It's said that many years ago when a curious Texan once enquired how the gardeners managed to get them so perfect, he was told that, actually, there was really nothing much to it. It was just a matter of choosing the right site and the right grass seed, and putting the one on top of the other.

And then rolling and mowing it for 400 years.

If I'd been that Texan, I think the patronising punch line of this story might have turned into something more literal on my side. At the very least it would have been the cue for me to go in search of a powerful weedkiller which – special relationship notwithstanding – a posse of your polite English bobbies wouldn't have stopped me dumping on the grass.

But that's Oxford for you. Personally, I've never had a problem with it. I realised long ago that the university's the sort of place you can only get to by being very intelligent or very stupid, and since one requires brains and the other an aristocratic lineage, my best chance of getting there was always going to be on a train out of Paddington like most people. So I don't hold Oxford's elitism against the place. Indeed, I have come to admire the effrontery with which it gets away with it.

As far as I know Tom Rolt never aspired to even a university education, let alone an Oxford one – which is probably just as well since from an early age his bent had been towards practical engineering, a subject which has hardly been Oxford's forte (or at least not at its university, that sort of oily rag stuff being left to the motor-wallahs out in the car factories at Cowley). Surprising this, when you think about it, because those of my generation – born in the years when the sun was setting on the British Empire, but before it finally had – were brought up to believe that the edifice had been built on the achievements of people from the top universities, the administrators through whom the blessings of Englishness flowed to an uncivilised world.

And yet it stands to reason that this can't have been true: administrators don't actually *build* anything. The people who do are engineers: men like Tom Rolt who function not in the realm of the intellect, and certainly not in the attractive medieval colleges of the old universities, but in the ugly physical world of labour where things have to be assembled and repaired and men have to roll up their sleeves and get a bit of dirt on their hands to do it.

Rolt did an old-style apprenticeship, five years long, which used to be the norm in British industry when we had industry in Britain. Afterwards, like any young lad with a brain and a practical bent, he'd have been able to build an engine from scratch, including being able to cast, turn and mill the main component parts of it. In return he was led to believe he had a job for life if he wanted one.

Not that Tom Rolt could have ever been happy spending his life in a factory. He was suspicious of too many contemporary values, and he questioned whether industrial progress was always for the best. Besides, those jobs he'd trained for didn't materialise in the Depression years. He spent some time running a garage which didn't suit him much either, though it gave him time to devise the practical and philosophical strategy which eventually took him to the canals. He called this his 'design for living' – essentially it was a template for how he could earn enough money to live on a boat without the support of an independent income.

This is where his book *Narrow Boat* fitted in. Though on one level it's just the simple account of the honeymoon cruise with Angela, on another it was Rolt's (ultimately highly successful) attempt to earn his living as a writer.

If any confirmation were needed that he'd made the correct decision it came in the autumn of 1939 when war was declared and he had to put the writing on hold and go back to engineering as part of the war effort. He and Angela were living on *Cressy* by then, and they based themselves in Cheshire where Tom worked for Rolls-Royce in Crewe, making the Merlin engines that powered Spitfire aeroplanes.

The experience nearly destroyed him.

By then it had been almost eight years since he'd worked for a large engineering firm, and he'd fondly imagined that with his skills he'd be assembling engines as he had during his apprenticeship. Instead he found himself mindlessly tapping an endless series of holes in cylinder blocks, even this soulless task reduced to nothing by the use of a jig which, as he observed bitterly, removed 'the last vestige of human skill from the work'.

Tom Rolt was no political fanatic, and if you plough through even a few of the thirty books and numerous articles he was eventually to write in his career, you can't help but be struck by the right-wing vein of much of his thinking. But he's a product of his time, an idealist and a sentimentalist too. *Narrow Boat* harks back nostalgically to a mythical sylvan age where honest ruddy-faced rustics toiled in village workshops and countrymen quaffed foaming pints of ale from pewter tankards in thatched country inns.

But frankly, who's to say we wouldn't all have been up for nostalgia after six years of being bombed by the Nazis? Towards the end of his life even Rolt himself recognised the book's failings, admitting that he found it 'too self-consciously Arcadian and picaresque' and its escapism 'slightly embarrassing'.

Tom Rolt only worked at Rolls-Royce for six weeks, but it scarred him for the rest of his life. It represented such a nadir that in his despair he even used to look forward to using the lavatory as a respite from the unmitigated tedium of the job. The episode led him to an odd conclusion, or a conclusion odd for a man who I can never visualise without a copy of the *Daily Telegraph* tucked under his arm. He wrote: 'After such an experience, the strikes that have plagued the engineering industry since the war are no surprise to me. No amount of money can make such durance any less vile.'

I was reminded of this during my time in Oxford. When I'd left London to start my trip I'd not expected to be in the city long; but the rain which had led to the boat being in Oxford in the first place continued unabated, and after two weeks I was still there with the Thames floods trapping me in one direction and floods on the River Cherwell trapping me in the other. As a result, I got to the stage where I couldn't endure the place a moment longer. I was moored on a stretch of canal a little way short of Isis Lock, which is separated from the river by just the width of the towpath. It's only a ten-minute walk from the city centre, and, with the overhanging trees giving the place the air of woodland grove, and the regular chatty stream of cyclists and pedestrians who use the towpath as a cut through, it's normally as pleasant and companionable a spot as you'll find in the middle of any major city anywhere.

But I felt I'd done Oxford after a week, and after ten days I was screaming to get on the move again. I'd visited the Sheldonian and the Bodleian and the Ashmolean; I'd poked about in as many colleges as they'd let me into; and I'd taken sodden evening walks along Christ Church meadow, and made even wetter bike rides to explore some of the university parks and outlying suburbs. One day I even cycled across Port Meadow to Godstow Lock on the Thames – which I might have enjoyed except that it was totally flooded and the path I was riding along was the only thing above water level, so I got the weirdest sensation of cycling across the surface of a lake.

The pitiless rain was bad enough, but the mud that it created on the towpath got to me in the end. After a couple of days it got churned like whipped cream; and after a week it was such a comprehensively infused mixture of old leaf mould, sludge and dog shit that I could have marketed it in Body Shop as a traditional facepack. What made it worse was that the weather didn't stop the pooches taking walkies, it just stopped their owners coming with them, so for the duration a sort of towpath anarchy prevailed with the canines taking over the world and crapping all over it with uncontained glee.

However much you wiped your feet and meticulously changed into slippers when you came into the boat, the mud always seemed to permeate by one means or another. Eventually I'd had enough of it, and one morning after I'd woken to find the rain hammering on the roof yet again, I turned the boat round and headed north, determined that if I was going to get constantly rained on, then at least it would happen nearer the Cotswolds where the onset of the lambing season would ensure that unaccompanied dogs met a hygienic, if brutal, end.

Of course – sod's law! – it stopped raining the moment I started the engine, and once I'd got beyond the colonies of New Age travellers that live on boats out towards Wolvercote, the sun had forced its way through the clouds and the sky had become the pale colour of blue lint, bringing in its wake a host of fishermen. This was unusual because I'd never before seen fishermen out in such force so early in the year, especially when such a large proportion seemed young blokes, and obviously not short of a bob or two either, judging from the quality of the tackle they were using.

The reason became apparent after I got chatting with a couple of them. It turned out they were car workers at Cowley, which had once been owned by Leyland until it had been sold a year or two before to the Germans, who'd subsequently become so sick and tired of the British motor industry that they were at that moment looking to offload the company to anyone who showed the slightest interest in making cars in Britain. Or making *anything* in Britain, for that matter. Or not even *making* anything, actually – as long as someone would just take the company off their hands quick, no questions asked.

The fishermen, it transpired, had been sent home for an enforced holiday under an arrangement for flexible working which the unions had negotiated with the management. Of course, I use the word 'negotiated' here in its loosest sense – the sense that if you gave someone your wallet after they'd held a gun to your head, you might be said to have negotiated a price for your life.

What this meant in practice was that in return for not demanding wages from the company which had contracted to employ them but hadn't got anything for them to do, the men would nevertheless get paid on the basis that at some stage in the future they would agree to work every last hour that God sent without the bothersome inconvenience of claiming overtime for it. I somehow guessed that this idea hadn't come about as a result of a spontaneous groundswell of rank and file opinion. What it seemed to mean was that when the blokes eventually got back to work – if they ever did – they wouldn't be taking another day off until about 2050.

The whole arrangement seemed yet another example of the protracted death of trade skills in this country, and reading Tom Rolt's account of working briefly for Rolls-Royce all those years ago, it all seemed such a depressingly predictable result of taking away people's pride and self-respect in their work.

FIVE

Thrupp is not what you'd call a big place – not unless you're one of those people who live on an isolated farm in rural Norfolk twenty miles from your nearest neighbour. Even then, I don't think you'd find it all bright lights and big-city bustle. It lies six or seven miles north of Oxford, just beyond Kidlington, which is hardly one of the world's major conurbations either, but which people have at least heard about because it's the headquarters of Thames Valley Police where Colin Dexter's Inspector Morse was supposed to have been based.

But Thrupp is about as different from Kidlington as a fictional detective is from the real thing. Kidlington at least has shops and offices and places where ordinary people live; all Thrupp has is a cruising club with a lot of moorings for boats, and a row of about a dozen tiny houses – 'artisans' cottages' – prettied up with white paint and red geraniums. Oh, and it has a pub too. Actually – officially – Thrupp has two pubs, but the other one is round the bend of the canal and to a purist like me not really in Thrupp at all and just another regrettable example of a small place getting ideas above its station.

I washed up in the place the way you do on the waterways, entirely by chance. Travelling north from Oxford there weren't many other boats on the move, and I didn't meet one until Wolvercote Junction where the canal branches off to join the River Thames. Single-handed boating is exhausting enough at the best of times with locks, but on this stretch of canal you also have to deal with lift bridges. With their distinctive upright balance beams, they're a feature of the Oxford Canal, and they may look twee and pretty enough on postcards; but believe me, they're a swine to get through on your own. You either rope them down or jam them up. Either way, as you go underneath, you find yourself praying that a ton and a half of Grade Two listed Georgian doesn't come crashing down on your head.

By the time I got to Thrupp it was as much as I could do to collapse into the Boat Inn and crawl to the bar. Then it was as much as I could do to drag myself back to *Justice* for an afternoon nap. After that? Well, after that it was opening time again, and I didn't see the need to move at all that day and so – as is the inexorable way of things on the waterways – I finished up staying at Thrupp for more than a month and a half.

As a place to wait for the floods to subside, it suited me perfectly. It was filled with canal people, a lot of them, like me, holed up by the weather, and most of them – like me too – happy enough to keep themselves to themselves during the day, but at night keen to assemble companionably around the bar of The Boat. By degrees I soon found myself drawn into a surprisingly lively social scene. On some nights there'd be an impromptu folk club where we were all expected to do a turn, or at least join in with the chorus; other evenings we'd play Aunt Sally, the idiosyncratic Oxfordshire version of skittles that's survived in these parts.

One Saturday the boat club even held an open day to introduce city kids to the waterways, and I somehow found myself roped in to help, sitting around a campfire by candlelight cradling a burnt sausage and yelling out the incomprehensible words to some song about cranky poohs and goolley goolleys. The kids were great, full of drive, energy and curiosity – though I must confess there were some of them I was happier to have sitting around singing with me, than following me up a deserted street. But no doubt I do them an injustice, and in this I'm typical of the English. As a country we aren't terribly keen on young people, being somewhat fastidious about the procedures necessary to beget them, and somewhat uncertain of what to do with them once we have.

In contrast to the nights, my days at Thrupp were spent in congenial solitude when I had the first opportunity for ages to spend time just contemplating life and where it had taken me. Most of the things I found myself thinking about were totally trivial and irrelevant. I spent hours staring at the fruit bowl, for instance: watching swarms of fruit flies congregate sociably on my browning bananas. Funny things, fruit flies – simple creatures, but infinitely complex too, as the American biologist Thomas Hunt Morgan found when he used them for the research which in 1910 led to him becoming the first scientist to pin down the location of a gene to a specific chromosome. So it's not going too far to say that in fruit flies lies the very meaning of life.

In the same vein I also spent a lot of time thinking about eggs.

I am quite fond of eggs, and one day I frittered away an entire morning working out how many of them I'd eaten over my lifetime. It came out at more than five thousand. Five thousand! Can you imagine it? Even allowing for periods when I didn't eat any at all, and other periods when I glutted on them (pickled eggs in pubs, for instance – I had a mania for them in my mid-twenties) I've probably consumed eggs at an average of three a week since the age of eighteen. That's 156 a year for 32 years – 4,992 of them, not counting the ones I ate as a kid. That is one bloody big omelette by anyone's standards.

Then I began to think about everything else I'd eaten: the tons of potatoes, the fields of vegetables, the herds of cows, the flocks of chickens, the shoals of fish... And what about my other consumption? What about all the raw materials I'd used, all the wood, metal and plastic expended on my behalf? All the energy I'd exhausted, all the gas, all the electricity... And this is only me, remember, just one insignificant soul among millions in this world – just one man who, admittedly, might be tending to plumpness around the midriff in his middle years, but one who hasn't exactly led a life of hedonistic excess.

What started me off on this train of thought was a sociable moorhen which pitched up outside *Justice* one morning as I was standing in the sunshine at the side door, sipping at the day's first cup of Ceylon and tossing crusts of toast into the water. Now, when I use the word 'sociable' here, understand it's only in the context of a bird which usually only has to catch sight of another species to flee in frenzied, uncoordinated panic. Moorhens have long, spindly legs the thickness of drinking straws. They do not run gracefully, especially when they try to do it on water. In fact, they don't walk particularly elegantly either, even on land. Come to think of it, their swimming action, which involves much redundant bobbing of the head, leaves a lot to be desired too. In short, this is not a bird endowed with much in the way of natural poise and assurance, and certainly not one you should ever consider as a household pet.

It swam around aimlessly for a while, and pecked haphazardly at the surface of the water before taking up a precarious position on a thin branch that trailed from a bush on the opposite bank; and over the following days it based itself here, disappearing at various times and returning with such predictable regularity that eventually it began to dawn on me what I was dismissing insensitively as just a branch was actually… well, this creature's home.

This was a bit of a revelation. OK, I realise there's a danger of becoming too anthropomorphic here; but all the same, the reduction of a concept so inexorably bound up in the British mind with bricks and mortar to something no grander than a twig took a bit of getting my head around. How many twigs had I inadvertently bulldozed in my boating life by inattentive steering? How many forests of them had I demolished on towpath walks by mindlessly snapping them off to hack at stinging nettles?

This was all a salutary reminder of how lightly some living things tread on the world, and how heavily does humanity. And it touched a deep chord in me when one day it swam nearer than it had ever done before and delivered one of those shrill cries which I'd always thought agonisingly mournful, like the shriek of the existential soul railing against the nihilism of the universe.

Actually, the damn thing began screeching at me regularly from then on, four or five times a day, until the penny finally dropped and I realised that his was less a cry of metaphysical angst than a demand for more toast for which it had obviously developed a taste.

Ah well… In the midst of a life-crisis there's a tendency to search too hard for deeper meaning. It serves me right for being too sentimental, I suppose.

Thrupp lies very close to the village of Woodstock in which stands Blenheim Palace, stately home to successive Dukes of

Marlborough; and towards the end of my stay when Em was up for the weekend we decided to drive there in the Debsmobile for an afternoon of heritage. The village is a Cotswold picture-postcardy-type of place, filled with tourist buses, listed buildings and fancy restaurants selling food at London prices. There's an expensive 'heritage hotel', and a lot of boutique shops as well. One sells knitting patterns and precious little else. Another sells shoes with genuine gold-plated soles – well, I took it that they *must* have genuine gold-plated soles at the prices they were charging for them. Another only sells goods from the Third World. With a facetiousness verging on the tasteless it's called One Village.

Blenheim Palace was built in the early eighteenth century after Queen Anne granted John Churchill, the first Duke of Marlborough, the manor of Woodstock and £240,000 for defending Holland and Austria from invasion by the French, so saving us – at least for a generation or two – from overpriced wine, sloppy kissing and Golden Delicious apples. It's as good a use for quarter of a million quid as I can think of – never mind that we got one of the most beautiful baroque houses in the world out of the deal too.

But it's probably as Winston Churchill's birthplace that Blenheim is best known. The tourists are told that he came into the world prematurely in the 'cloakroom' after his mother had been taken in labour following a bout of dancing – though I've always suspected the more prosaic truth was that he was born in the lavatory after she got caught short. Churchill had heard this said himself. He used to joke that he couldn't confirm it one way or another. Although he was present at the event, he said, unfortunately he had no personal recollection of it.

The curious cocktail of the military, the royal and the political which characterises Blenheim was summed up for me neatly in the menu of one of Woodstock's many tearooms where we were eventually forced to seek sanctuary from the rain which, in this most appalling of summers, had begun bucketing down yet again. There, for a light morning snack, you could have Colonial Rarebit (cheese on toast with a pinch of curry powder), Churchill Rarebit (cheese on toast with parsley) or Rarebit Diane, which I assumed was misspelt, but named after the late princess. Actually I was wrong and it turned out to be named after Diane the owner of the tearoom who – the waitress informed us with the deference the ordinary show to those in whom they instinctively recognise greatness – had actually invented the dish.

'And is it a secret?' I asked.

'Secret?'

'The recipe. It's cheese on toast, I suppose. But do I get to know what makes it so special?'

The waitress leaned over to me conspiratorially, as if imparting some nugget of information bearing on national security. 'It has a tomato on top,' she said.

Now call me old-fashioned, but I find it difficult to reconcile myself to the fact that the country that developed parliamentary democracy, invented the jet engine, and dreamed up the format for *The X Factor* can have fallen so low in its own estimation that it feels the need to celebrate the originality of adding a slice of tomato to a toasted cheese sandwich. Apart from this unsettling burst of innovation, the tearoom was reassuringly predictable, for when our beverages eventually arrived they were cold in the way that has become as much the endearing hallmark of the contemporary English tea shop as the grubby packets of sugar and pots of UHT milk which arrived with them and which similarly have come to represent a benchmark for everything that is tacky about us.

It was still raining when we left, and by now we'd given up any idea of visiting the palace itself, having discovered how much it would cost to get in. A much more pleasant proposition even in the rain, we decided, would be to turn up our collars and walk around the grounds where we could avoid the crowds and enjoy one of Capability Brown's loveliest creations in relative solitude. Even this cost us an arm and a leg though, since I didn't discover until later that there's a public footpath running through the place to which you have right of access if only you approach the gatehouse without waving around five-pound notes like I did. Inside, we hardly had the place to ourselves either, for considering it was such a miserable day, the grounds were surprisingly busy – a fact I put down to a characteristic of the English to persist with whatever it is we have planned for our leisure hours regardless of what the weather may be on the day.

You see it on seaside beaches where families in swimming gear sit huddled behind gaily coloured windbreaks as Force 9 gales sweep in from the Atlantic. You see it in parks where young dads doggedly continue kickabouts with their kids way beyond the point where even a hardened Premiership pro would be looking to the referee to abandon the game. And we saw it in the grounds of Blenheim that day in early April where we found ourselves stepping over families wrapped up like trawlermen but still battling gamely to have picnics though they'd long ago given up any pretence to pleasure in what they were doing.

Mind you, I suppose we were doing much the same ourselves, walking around in what by now had become a storm.

Eventually we gave up the struggle and visited the palace after all. Well, we visited the gift shop – which apart from the cafe is the only place in the dry they'll let you in for free. But it was a good gift shop, classy: the sort of thing you'd expect in a stately home like Blenheim. It was filled with posh presents like cut-glass whisky tumblers and expensively woven tartan – which must confuse the Americans something rotten since they associate both with Scotland and don't realise that all the best bits of that country are owned by the English aristocracy. The 'traditional' limited-edition teddy bears must baffle them too. You find them in every country house gift shop – and they baffle me as well. I've never been able to work out this connection between furry toys and the aristocracy, over and above suspecting that at the root of it is some illicit sexual practice into which I've never been initiated, being too much of a proletarian.

Everything English seems to be 'traditional' nowadays. God knows, you can't even walk into a high street supermarket without being regaled by shelves of 'traditional' goods, whether it be packets of ginger biscuits or bars of soap. And everything you buy besides, from a table lamp to a digital clock seems to be modelled on 'traditional' lines – which generally means it's been given a wood-look plastic fascia and brass-effect finish.

All this is not helpful for us as a nation. It's bound to affect the way we see the modern world. All it takes is for someone to drop a cheese on their way home from a market and for the next 300 years there's a cheese-rolling contest at the same spot. Or some creepy-crawly falls into a mixing bowl in Burslem, and the traditional Potteries Spider Cake is born. And it's getting worse too; nowadays we seem so hell-bent on establishing new 'traditions' that if a couple of blokes get together for a drink in a pub a few weeks running before you know it people are weaving tapestries of the scene and sticking their fingers in their ear and singing folk songs about it.

The concept of 'heritage' is just as bad. The idea's become meaningless; or if it has any meaning it's not in the general sense of being what we've inherited from history, but rather, very specifically, what we've selected from history to define what we think of ourselves. So all this Black Rod bollocks thumping about in the cellars of the House of Commons pretending to look for explosives at the start of every new parliamentary session – now that's defined as 'heritage' because it's all bound up with the Gunpowder Plot and thought to be important because of what it says about our attitude to parliamentary government.

But what about other aspects of our past where England has an unparalleled track record of exploitation, whether it be sending kids up chimneys at home or getting coolies hooked on opium in China? You don't see many Wedgwood plates commemorating that, do you?

Heritage! Tradition! Doncha just love 'em both? In the gift shop in Blenheim they were selling boxed sets of coins from 1966 with pictures of the then England football captain Bobby Moore emblazoned all over them.

1966, for God's sake! The year we won the World Cup! The *only* year we won the World Cup!

Part of our heritage maybe, but sadly far from being traditional.

★

Back on the boat Em was the first to notice that the moorhen wasn't in its customary place on its twig and that the bread we'd left for it that morning remained untouched, even by any of the flocks of scavenging ducks that can usually be relied upon to patrol any patch of English water on the off-chance of finding floating carbohydrate.

I took this as a bad omen, and now that the floods had finally abated and the river was open once more, I determined to move back to the Thames and head for Bristol at the first opportunity. I'd anyhow stopped on a mooring restricted to a 14-day maximum and I was overstaying my welcome. As I made preparations to go the next morning – as sad to leave Thrupp as I've ever been to leave anywhere – I noticed a moorhen a little further up the canal hovering about another trailing branch. Now don't get me wrong. I'm not saying it was the *same* moorhen, but this one did seem inordinately interested in my departure and – was I imagining this? – did it seem a little sad to see me go?

'Of course it isn't sad,' said Em, when I pointed it out to her. 'And yes, you *are* imagining it. It's just a bird – and a particularly dumb species of bird at that. It wouldn't even recognise you if you were its mother, let alone an anthropoid like you in the equivalent of an ocean liner.'

Later I drove her to the station, and, as she left me, she kissed me lightly on the cheek. 'Get a grip, Steve,' she said. 'Or at least make an effort to get a grip.'

I cast off as soon as I could, feeling a new lease of life now I was on the move once more.

It was two hours before I realised I was travelling in the wrong direction.

SIX

Reading *Narrow Boat* you'd think that May to September 1939 had been the perfect English summer. Except that if you go back to the facts, you find it wasn't actually that good. During three of those five months, temperatures at Kew were below the average for the time of year; and in one month – August – it was exceptionally wet with rain falling pretty much every third day.

My stay at Thrupp had given me the chance to finish the book again and I'm not embarrassed to admit that I found it as emotionally affecting as when I first read it. There was something strange and haunting about it which was compulsive; and I was attracted by its style too: its curiously stilted language that could sometimes be lyrically beautiful, sometimes archaic. It surprised me that after so long the book was still capable of capturing that mystical sense of the English canal landscape I'd first felt on holiday with Dave all those years ago when the waterways had resonated so deeply inside me.

Yet even as my heart warmed to it, my head was warning me there was something inherently dangerous about its sentimentalisation of the canal environment and its appeal to a lost and better England. It was like Rolt's version of the weather: it wasn't objective truth, more a reflection of what he was *feeling* at the time. War was declared in September; and the summer was the last period of peace for six years. He was on his honeymoon. He was in love and ecstatically happy. Of *course* it was sunny. How could it have been anything else?

Not that you'd know much of background events from the book. It's not until you get to the conclusion you find out about the war, and the honeymoon isn't mentioned at all. Indeed, Angela herself only merits a couple of references in the text, one of them when she brings up curtain fabrics from London while they were fitting out the boat – a role that hardly does justice to her importance to the whole project, let alone her independent spirit.

The truth is that the love affair that most inspires *Narrow Boat* isn't the one with Angela, but Tom's romance with England, the English landscape and English tradition. It jumps out at you from every page. Which is curious really, because this obsession with the past stands starkly at odds with his job as an engineer where he was involved in the cutting edge of the contemporary world.

It was a paradox he recognised himself, and as he got older he finally came to realise that he despised much of what modern life stood for. His England was an England in which people's self-worth grew organically out of the work they did and the pride they felt in that labour – something he believed had been lost by modern industrial processes. This is why the boat people so captivated his imagination, even though their way of life was on its last legs. For Tom Rolt, the life of the boat people *was* their work, and that engendered its own culture in the songs they sang, the stories they told and the pubs they drank in.

Never mind that what they did was mostly grinding and repetitive labour carried out in filthy weather at all times of the year. Never mind that even then most of them were reduced to virtually begging for work, and that to get any at all, they – or the companies that employed them – had to cut margins so low that what could be earned was only just enough to keep a family above the breadline. Never mind either that given the opportunity, most canal people would (and did) abandon this relentless treadmill as soon as there was a viable alternative open to them.

Despite its lack of documentary realism, it's not difficult to understand how a book the tenor of *Narrow Boat* – written as the curtain came down on an age of colonial certainty – should have such a hold on the imagination of those facing the insecurities of a new age in which the very nature of work itself would change. No, what's more difficult to comprehend is that it *still* has that allure in today's cynical world. For a start, even the events the book describes didn't happen, or at least not in any real sense. Yes, of course, Tom and Angela actually travelled the route, and it would be silly to claim that there isn't at least a loose relationship between things that happened and the description of events in the book. But what appears in the book is embellished and selective: it's artefact – fiction not fact. For the most part *Narrow Boat* is just a confection constructed out of nothing more tangible than Rolt's fanciful imagination and his regret for times past.

The world of the book isn't a real world any more than those fantastic castles of traditional narrowboat painting are real. Both are idealistic representations of a romantic dream. This sort of stuff can be comforting for a while, but I got to the stage where I couldn't stomach any more of it. The relentless whimsy was bad enough, but I realised that I was trying to find Tom Rolt in the book, and Tom Rolt wasn't there. Instead there was just a vague shadow, evocative enough of the real man for me to recognise it as him, but without enough substance for me to grab hold of him.

I imagined him sitting writing at the desk he'd built specially on *Cressy* for the purpose, his shoulders stooped and his head slightly hunched over the keyboard of his typewriter, smoking as he always smoked. Sometimes in the book it's as if you can hear the very intonation of his voice across half a century. Yet even so, you can never get to him or his world, which seems another age away, as far removed as if he'd been a Victorian.

Thankfully for my purposes, *Narrow Boat* wasn't the only thing Tom Rolt was writing that summer. As he and Angela travelled slowly northwards, winding through the Midlands' counties and into Derbyshire and Staffordshire, he was also keeping a log of the journey which he'd begun the day he left Banbury, and which would become his major reference years later when he came to write his autobiography. He kept this log for the whole of *Cressy*'s cruising life, writing it every evening in his neat handwriting in an unremarkable red hard-backed notebook. This is an altogether more mundane piece of writing than *Narrow Boat*. It is factual and unadorned, filled mainly with details of distances covered, and locks passed, though there are occasional mentions of the weather experienced, and – sometimes – the meals he and Angela ate.

But it's no less powerful for that, for in the artless way of these things, the small details of personal narrative it records become part of the great tide of history itself. They were approaching Stoke-on-Trent, for instance, when they heard that Hitler had invaded Poland; and they were close to Middlewich in Cheshire on September 3rd when, confirming their worst fears, they heard the 'solemn' voice of Neville

Chamberlain on the radio announcing that Britain had declared war on Germany.

You won't find it recorded in *Narrow Boat*, but Angela broke down at the news, convinced not just that her and Tom's immediate plans had collapsed, but that their whole life together would suddenly fall apart too. Angela had reason to worry about being left high and dry by the war, since she had a good deal more invested in the relationship than Tom. It's said she was from royal stock and could trace her ancestry back to William IV. Whatever the truth of this, one thing was beyond dispute: in marrying she'd been compelled to confront the hostility of her father who'd harboured ambitions she might marry into a titled family, and who had turned his back on her when it became clear this wouldn't happen.

When he discovered she was planning to marry Tom he'd acted like a Victorian paterfamilias, summoning the Rolts to a meeting at the Cafe Royal in Piccadilly in London and demanding they make a settlement on his daughter.

It's hard not to believe this matter of Angela's estrangement from her family and the potential isolation to which the war could condemn her wasn't discussed between them the night war was declared, since immediately afterwards – and with a new purpose to their cruising – they moved to a mooring in the small Cheshire village of Church Minshull. It was from here for two months that Tom travelled to the job as a fitter that so nearly destroyed him at Rolls-Royce – but which, as a reserved occupation, at least kept him out of the army.

Again, there's none of this in *Narrow Boat*, where the most we're told as readers is that they made a 'prolonged stay' in the village. Because nothing, absolutely nothing – not even a world war – could be allowed to destroy the book's carefully nurtured alchemy of an idyllic English summer.

*

There was a change in my own plans too after leaving Thrupp. Well, there couldn't help but be a change seeing that I was travelling in an entirely different direction to the one I'd intended. But what the hell? Who ever *really* makes decisions in this world? Decisions are things that just happen to you while you're working out what to do next. So I decided to keep pressing on the way I was going.

Not that it mattered a lot. Em telephoned me as soon as she got back to the Crumbling Pile; there was a note of concern in her voice. Some drainpipe had started leaking while she'd been away, and the living room walls were soaked and mould had started growing across the paintwork. Or maybe I'm thinking of some other time she rang. Maybe this call was when she'd discovered that the roof had been leaking and that there was a wet patch in the bedroom and fungus sprouting across the ceiling. One way or another, the message was clear: I'd have to go back to London.

I cruised to the small village of Lower Heyford where a boatyard lies adjacent to a station, and where I could leave *Justice* and the Debsmobile safely. Frankly, at this point I wasn't too unhappy to get away from canals. All this obsessing about the weather of 1939 had only served to accentuate the fact that the weather I was experiencing was wretched. April had been the wettest on record; May the rainiest for seventeen years. Altogether the world seemed so waterlogged that it was a wonder *I* wasn't covered in mould, let alone the house.

The journey home was painless, though, predictably, the minute I arrived at Marylebone and adjusted to the pace of traffic, and the smell, and the noise, and realised just how unpleasant a city London can sometimes be, the weather changed dramatically. The thermometer hit 80, making London even more abhorrent than usual, and making me wish I'd never left the canals at all…

I live in Blackheath, which is south of the river and one of London's 'villages' – only unlike most of the others which are the contrivance of estate agents, this one's genuine. It has genuine village pubs, and genuine narrow village streets, and genuine village shops – which in the spirit of genuine village commerce charge premium prices for everything. Not that you can blame them, I suppose. With rocketing rents and rates in this part of the world, it's been a struggle for any traders who sell anything useful to keep going at all. So over recent years there's been a tendency for utility shops to close, replaced by restaurants which have spawned in such concentration that it would take you the better part of a month to eat your way round here.

*

All told, Blackheath's a pleasant enough area to live considering you're in one of the biggest cities in the world. The air's hardly alpine but it's cleanish all the same; and the area's green, and there's an overwhelming sense of history about the place which seems to guarantee you a role, however insignificant, in the great tapestry of events which have shaped England's past.

The 100,000 followers of Watt Tyler protesting against the poll tax in 1381 assembled on the heath, for instance; and Henry V was welcomed back from France here after his victory at Agincourt. Neighbouring Greenwich Park is one of the few places we know for certain that Shakespeare performed as an actor; and Henry VIII and his daughter Elizabeth were both born in the royal palace of Placentia which stood on the site of what used to be the Royal Naval College and is now Greenwich University. Elizabeth came to love Greenwich as her favourite palace and she spent a lot of time there. In fact, it was at Greenwich that Elizabeth signed the death warrant for Mary, Queen of Scots; and at Greenwich that news was brought to her of Mary's execution.

With its National Maritime Museum and its Royal Observatory, Greenwich is one of Britain's World Heritage sites, and there's so much heritage in evidence as you walk around that when you get to my age you sometimes fret about spending too long in any one spot for fear of someone slapping a preservation order on you. But Greenwich is that sort of place. Walking around its 'antiques' markets on a Sunday – and on a Sunday the *whole* of Greenwich becomes an 'antiques' market – is an object lesson in how to make a fetish of the past. There's stuff on sale here you couldn't have given away at a church jumble sale when I was a kid. Utility war furniture built out of plywood, flouncy 1950s standard lampshades in ruched pink nylon, pairs of patched and faded 1970 denim loon pants. Today it fetches a fortune.

What I always thought would benefit Greenwich – what I thought would benefit Britain – was something to counteract all these dusty reminders of our bygones: something uncompromisingly modern which could stand as a radical symbol of national growth and rebirth; some great project that would bind us all together in common purpose and proudly emphasise to the rest of the world the essential qualities of our national character.

Then they built the Dome.

The place has been the bane of my life ever since. At least in the past, if people knew where Greenwich was, they knew for the right reasons. Now, they only know it for one reason. And despite the fact that the Dome's become the O2, and the O2's become the most popular musical venue in the world, mention of the place is still the cue for elephants to start blanching, and for normally law-abiding citizens to pin you against the wall, the better to bend your ear about government profligacy.

It's a shame really, because as a building the Dome is an amazing structure, and I feel for it as I do for kids you've watched grow up. From the top of Greenwich Hill, close to the Observatory, is the best view of London you'll find anywhere, and from here I watched it gradually being built. One afternoon, spellbound, I gazed in disbelief as groups of men played out a sort of aerial ballet on the struts, swarming around the structure like flies and trailing behind them the massive cables which would support the roof but which in the distance looked as delicate and insubstantial as the threads of spiders' webs.

So after all this I couldn't get away in millennium year without visiting the place, could I? Though given the debate that was raging at the time, even this inconsequential resolution was ascribed the weight of ideological political statement. 'What! You're thinking about going to the Dome? Actually *going* there?' friends would gasp, a note of distaste in their voice as if I'd just announced I was inviting Osama Bin Laden for tea.

If I was told once that the cost of building the Dome would have built six hospitals, then I was told it a thousand times; though precisely what I was to do with this information and why it was imparted to me, I never properly discovered. Perhaps the idea was that once I got inside, I should surreptitiously establish a bridgehead for some massed SAS-type attack by the white-coated forces of the NHS determined to improve the quality of the country's primary healthcare. More likely it was mentioned in some dog-in-the-manger way so as to ensure that if by any accident I happened to actually enjoy anything I saw in the place, I should feel guilt that my pleasure had been achieved only at the expense of dying cancer patients.

Being cussed the way I am, this made me more determined than ever to visit; and so one morning, with a sort of jaunty V-sign to political correctness, I hopped on a 108 bus from the top of the road and sat somewhat self-consciously surrounded by groups of pensioners with heavy shopping bags who eyed me suspiciously, every one of them no doubt scheduled for a hip-replacement operation and holding me personally responsible for their low place on the waiting list. Fortunately I'd brought a newspaper with me, and so I was able to lose myself in the sports pages. In fact, I became so engrossed in them that the next thing I knew everything had become dark as if night had fallen. The only light now came from the glare of car headlights which were dazzling me through the bus window.

What had happened was that despite it being the biggest thing in these parts, twice the size of Trafalgar Square and an icon of international repute, I'd only gone and missed the Dome completely. I was now speeding through the Blackwell Tunnel towards the East End.

I got off the bus at the first opportunity, intending to cross the road and hop on another one going in the opposite direction. It seemed a straightforward enough thing to do; how was I to know it would all go wrong? How was I to know that the 'road' at this point is the A102 (M) – the critical designation (M) signifying a clamorous six-lane highway, solid in each direction with queues of commercial traffic belching thick exhaust fumes and kicking up the sort of racket that threatens to shred your ear drums? Take it from me, you don't negotiate roads like this with the sort of quick right-left-right they teach you in the Green Cross Code.

What you have to do instead is navigate yourself up and down a series of staircases decorated with X-rated graffiti until you emerge at a complex of traffic lights and roundabouts with roads splaying off in all directions. From here you keep catching brief and tantalising glimpses of your destination as you follow a pedestrian one-way system which takes you round on yourself by a route that spirals so much you eventually come to think that the only way you'll make further progress is by crawling up your own colon.

Eventually, when you've reached the point of despair and want to sink to your knees and die, you come across some ramps which lead to the opposite side of the motorway where you emerge at the roadside through a tiny hole in a twenty-foot-high concrete wall.

This – believe it or not – is the bus stop for the 108, Greenwich direction, and it is without doubt the ugliest and most unpleasant bus stop you're ever likely to encounter anywhere. It's just a lay-by in an underpass with the traffic spewing crap all over you while you're forced to stand terrified, only a kerbstone away from the traffic. Its design is so bad it is sadistic – which is rare, even in this country, where it sometimes seems we teach sadism as a course option in architectural schools.

Did any of the people who conceived this set-up ever spend one moment considering how human beings would feel using it? Did any of them ever wait for a bus there? Did they feel proud at what they'd built?

It was a freezing cold day, and with me were an elderly woman in her seventies, and a young black guy who was late for work, judging by the way he kept looking anxiously at his watch. The buses were officially scheduled to arrive at ten-minute intervals, but it was nearly half an hour before one finally turned up that day. When it did it went flying past us with its 'Not in Service' sign proudly displayed in the manner of a talisman intended to protect the driver from evil spirits. I made some involuntary cry of frustration, and the old lady smiled sympathetically as if to lend me moral support. The black guy pursed his lips and looked to the sky for deliverance.

It made me angry. Angry at the pitiful state of public transport in this city, yes; but even angrier at the stoical, uncomplaining forbearance with which people accept the situation when what they should do is riot, cause mayhem, spread civil dissent and foment revolution. Or at least get cross and complain to someone.

But perhaps nowadays people are just cowed. Perhaps they don't expect better. When a bus did finally arrive, the old lady was so full of amiable chat to the driver as she climbed on that I wouldn't have been surprised if she'd invited him back to her place later for a cup of tea. Even the black guy risked a smile as he flashed his season ticket. At this stage he was probably so relieved that he was actually going to get to work that day that inside he was doing an ecstatic song-and-dance routine.

I just said: 'Why have we been waiting so long? Is there a problem?' And frankly, if I'd caught the Queen farting at a royal garden party I couldn't have been made to feel more embarrassed for admitting I'd noticed anything amiss. The driver looked me up and down as if I was something that he'd just picked up on the sole of his shoe.

'Traffic,' he replied, as if this were some calming mantra which explained everything from the meaning of life, to Jonathan Ross's sense of humour.

I just thought, 'Sod the twenty-first century,' and I stayed on the bus and went back home.

SEVEN

Sorting out the problems at home took me a week; afterwards I returned to the boat at Lower Heyford. But I'd hardly been back an hour than I was beset with new difficulties. Driving to the supermarket to stock up the larder, the Debsmobile suddenly lost power. Without thinking I automatically started pumping the accelerator, and it was as if something that had become disengaged became suddenly connected again, for the car surged forward with such an alarming burst of speed I thought the most sensible thing was to put my plans for shopping on hold.

I turned tail and just about managed to splutter back to the boatyard before it gave up the ghost. Afterwards I sat for a moment or two cradling the wheel, pondering my next move. Nothing was clearer to me than that the Debsmobile required serious professional attention. This just about took the biscuit, coming on top of the hassles I'd had at home with the Crumbling Pile – ones I'd managed to address only by the application of great wads of currency to the greasy palm of some dodgy builder I'd found through the Yellow Pages. I felt everything was against me, and that the car had joined the Provisional Wing of the Army of Inanimate Objects in what seemed to be a war of attrition being personally waged against me by Fate itself.

I lifted up the bonnet and prodded around a bit. This might have been more profitable if I'd had so much as the first idea of what I was doing. It gave an impression of expertise though, and pretending to a know-how you don't possess is always a good strategy with a broken-down Triumph Herald. It was once such a common car that sooner or later someone who has taken the thing apart a dozen or more times is bound to appear out of the woodwork and diagnose exactly what's wrong with it.

Sure enough, after a few moments one of the engineers at the boatyard emerged from a workshop, rubbing his hands on an oily rag, which is an infallible sign of someone who knows what they're doing.

'The main cylinder on the clutch, I should say,' he announced after a cursory glance. 'Buggered,' he added, if I hadn't quite grasped the technical point he was making.

'Exactly what I was thinking,' I nodded – an assertion that, admittedly, may not have been the epitome of truthfulness, but which at least was voiced with the right degree of professional panache. The nodding helped too, because I don't know if you've noticed, but people who deal a lot with machinery always do nod a lot. They spend a lot of time spitting on the floor too. And they smoke those rancid roll-ups with wet ends which gives them an air of proficiency even if makes you want to throw up looking at them.

Unfortunately I then blew it completely, for instead of taking off my jacket and proceeding to fix the said problem by recourse to a new main cylinder which I should have been able to produce routinely from my back pocket, I said somewhat timidly, 'I think I'll just call... er... the RAC.'

When he arrived the RAC man was absolutely delighted to see the Herald, and you can understand it really since how would you feel if you'd spent a lifetime learning how to repair cars only to wake up one morning and find they'd turned them into computers so that fixing even a jammed window needed programming skills? At least with a Triumph Herald, if something goes wrong you've a fair chance of being able to patch it up with a pipe cleaner and a blob of chewing gum.

Not this time, though. This time it was more serious. This time the car would have to go to a garage.

'Main cylinder on the clutch,' the RAC man explained.

'Buggered,' I interjected confidently.

He nodded, spat and reached into his inside pocket for a packet of Old Holborn.

He'd got me down as a pro by then, you see.

*

Without a car to get me to the supermarket I was in trouble in Lower Heyford since it's hardly a teeming metropolis. In fact, it's not even a proper village really. Most people who live in the place either work in London and commute by rail, or they don't work at all since Lower Heyford is one of those pretty Cotswold hamlets which people retire to when they've made their pile. Though it has a delightful church, a quaint village green and a hundred picturesque cottages trailing honeysuckle around the door, it's only got a couple of shops. OK, I grant you, this may be two more than you find in most villages nowadays, but it doesn't exactly provide untold opportunities for culinary creativity. Especially for someone like me who fancies himself as a bit of a chef.

Nevertheless I managed to hunt down a chicken joint and a couple of onions so that along with some garlic and ginger left over from my last stay, I was able to knock together a chicken and lentil curry: a sort of soul food that makes you so as you couldn't care less that your car's just been towed off to a garage where you just know you'll get a bill so steep it'll make your eyes water.

Make them water instead with the food. Try it; it's a version of a Madhur Jaffrey recipe, one of those one-pot curries which is perfect for cooking in cramped spaces and which tastes just as good in June as it does midwinter.

A Recipe
(For two people)

Skin and cut up a couple of chicken joints, and put them in a pot with a small teacup of red lentils, a roughly chopped onion and a teaspoon of turmeric if you've got it handy (but don't worry if not, since its function is mainly cosmetic, making the dish look a fabulous yellow as opposed to a murky grey). Chuck a couple of sliced green chillies in there too if you have them.

Cover all this with about three-quarters of a pint of water into which you've crumbled a chicken stock cube. Or use genuine chicken stock if you want to be posh.

Bring to the boil and simmer for 20 to 30 minutes, ensuring that: 1) the chicken cooks through so you don't kill yourself with botulism; 2) the lentil sauce in which it's cooking attains the consistency of a purée (add more water if you think it needs it, or boil some off if it's too liquidy); and 3) the sauce doesn't burn on the bottom of the pan as it's prone to do.

Stirring occasionally helps all round.

When the dish is getting near to completion, thinly slice a couple of garlic cloves and fry them in a little vegetable oil until they brown lightly. Stir them into the pot along with the oil in which they've been cooked. Sprinkle in some chilli powder according to taste, and add a handful of chopped fresh coriander leaves if you can get hold of them because it really does add to the flavour. Don't fret if you haven't though – a bit of chopped greenery of any sort will make the dish look pretty on the plate.

Serve with plain boiled rice.

Puzzling, isn't it, this love affair we English have with Indian food? It's reached the stage where chicken tikka masala has taken over from fish and chips as our national dish. Sometimes I have to pinch myself to believe that I'm not dreaming, so much have the English changed in this respect over my lifetime. The word 'revolution' hardly describes it. When I was a kid, English food was watery mashed potatoes and overcooked cabbage; it was bland slabs of meat fried to the consistency of leather, or stewed to a mush. The idea of eating anything spicy was an abomination, and anything with garlic put you outside the bounds of polite society.

Like olive oil, garlic was one of those ingredients categorised under the disparaging heading of 'foreign food'. But these were the days when recipes for a Continental Salad advised you to rub the bowl you were going to use with half a clove of garlic – a practice which was fine if you were going to eat the salad bowl.

My parents were typical of their time. They were suspicious of anything unfamiliar – which was probably why, being the cussed sort, I first got interested in cooking. An added incentive was when I got interested in girls. As a bloke, it was true, my stomach was the quickest way to my heart. But it wasn't that different for women. I learnt soon enough that a good meal was the quickest way to get them into bed. My mother and father probably suspected as much, since they'd always be sniffing around me apprehensively whenever I took a girlfriend out.

'You've not been eating any of that *smelly stuff*, have you?' my dad would ask, reluctant even to name the offending ingredient. And then, before I could answer, my mum would add: 'You've not been forcing Liz/Susan/Judy to eat it too, have you?', as if my idea of a wild night out at this juncture in my life was pinning young women to the floor and popping garlic into their mouths. Believe me, with their prejudices I reckon my parents would have preferred me to give my girlfriends babies rather than the sort of foreign filth flavoured with an ingredient they associated less with cooking and more for its faculty to deter vampires.

Remarkable then that before they died they'd both acquired a taste for garlic and were shovelling the stuff down their throats as if it was going out of fashion. And not just in curries, either. Or even in foreign food. My mother was particularly addicted to it and put it in traditional English dishes like Hot Pot, and Liver and Bacon. I swear that at one stage it was even finding its way into her breakfast cereal since she used to walk around first thing in the morning reeking of the Paris Metro.

It was the same with chilli. In the past my mother only had to detect a trace of the stuff in food to go pogo-ing around the table, waving at her mouth as if her sincerest desire was to wish it a speedy departure from her face. Towards the end of her life though any of her recipes could come in what she called 'Delhi-style', which was another way of saying the food had so much chilli in it you'd suffer third-degree burns swallowing it.

It makes you wonder what English cooking actually *is* nowadays. There's a sixteenth-century village pub in Lower Heyford, a chocolate-boxy thatched building with a flagstone floor and windows which look out across the village green to the old village church and the River Cherwell. Nowadays it's more of a restaurant than a pub, and not a bad restaurant at that, except that you'd be hard pressed in this most English of villages to find a genuinely English dish on the menu.

It's almost as if, having embraced food from other countries, we've discounted our native cuisine to the state where we lack any confidence that we've actually got one. This has led to the crazy situation where supermarkets stock produce from the four corners of the earth, yet can't find shelf space for a locally made pie. In France supermarkets are forced by law to sell regional cuisine, and I can't help thinking that if village shops in England did the same thing, they could get ahead of the game by offering customers something which the big stores won't.

We undervalue food as part of our national identity. Standing on the heights of Lakeland, the Malvern Hills or the Long Mynd in Shropshire, we're understandably proud of our landscape; yet we curl up in embarrassment at the mention of faggots, chitterlings or brawn, the Bath chap or the Bedfordshire clanger. Yet in their own way both landscape and food have made us what we are.

*

Just down the towpath from Heyford church – beyond Heyford Bridge where the main village road crosses the River Cherwell

– is Rousham Park House, a splendid country pile built for Sir Charles Dormer in the early part of the seventeenth century and amazingly still in the same family today.

It's built in the Tudor style, the main wing with three bays, the centre one proudly crowned with a leaded cupola, and the whole thing topped with a battlemented parapet which gives the building a gracious, solid feel. Apart from the replacement of some of the original glazing by sash windows in the nineteenth century, it remains pretty much unspoilt; and since subsequent extensions have been built in the same style, there's a pleasing unity about the place which is the sign of good architecture.

Rousham Park House is open to the public a couple of afternoons a week throughout the summer, and the garden – which is far-and-away its best feature – is open daily. However, don't expect to be pandered to, for the place doesn't make many concessions to modernity. You visit the house on its own terms, not yours; and this means that Rousham is never going to be the sort of place to attract the coach parties like Blenheim, since it doesn't encourage rowdy kids chasing about disturbing its calm. In fact, it doesn't encourage kids at all, so if you're a theme park sort of family on a search for a fun experience, I'd give this one a miss since there's not so much as a cafe or gift shop here, let alone the hint of a white-knuckle water ride.

Instead you're invited to bring a picnic and treat the place as your own. Fortunately, not a great many people do this, so that as you wander around in isolated tranquillity, you have it to yourself and can almost imagine that it *is* yours. I visited on one of those dog-day afternoons you sometimes get in June when there's hardly a breath of air to disturb the exquisite stillness of the day, and when the sun is so high in the sky it throws shadows as sharp as knives across the green, luxuriant countryside. It's only a short distance from the canal, but I cycled there for the ride. The extra height of the bike allowed me to see over hedges and walls so that long before I arrived I caught tantalising glimpses of the house through the open parkland which surrounds it.

My route took me down a narrow private lane which leads to the tiny village that is part of the Rousham estate. At the bottom there's a compact church, surrounded by bulbous close-cropped yew bushes; and what was once a small school and a clutch of cottages which were built as homes for estate workers, and which probably still are since today Rousham is a substantial working farm around which – a final charming touch, this – wanders an impressive herd of rare-breed long horn cattle.

Such was the extent of my poor preparation for this trip that although I knew of the existence of the house, I wasn't sure that it was actually open to the public so I wasn't confident approaching the place. I made myself as inconspicuous as possible in the hope that if I got stopped, it wouldn't be before I'd got close enough to the house to at least be able to say that I'd seen it.

But it isn't easy to be inconspicuous riding a bike down a country lane. Especially a bike like mine which has so many chips and scratches on it, repaired with so many daubs of different coloured paint that Joseph's dreamcoat is a bit on the dowdy side compared to it. All the same, imagine my surprise as I was making my way around the side of the house to be confronted by someone screaming at me.

'Two pounds! Two pounds!'

The voice belonged to a woman who stood at the top of a small flight of steps leading up to the main door of the house. She was batting balls across the lawn with a warped wooden tennis racket for a couple of mangy Collies. I could only imagine this was an unconventional way of exercising them. Either that or she was stark raving mad. Or maybe both. She had wild flyaway hair the colour and texture of a starched sheet, and she was wearing a shapeless Indian skirt of 1970s vintage, with a torn grey cardigan draped across her shoulders. 'Two pounds! Two pounds!' she shrieked again. And then, as if anticipating what was in my mind, she said, 'Saw you coming down the drive. Thought you looked a bit shifty. Thought you might be trying to avoid paying.'

She seemed to find this prospect highly amusing for she broke out into a long, throaty laugh. Another tennis ball went skidding across the lawn and the dogs raced off in pursuit, snapping at each other as they ran and scattering in their wake two or three of the miniature chickens which I'd noticed for the first time were scratching about the grounds in great quantities.

They were very peculiar creatures. They seemed to be wearing little pairs of flared trousers made of feathers.

'Belgian Booted Bantams,' the woman barked, making much of the explosive alliteration of the words. 'Supposed to have come over a couple of hundred years ago in a crate of furniture,' she explained. 'Been here ever since.'

Paying over my entrance fee, I wandered into the recesses of the garden which is built on a steep bank of the River Cherwell. It isn't actually a very large garden, but it gives you that impression because new and startling vistas constantly open up as you walk around. The design is the work of William Kent, who may be a household name to anyone interested in this sort of thing, but who isn't exactly up there with the Capability Browns of this world for an ordinary Joe like me whose horticultural knowledge doesn't extend much beyond knowing the route to the local garden centre.

It's all very classical with Italianate porticoed temples and meaningful statuary of dying gladiators and the like, but it's arranged so that you keep seeing things from different perspectives. This is OK as far as the statues are concerned since on the whole these tend to be predictably located and not much given to ambulation. But trust me, the illusion it creates can be spooky if there's anything around that actually *is* moving.

I kept seeing people dressed in the same clothes. I thought there'd been a job-lot of flowery blue skirts and cavalry twill trousers on sale in the local Oxfam shop. It was the only way to explain it. Finally it dawned on me that the retired couple who I first saw sauntering around the pond was the same couple I'd seen earlier on the terrace, and the same one that moments before I'd glimpsed close to the wood. In the confusion of the garden's twisting paths it just didn't seem possible.

Mind you, the bottle of ice-cold wine I brought with me in a flask and sipped with my sandwiches didn't help my grasp on reality that day. Afterwards I dozed off undisturbed on one of the lawns, sheltered by a wide chestnut tree until suddenly it seemed to be evening; and a perfect evening at that, still and balmy with the failing light luminous above the fields, and choruses of wood pigeons softly serenading me as I cycled back to the boat. I took an indirect, meandering route, and in one of the villages I passed, I stopped for a couple of pints of Hook Norton bitter which I drank gazing through the bar window as a perfectly spherical, shimmering sun sank behind the horizon.

I must have looked glazed when I turned back towards the bar. The landlord looked me up and down appraisingly as if weighing up his options were I to be so unwise as to order another drink.

'I take it there are no drink/driving rules on pushbikes then?' he asked pointedly.

EIGHT

A few years ago you'd have moved heaven and earth to avoid staying on a boat a moment longer than you had to in Lower Heyford or its sister village Upper Heyford, a mile or so north up the canal. The waterways guidebooks warned against it, and there were signs posted along the towpath for those rash enough not to take them seriously. Nevertheless, every so often you used to hear of people who'd stopped there for an afternoon nap, or worse, attempted to moor there overnight.

Their lives were never the same again.

Never mind that beforehand they might have been one of those impassive, steely nerved types who become Olympic marksmen or bomb disposal experts: afterwards they'd mutate into excitable hysterics – the sort who go for a high jump record whenever they're startled. The kind that look at you as if you're Hannibal Lecter when you approach them on the street to ask directions.

You can blame the Americans for this. Until 1994 Upper Heyford was a base for the United States Air Force strategic air command and its fleet of F1-11 supersonic fighters. It was one of the bases that in 1986 was used to launch Operation El Dorado Canyon on Tripoli from which the Libyan leader Colonel Qaddafi only just escaped with his life. Which is a strange thing to contemplate, and as good a demonstration as I can cite of how small a world we live in; for as you quietly slip past the village and navigate Allen's Lock, which is really the only thing that identifies the place from the canal, it's difficult to believe there could be anything conceivably linking this secluded Oxfordshire hamlet with the hot and dusty North African capital.

Yet it's the reason you never stayed around this area. It was common sense really, since the skills a pilot needs to reduce Tripoli to rubble inside an hour aren't ones you get sitting in bars drinking Bud and popping pretzels. When the base was operational, pilots would be out most days honing up their flying technique with an enthusiasm that took the Anglo-American relationship to a new level.

Such a close level, in fact, that they'd fly over this part of the world taking the heads off the daisies. It was bad enough if they buzzed you during the daytime while you were cruising, since you half expected it. And anyhow, they travelled at such speed that they'd be gone before you knew it – even if they did leave your ears resonating for hours afterwards. But it was worse if you *weren't* expecting it, and much worse by far if you'd been incautious enough to moor for the night and were asleep, so that the shock of the experience could leave your nerves very badly affected.

Not to mention your bed linen in need of laundering.

I often used to wonder whether the people flying the planes were actually aware of the boats and whether they were playing games with us. After all, it must get pretty boring skimming across the top of the world so fast your face distorts. Much more entertaining surely is to pass the time with amusing diversions – *Enemy narrowboat armed and proceeding at 7 o'clock. Request permission to attack* – that sort of thing? But then I met a man who knew about these things, and he told me that those babies (by which I take it he meant the F1-11s) travelled so fast that even if they were looking out for a boat and spotted one, they'd be over Belgium before they could react to it.

For all I know the decision to halt regular flying from Heyford could have undermined the very security of the western world, but I was still delighted when the decision was taken, for it re-established this section of the canal as one of the loveliest and most rural stretches of its whole route; and in particular it made it possible to tie up overnight peacefully at Somerton Deep Lock, which to my mind is the epitome of a perfect waterways mooring, and a place I've stayed so often I've probably got squatters' rights if I was ever to assert them.

The lock, four miles or so north of Upper Heyford, takes its name from nearby Somerton village, and it lies in the shallow valley where the River Cherwell and the canal are so close together they're only separated by a narrow water meadow. It's an enchanting spot with a view which in any other country in the world would be called spectacular, only in England a place only ever merits being called that if it's associated with mountains and high forests. This is sad because in its own way the gentle 360-degree patchwork panorama of undulating pastureland that you see from Somerton Deep Lock is just as breathtaking.

A simple cottage adjacent to the lock is the only sign of civilisation – but far from detracting in any way from the attractiveness of the spot, it adds to it, dovetailing into the landscape naturally as if it's always been there and was always meant to be. It's an example of what nowadays is given the grand name 'vernacular architecture' – which is just another way of saying that it's the sort of unconsciously elegant design that was created by people whose first concern was to build houses people could live in.

This is very different to contemporary architects who build places no one in their right minds would want to live in. This should be given a grand name too: it should be called 'crap architecture'.

The cottage at Somerton is a very simple two-storey structure, with eaves at a steep angle which makes the building seem larger and more dominant than it actually is. A lot of canal architecture is attractively functional like this. Old warehouses, for instance, which are almost classical in form; maintenance yards, which sometimes take your breath away with their harmony; or even the charming but commonplace humpback bridges which crop up all over the country.

As far as I know the lock cottage at Somerton, being so remote, still has no mains electricity, and is lit as it has been for years by a 12-volt system powered by a wind vane. There used to be no mains running water either, and what fell onto the roof was collected in large butts. In those days the place was totally self-sufficient since it wasn't attached to the sewers either, and all its waste 'grey' water went straight into the canal and everything else into a cesspit.

For many years, despite its remoteness and lack of mod cons, it was occupied by a couple who used to work in London. Since there's no road anywhere close, they used to moor a skiff with an outboard motor below the lock and they used this to cruise to the nearest road bridge where they kept their car. If ever you moored at Somerton – and there was a period I could never travel up the Oxford Canal without spending a night or two there – you'd see them when they got back. On fine evenings they'd invariably take a walk along the towpath accompanied by their three enormous cats which would follow at their heels like spaniels, and which would even answer to their names the way dogs do.

They were fearsome brutes, these creatures, totally unlike your normal domestic moggie. They were the size of small rottweilers, and they had the same temperament. Normal cats might aspire to the odd mouse as a reminder of their feral past; these were satisfied with nothing less than the ferocious mink that populate these parts, which they hunted down in a pack. One of them was even said to have chased and killed a fox on its own – which, knowing the creature in question, I can easily believe. Trust me, if you stood too close to it, you could sense it sizing up your leg with the sort of rapt attention that cats normally reserve for cans of Whiskas.

The cats and their owners left Somerton a few years back, probably forced out by the floods that regularly swamp the countryside here and which must make commuting a pretty unreliable business. With so much rain, the fields were in flood when I passed and I didn't feel comfortable stopping. Instead I pressed on a few more miles to Aynho Weir Lock where the canal and the river, after having carried on a flirtatious on-off affair for so long, now consummate their relationship in a brief and passionate union as they cross at right angles.

It's another lovely spot, and an unusual one too. Eighteenth-century canal engineers were building arterial highways for haulage transportation, and they didn't trust the unpredictability of rivers which they avoided as far as they could, so that this sort of thing only happens at one or two places in the whole country. The lock here is odd as well: it's a lozenge shape, designed to be bigger than it need be so as to feed water from the river into the canal. Water supply was always a problem for the early canal architects. Nowadays the lock itself is the problem – or at least it is to single-handed boaters in craft more than fifty-foot long which for some reason always seem to get slewed across the chamber or jammed against the odd angle of the walls.

Getting through Aynho Weir can be a bitch. My tip if you ever get stuck there is not to panic. Don't automatically rev the engine up as high as you can in the hope you can somehow force your way against the natural elements. Instead, take stock of the angle at which you're jammed and the relevant forces which the boat engine will create against the rudder. Consider whether the propeller might be fouled. Examine whether you're caught in the cross current, or held by wind, or somehow impeded by floating detritus under the water. See if the brass on the boat is clean. Water the plants. Floss your teeth.

Then rev the engine up as much as you can. More often than not you'll find the problem has solved itself.

Otherwise you could try screaming at the boat: 'Come on, you bastard, move... MOVE!' is a favourite of mine. Or alternatively: 'Shift, you useless heap of moribund pig iron! SHIFT!' – something of that sort. It may not help you get away from the lock any quicker – certainly not as quickly as a more powerful engine would. But who knows? It might make you happier, depending on how you're feeling about yourself at the time.

We single-handed boaters have to develop specialist techniques like this to make up for what we lack in... well, for what we lack by being stupid enough to cruise single-handed and not have anyone around to help us when we get stuck in places like Aynho Weir Lock. Travelling on your own, even the most mundane of tasks – things you'd hardly think about with someone else on board – can become major logistical operations.

Take tea-making, for instance. Normally as a bloke this is an easy one. You just bark out a demand to the nearest female in the sort of confident manner you use when you're a pig who rules the world. But even as a woman, getting a cup of tea on a boat is hardly the most difficult thing in the world. You just fix a bloke in your gaze, lower your voice an octave or two and start to whine through your nose, adding the word 'luv' to everything you say.

That's 'luv' as in 'Make us a cup of tea, luv,' or 'I could murder a cuppa, luv.'

You can't do this cruising on your own though. On your own there's nothing for it but to stop the boat, moor up and put the kettle on. Except that if you're under way and making good time, or if you can't moor because it's too shallow – well, there's no alternative but to brew up on the move, which is a tricky operation requiring precisely the right knack.

We used to have a boat where the cooker was just a step or two under the steering position so you could leave the boat to its own devices for as long as it took to rush downstairs, fill a kettle and strike a match. The worst you risked was a bout of embarrassment if you crashed into the bank while a fisherman was watching you. With *Justice* though – an altogether grander vessel – the kettle and teapot are in the front cabin nearly fifty feet away, so you have to use a different technique. You have to slow the boat down gradually, bringing it to a halt in midstream. Then you have to run up the narrow side gunnels as fast as you can before the wind, or the current, or what's left of your momentum, drives you off course; or worse, before some other vessel appears from around the bend to find this inland *Marie Celeste* blocking the way ahead.

Take it from me, this is not an easy manoeuvre – and sometimes it hardly seems worth it just for a cup of tea. I mean, you can survive without a cup of tea, can't you?

But what do you do when you're desperate for the toilet?

If you're a bloke, then there's just too much of a temptation to cut corners. I don't know many men in the middle of the countryside who won't try it on the move, regardless of the fact that they're attempting to control themselves and 20 tons of solid steel at the same time.

It's a recipe for disaster.

Even in the middle of nowhere, miles from the nearest village, you can count on the fact that at the very moment you've got things underway you'll be disturbed by some farmer's daughter out riding, or by a gaggle of ramblers on a country walk. Tell me, why is it that ramblers always seem to be inexorably cheerful people? And why is it that they always seem to come down to the towpath on the blind side of a bridge? You may think that because canal boats move gracefully and slowly, so do those navigating them; but let me tell you that there is nothing in the world that moves faster and with less elegance than a single-handed helmsman caught short at the tiller with his privates on parade.

*

It was getting on a bit by now, past eight o'clock and way beyond the point I should have found a mooring for the night. I was close to Kings Sutton, which is a devil of a place to get to from the canal, but which is an appealing village scattered with clusters of thatched cottages fringing a wide green. At one end there's a pub, and at the other a handsome church which has a main spire buttressed by four smaller spires that give it the appearance of a space rocket. The canal here used to be a favourite overnight mooring of mine, but sadly not any more. Nowadays, appealing or not, tying up at Kings Sutton you face the same sort of discomforts you once did at Lower Heyford – only the problem isn't the noise from American planes but the din from our very own, home-grown, M40 which at this point skirts so close to the canal that it's like being on the central reservation.

It's heartbreaking because as you approach Kings Sutton from the south, there's an ideal mooring on a bend opposite a lush meadow where an old oak tree spreads lazily across the towpath. Manthe afternoon I've spent there, stretched out on the roof of one boat or another, shielding my eyes against the hot summer sunshine listening to the cricket or Wimbledon on the radio. Many is the evening I've spent with friends sipping chilled wine while the smells of the barbecue fused with the heavy scents of the evening air.

Gone. All gone now. Gone in the name of progress. Like the peace of the Birmingham and Fazely Canal as it edges towards Staffordshire, shattered by the roaring M42. Like the calm of the Trent and Mersey Canal, fractured by the A38 thundering towards Burton upon Trent. Like the aching serenity that was once the River Soar in Leicestershire until they upgraded the A6 and destroyed the whole valley. Gone. All gone for the sake of ten minutes or so off a journey between one ugly conurbation and another, from one no-hope suburb to the next.

Cruising the canals is the fastest way of slowing down; it gives you time to think about things and I've often found myself musing about what happens to all these saved minutes of motorway time. There'd be hope for the future wouldn't there, if all these movers and shakers of the modern world were to spring from their BMWs to devise new and better systems of justice or more equitable financial structures to rid us of poverty and obliterate hunger and disease? But don't you just know in your heart of hearts that they'll be flopping in front of the box like the rest of us once they've got home, so exhausted at the stress of their journey they'll need twice the time they've saved just to recover from it?

I pressed on for a mile or so towards Twyford Bridge to get some peace and quiet. But even here the wind was in the wrong direction, carrying the sound of the traffic my way so that there was this annoying low burr in the air as if some demented insect was flying around inside my head. It was the same at Grants Lock another couple of miles further on where the pretty lock cottage was once in the middle of nowhere until they built the motorway on the hill overlooking it. In fact, the sad situation today is that a stretch of canal which the guidebooks once described as amongst the prettiest and most rural of the whole British canal system has been so sacrificed to the motor car that there isn't a decent rural mooring to be had in the eleven miles between Aynho and Cropredy.

Oh well, you might think, not much of a world crisis there, then.

But surely you don't have to feel particularly concerned about boats, or canals, or even Oxfordshire, to see that something fundamental and irreplaceable is being gradually lost. Take it from me, for I've seen it pottering around the waterways year after year at 3 mph, this destruction has been duplicated in a thousand different places in a thousand different ways over the last twenty years. An ugly new estate here, a by-pass there; a formless concrete bridge in one place, a vile new supermarket somewhere else.

If we're at all concerned about the landscape of England then it must be apparent that we're not so well endowed with beauty spots in this overcrowded island of ours that we can afford to lose what few we have in the surreptitious way that is happening. We pay lip-service to conservation but in practice what this really means is just the gentrification of certain parts of the countryside while so much of the rest disintegrates under stress from the modern commercial world.

I've seen too much of this sort of thing on the canals – the creation of a sort of national theme park, a *Reader's Digest* England where certain segments are designated 'areas of outstanding beauty' or 'sites of special interest' – parks that lie across the land like so many sterilised, lifeless laboratory specimens. Meanwhile the rest of the country's left so much to its own devices that even when our most common species of flowers and birds are threatened by pollution and overdevelopment no one seems to give a damn.

Eventually I finished up mooring in Banbury town centre, just above Banbury lock. It was dark when I arrived, and as I was tying up I was somewhat startled to catch sight of a shadowy figure standing against a wall watching me. It was a man in his twenties, perhaps a little older. Once my eyes had adjusted I could make out a dog at his feet which I concluded he must have been taking for a walk before I'd arrived to distract him.

'Bit late to be boating,' he said.

I smiled and nodded noncommittally, not keen to encourage conversation. I didn't want to be rude, but I was tired. I'd much rather have been inside the boat with my feet up. I'd much rather have been half-way through a bottle of beer.

'Come far?' he asked.

Still fiddling with my ropes, I grunted something which at first I didn't think he could have heard for he launched himself into a nostalgic eulogy on the beauty of the route I'd just travelled. It took me a while before the penny dropped. When it did, I realised with some surprise that he knew the canal very well, very well indeed. But not because he'd ever cruised it himself, or even walked it; but because he'd seen bits of it a hundred times as he'd driven down the motorway in his car.

'Surprised you've decided to stop here,' he said at length.

'Here?'

'Well, you know, in a town. After passing through all that terrific countryside, I mean. It's… well, it's a bit of a noisy place to stop, isn't it?'

And at that moment, as if to give force to what he was saying, a massive bread lorry turned at a nearby set of traffic lights, making the boat vibrate as it changed gear.

Yes, there was no denying it: Banbury *was* noisy.

But at least you *expect* a town to be that way.

NINE

So after all that soul-searching about where this trip should start, I'd finally washed up in Banbury, where it should have begun in the first place. Mind you, when I woke up the next day it didn't *seem* like Banbury. It had been at least a year – longer – since I'd been back, and as I gingerly prised open the front doors of the boat and poked my nose into the morning sunshine, I was regaled with the startling sight of a massive new shopping centre which in the interim they'd built around the lock. It was so close to where I was moored I could read the bargain offers on the price tags in Woolies.

Well, that's Cherwell Council for you.

Cherwell Council has a complex relationship with the Oxford Canal. As the local authority for Banbury, it's responsible for a town that owes a massive debt to this waterway which once brought it prosperity. But for years now it's given every impression of hating the canal.

Now I call that a complex relationship. I certainly don't understand it anyway.

In the late 1700s when they were building the canal to connect to the River Thames and London, the promoters ran out of money when they reached Banbury, and so for twelve years it ended at a basin near the centre. This was the municipal equivalent of winning the lottery. Soon the place became a busy inland port which prospered beyond anyone's wildest dreams. Canal basins like this aren't uncommon in towns, and they can provide a focus for urban renewal, as they have in Wigan, or on a larger scale in Birmingham and Manchester where whole new districts of cafes and restaurants have been fashioned out of what was until recently derelict land.

Not in Banbury, though. In Banbury they filled in the basin. To build a bus station.

This imaginative spark of town planning didn't exactly bode well for the canal when the idea for a shopping centre was first mooted, especially since some of the early proposals for the development would have threatened the small dock which for more than two centuries had been located in the town. It was known as Tooley's, this dock, after the Tooley family who'd bought it in 1900 from a man called Chard who'd got it from a family called Neal who'd bought it in 1864 from Benjamin Roberts who'd acquired it from someone called Evans who'd been running it since the 1790s when it was first built.

History notwithstanding, you got the sense that Cherwell Council would have preferred to have bulldozed the place along with the basin, except that it was listed as an historic monument and protected.

When I first went to Banbury, Herbert Tooley – Bert, as he was known – the son of George Tooley who'd bought the dock at the turn of the century – was still living on the site in a small, shabby caravan. You'd see him sometimes pottering about, an old man stooped with age and not in the best of health; though he always seemed contented, and determined to die where he'd lived and worked for most of his life. The place then was still a focus for anyone with an interest in boats or inland waterways. It was a working dock – one of the precious few where there was still the equipment and expertise to repair wooden boats. But it was also something of a shrine to the survival of the waterways, for it was at Tooley's that Tom and Angela Rolt fitted out *Cressy* before the honeymoon cruise of *Narrow Boat*, and it was there they kept returning whenever the boat needed repairs.

They did so in the winter of 1940 as they were taking the boat to Berkshire, where Tom had managed to get a job that allowed him to leave the hated Rolls-Royce. His new work was in a foundry in Hungerford, and though it paid less than he'd been earning, the priority for him wasn't money, but to get away from the nightmare of factory life which had so horrified him. The stop at Banbury was only scheduled to be a short one for maintenance, but in the event it lasted far longer than anyone could have predicted for the weather suddenly turned very cold and *Cressy* became trapped in thick ice which was to paralyse the whole waterways system for months.

Tom had begun writing *Narrow Boat* during the honeymoon cruise, provisionally entitling it *Painted Ship* after the reference in Coleridge's *Ancient Mariner*; but he'd found it impossible to carry on with the project while he was working and had laid it aside. Now, with time on his hands, he returned to it with a new enthusiasm, writing at his desk in the cabin through the long winter evenings. Sometimes he read what he'd written to Angela. 'Very occasionally I would make a tiny suggestion or criticism,' she commented years afterwards. 'They were not well received.'

The enforced stop in Banbury gave Tom a perfect opportunity for sustained work and when he left in March 1940 the book was all but finished except for a concluding chapter or two. Angela has left us a description of him working on *Cressy*, hunched over his desk, his face creased in concentration, tapping away fast and fluently at his typewriter using just two fingers. Occasionally he'd get stuck and he'd sit 'chain smoking, lighting one cigarette after another until suddenly the words flowed again'.

Brief though it is, reading her account of Tom at work always sets my imagination racing. I picture them at Tooley's, where in my mind's eye it's a cloudless frosty night, and there's a hazy winter moon casting a pale light over the ice, highlighting the thin pall of smoke which hangs over the basin from the chimneys of *Cressy* and the other boats moored there. Sometimes it's almost as if I can taste the acrid coal burning in the boat stoves which is bitter in my throat; but it's mixed with sweeter smells too – the odour of different woods: the sawdust of rich elm like almonds, and the sweet resins of pine shavings rising from the dock.

At first, so quiet is it, and so dark, I think it must be midnight, or maybe even later; but then I become aware for the first time of the clamour of the town which seems so far away, even though it's so close; and I catch fragments of drifting conversation from women in headscarves queuing for buses. Gradually it dawns on me that it must be earlier than I think. I hear the deep, hollow echo of a caulking hammer ringing against the planking of a boat. It is coming from the dock where men are still at work. Finally I realise with a faint yet disturbing sense of disorientation that it's still only the afternoon, not yet five o'clock and maybe even earlier…

★

Actually, it wasn't much past seven in the morning but I realised as soon as I stuck my head out of the boat that I wasn't going to be able to get much of a lie-in that day, for the shopping centre wasn't finished and workers were swarming all over the place, banging and crashing together anything that looked as if it might raise the general sound level a decibel or two. I washed, threw on some clothes and walked over to examine the new development which I'm pleased to report was nothing like as awful as I'd anticipated. Even Tooley's was better than I thought it would be, since after a good deal of protest the planners eventually conceded to it being kept as a working boatyard, albeit a somewhat unusual one in that it's clean and orderly and covered with an ugly framework that makes it look like a greenhouse.

Tom Rolt would have hated it. I think he would have found its orderliness too antiseptic. OK, the old place was always a bit of a mess: a cross between a junk yard and a back-street garage. Yet for all that, it was comforting and reassuring, and spoke of another, kinder world governed by a different set of values than those of today.

I visited the museum up by the famous Banbury Cross where I was looking for pictures of old Banbury. Staff there were aware of how important the Oxford Canal once was to the town, and how crucial Tom Rolt was to the survival of contemporary waterways, but for a long time they didn't have any pictorial record of how it used to be around the canal when *Cressy* was moored there that first winter of the war.

Luckily, a short time before my arrival, someone had walked in off the street and donated a set of black and white photographs of the area taken around that period. They'd been shot with nothing more distinguished than a box Brownie, but you could see by the value ascribed to them by the staff that they'd been pounced upon as if they'd been Daguerre originals.

In the old days, the area adjacent to the canal on the town side was a confusing maze of small streets lined with higgledy-piggledy workshops and warehouses, two- and three-storeys high – most of them dating, I guess, from Georgian or early Victorian times. Factory Street, where Tooley's was, led from the Market Square to a lift bridge over the canal. It was an extremely narrow thoroughfare – so remarkably constricted that Tom Rolt even commented on it in *Narrow Boat*.

So it wasn't as if I had no mental picture of the place.

Even so, back at the boat, examining the photographs properly, I was still astonished at the gulf that existed between my imagination and the reality. Factory Street was narrow all right – but much, much narrower than I'd thought. In fact, it was more like an alleyway than a street – no wider than a car in places. And yet I'd always known it was like that, hadn't I? Why should it have surprised me so much to see pictures of it? My mind began racing as I played over every scene I could recall that had ever taken place there, painfully struggling to re-impose the characters of my imagination onto their new backdrop.

There was one photograph in particular that I kept staring at: a picture taken looking down the street, past Tooley's and the row of half a dozen cottages which used to stand at the side of it – one of them, incidentally, where the Tooley family had once lived. It dated from sometime in the early 1960s, later than the other pictures, and not long before the area was demolished. The cottages are virtually derelict and some of the upstairs windows are swinging open so that you can just about make out the ragged edges of broken glass clinging to the surviving frames. Downstairs some of the windows haven't even got frames and have been ripped out; and the vandals have even pulled away parts of the wall underneath, revealing raw courses of brickwork gaping like open wounds.

I found this image oddly compelling. Yes, the mental picture I had of Factory Street wasn't entirely divorced from the reality of what Factory Street was; but the reality as depicted in the photograph was nevertheless a different sort of reality. Like all photographs, it was a moment frozen in time; a single instant in the infinity which surrounded it. But this gave it a strange and melancholic quality that obsessed me in a way I can't account for fully even now.

It was taken in bright sunlight, and the poor contrast this created makes the image difficult to see. The foreground is dark and slashed with ominous shadow, while the brightness of the background burns out the detail of the lower part of the street in a sort of ghostly, blanched hue. For me the power of the image is that it catches Factory Street at the very point of its demise, for within a month or so there can't have been much of it left, and today no remnant of it survives.

You can just about make out its balance beams at the bottom of the street, beckoning you like a pair of open arms. I can never think of that lift bridge without sadness for eventually it was to become the setting for the final act of Angela and Tom's relationship – the very spot where she finally left him and where their idealistic dreams of an alternative lifestyle ended in what must have been heartbreak for them both. The two of them must have crossed over that bridge a thousand times during that first winter of the war when they were trapped in Banbury by the ice. They'd struck up a friendship with a boatman called Alfred Hone who was moored with his wife immediately opposite, so the bridge would have been the quickest and most obvious path between them. It's been rebuilt recently as part of the redevelopment, but for years there was nothing to mark it except the narrowing of the stonework of the towpath where it used to be.

Coincidentally it was there that I moored *Justice* on my second night in the town.

And a strange night it was too, very disturbed and restless. I'd not turned in until late, my mind burdened under the weight of where I was, troubled with so many imaginings of half-remembered events of long ago. I tossed and turned until the early hours, unable to sleep. When I finally did, I fancy I must have dreamt about Tom and Angela. I certainly recollect listening intently to some mundane exchange between a man and a woman I took to be them. It was about food, or shopping, or something like that. But then the conversation was suddenly an argument, and there were raised voices, and harsh words, and I heard an angry tearful outburst – though despite the volume, I couldn't make out clearly what was being said, and I couldn't understand what had provoked this clash between them. It made me unaccountably anxious, as if the antagonism between them was being directed at me.

At length I woke. I sat up suddenly, and became aware that my dream was actually real – or real in the sense that the voices were real and the argument was real. It seemed to be coming from the towpath, immediately outside the boat. Yet strangely, when I peered out of the windows into the gloom of a night illuminated only by the eerie sodium glow of streetlights, there was no one at all on the towpath. The only people around were two people in their early twenties, a man and a woman. But they were on the *other* side of the canal some distance away, standing against the water's edge in the pallid night-time shadow of the new development. However, seeing them was unnerving enough at that time in the morning, when you wouldn't expect anyone to be up. They were facing each other eye-to-eye and playing out some peculiar mime which seemed to involve the slow and mystifying movement of their limbs like a t'ai chi dance.

Strange, very strange. I went back to bed but I couldn't get back to sleep again for a long time, turning things over in my mind.

*

Sadly, the decision of Banbury Council to sacrifice its canal basin for a bus station wasn't untypical of the place. The town dates from Saxon times, but there are few buildings today much older than the seventeenth century, so one way or another a lot of Banbury has been replaced over the years, including its famous cross, which is a Victorian replacement for one pulled down in a fit of Puritan zeal during the Reformation. You can hardly blame the council for this though. Or for two Civil War sieges which left its castle in ruins. Even so, it says a lot for the town's sense of civic pride that the residents pulled down what was left of the stonework to rebuild their damaged houses.

But that's typical of the place too. People in Banbury don't seem as concerned about their past as people elsewhere. In the eighteenth century they even blew up their parish church rather than spend money restoring it. Predictably, given the importance it ascribes to such things, Banbury's new shopping centre incorporates a replacement bus station – which is a good deal more attractive that the old one. Mind you, it would have been difficult for it *not* to have been more attractive. The only thing that could be said in favour of the old bus station – apart from the fact that it was the best place in Banbury to catch a bus – was that it had a cafe which served a formidable mug of tea.

Soon after *Justice* was built, when she was no more than a steel shell, we ballasted her at Tooley's after having had a couple of tons of paving stones delivered from a nearby garden centre. It was tough work which involved manhandling the slabs one by one onto the boat up a narrow gangplank. In the specialist jargon of the inland waterways this is known as 'a bastard of a job', and Em and I wouldn't have survived it but for the sustenance afforded by the regular input of bus station tea.

Nowadays, with the old bus station demolished, if you want a good cup of tea in Banbury you are constrained to explore the cafes in the centre of the town where the general tendency is to serve you delicate china cups of hot water with what appears to be bags of wood shavings floating in them. Actually there is one place in Banbury where you can still get a fortifying cuppa, but it's brewed to such industrial strength you can feel the enamel dissolving on your teeth as you sip it.

It's tucked away in a back street which I had some difficulty finding, because recently – like most English market towns – Banbury has become almost unrecognisable in the summer months due to an annual outbreak of that pernicious disease *geraniumitis*, the main symptom of which is the appearance of a rash of brightly coloured bedding plants on every accessible inch of civic space. In its earliest manifestations, this condition was most apparent in concentrations of inconvenient pavement tubs, placed about knee height and ingeniously positioned to catch your shins as you were passing. Recently though the contagion has shown an alarming tendency to spread upwards, with plants colonising low walls and window sills, or any area at all which might comfortably accommodate a window box; and then afterwards – as they have in Banbury – spreading higher yet. The current fashion is to suspend hanging baskets from every available lamp post, slinging them so low that if you find yourself in the vicinity of one without knowing it and turn inadvertently in the wrong direction, you're in danger of losing an eye to a trailing lobelia.

Since I last visited, Banbury had become such a riot of plants that you needed a machete to hack your way up the high street. Mind you, a machete is a pretty useful tool generally in Banbury, especially on Saturday nights when the streets become awash with mobs of strapping farm-workers from the adjoining villages out for a night on the piss. Even for someone like me, used to kids in London, Banbury at the weekend still strikes the fear of God into your heart.

One night five or six years back I was having a quiet pint when a brick came crashing through the window and landed at my feet. Being an outsider I wasn't used to this sort of thing, though barely anyone else in the place even noticed what had happened. It was as if this sort of thing happened in Banbury every day of the week – which it probably did, and probably still does for all I know.

I remember there was a man standing at the bar who had his beer glass to his lips, and who – with the sort of indifference that passes for panache in these parts – finished his long draught without missing a swallow. My companion that night was a man with royal connections, and he seemed similarly blasé about what had happened – a response I put down either to his familiarity with the realities of contemporary England, or his sense of detachment from them born out of generations of good breeding.

I suppose I shouldn't blame Banbury for this. Its ambition to transform itself into a garden centre in the summer months is a common feature of English towns at the beginning of the twenty-first century. Sadly, so too is the propensity of its young to get arseholed on Saturday nights and start throwing building materials about. It happens all over the country, and Banbury's no worse than a hundred other places in this respect. Though I grant you it somehow *seems* worse because there's something about Banbury – the very name Banbury – which is so connected to nursery images of Fyne Ladies on Cock Horses, and so redolent of a better, less threatening past, that it somehow epitomises the genteel traditionalism that we have come to associate with towns of rural England.

And here's a funny thing: we still want to believe this survives, even when we live in rural areas ourselves and know better than most that it's a busted flush – a concept as dead and outdated as saving your virginity for your wedding night.

But Banbury. Banbury! Surely not Banbury, of all places? It's like a redoubt of Middle England falling to the invading hordes. The very idea of it pains me.

They really should have looked after their castle better.

TEN

So if we expect more from a place like Banbury because it's called Banbury, is there really something in a name then?

Take 'Zobo', for instance. As names go it's hardly a grabber, is it? It doesn't sound right for anything, notwithstanding the fact that on narrowboats we use a grate cleaner on our stoves called Zebo. It's a thick black paste and comes in a container so much like a toothpaste tube that knowing how stupid people are, I can't believe that at least one sad soul in this rich and colourful world of ours hasn't ballsed up at some stage and finished up with incisors the colour of coal.

A zobo is actually a sort of crossbreed domestic ox, related to the yak. It's not what you'd call a glamorous animal. Not a particularly speedy one either so you'd think it unlikely it would ever be appropriated as the name of a car. The Ford Zobo – 'Your passport to driving luxury'. It doesn't sound right, does it? It doesn't *feel* right.

Except that – improbable though it may seem – the name Zobo *was* used as the name for a car. Or at least for a time it was. It was a very commercially successful car, a vehicle still lauded for its elegant, racy lines and sophisticated engineering.

The car was the Triumph Herald, of which the Debsmobile – last left languishing in a garage in Oxfordshire with a crocked clutch – is an example.

'Zobo' was chosen as an early designation for the Herald after one of the staff was tasked to find a four-letter project code for a small car the company was developing. Given that any fool could have seen it was totally unsuitable as a name for a car, it was, paradoxically, an inspired choice because at this point in its history most of the vehicles being manufactured by Standard Triumph were hardly capable of being called cars either, being no more than the equivalent of large sardine cans with windscreen wipers.

The very names of the Standard range at this stage in its history smack of post-war austerity when the words 'British' and 'design' harmonised with about the same compatibility as 'Japanese' and 'prisoner care'. There was the Standard Eight, for example. And the Standard Ten. There was the Pennant, for heaven's sake – a vehicle that can genuinely be said to have defied all known concepts of aerodynamics, being modelled on the lines of an unmade bed. Sadly the Zobo wasn't much of an improvement, and one of the designers described the prototypes as looking like a 'mechanised bathtub'. Actually, I think he was just being kind. I've seen pictures of those prototypes and they do an injustice to the elegance of a bathtub.

Perhaps it's wrong to laugh at those early attempts of the British car industry to pull itself up by its bootstraps after the war. A lot was achieved at Standard under the chairmanship of Sir John Black who's remembered now as an autocratic dictator, but who nevertheless (or maybe as a result) managed to improve efficiency exponentially by introducing bonuses and paid holidays. Under

Black's leadership Standard went from producing 8,000 cars in 1931 to five times that number – 40,000 – by 1937. But times were changing across the whole spectrum of British life and a new generation forged in the war years was beginning to take over key roles in the country's industrial infrastructure – at Standard no less than anywhere else. In 1954 there was a boardroom coup and at what was to prove a significant period in its history the company fell into the hands of a group of men who weren't just talented managers but talented engineers too – men who'd been brought up with cars and engines, and actually liked them and knew what they were talking about when they discussed them. Men in their own way not entirely unlike Tom Rolt.

The new managing director was Alick Dick, who'd joined the company as an apprentice twenty years before. He was 37 years old and his appointment to the top job precipitated a whole host of changes as he promoted a group of younger, more enthusiastic men to be part of his team. One of the most important of these was Harry Webster who was appointed chief engineer, replacing the funereal Ted 'Grizzly' Grinham, who it was said couldn't see the merit in designing advanced cars. Which is, I suppose, a bit like saying of an Olympic sprinter that he can't see the merit of running quickly.

Webster was the same age as Dick and like his MD he'd joined the company as a young apprentice. George Turnbull who took over as boss of the company's experimental department was in the same mould; and though at 30 he was younger, he was another former apprentice for whom promotion represented the beginning of a long and renowned career, one that would eventually take him to Korea where he played a key part in launching Hyundai.

These and others like them at Standard Triumph seem to embody what England was in those days and looking at pictures of them with their thick-rimmed glasses and their fashionably narrow Italian ties I can't help but be thrown back to my childhood when all men seemed to look a little like this: when they all smoked untipped cigarettes such as Players or Park Drive and had swept-back hair held down with thick swathes of Brylcream, and when they all smelt reassuringly musty in the solid, dependable way that damp tweed does.

My own father was in the hosiery industry and an engineer too, though he wouldn't for one moment ever have used that term of himself since as far as he was concerned the only people who warranted that designation were men like Brunel or Telford – civil engineers responsible for projects which changed the world forever. At the very least they were academics who'd been to college and wore suits to work – which was something my father would never have dreamt of doing even though like most working men of that era he'd never venture beyond the front door without a collar and tie. In those days what you wore made a statement about you; it was a signal of where you lay in the hierarchical structures that characterised post-war Britain. My father always went to work in a casual jacket but as soon as he arrived at the factory he'd don a calf-length khaki overall which was a badge of his trade.

Regardless of what he called himself, my father was still capable of diagnosing and repairing those fearsomely complex knitting machines that were being installed all over the East Midlands during the 1950s. After years of low investment, industrialists had finally realised they had to do something to compete with Far Eastern countries which were beginning to export cheap knitwear into Britain. So they bought these monstrous things called Comets which were supposed to be the last word in new technology. My father used to take me into work with him from time to time at whichever Victorian mill building he was based – for skilled employment in the hosiery industry was easily had then and he used to move around a lot, sometimes even leaving one job on the Friday afternoon and starting a new one on the Monday.

As a child I found the factory environment overwhelming. The din terrified me and I couldn't understand how my father could show such astonishing detachment controlling these banks of machines that raged and screamed around us. He'd be on his feet constantly, literally running between the narrow aisles that separated rows of them while they spewed out great colonic tubes of what, he explained, would eventually become socks once they'd been separated and sewn up.

It was a numbing and repetitive process, carried out against such a brutal wall of noise that I wondered how anyone could stand it – except that like the people who worked in the place I soon stopped hearing anything after a while. Even so, my father could diagnose by sound when there was something wrong with any of the machines under his charge. He had the skill of being able to predict the advent of a problem by some minute change in tone or some scarcely audible whine; and when that happened he'd cock his head, concentrating intently for a few moments until he could identify the source of the trouble and decide which of the bank of red switches that controlled their power supply he needed to switch off in order to allow him access to repair the fault.

Sometimes if he thought he could get away with it he wouldn't even bother turning them off and he'd dive fearlessly into the very heart of the beast, emerging later with his face covered in grease and with flecks of fabric clinging to his hair, his task achieved as gloriously as if he'd been some knight in shining armour laying siege to a citadel for the sake of a maiden's honour.

Even as a kid I was aware of the danger he was courting, but at the time this just seemed the way that life was. Or at least the way it was when your only experience of it was through the TV and books. Everything seemed like a game and the world of grown-ups was the most exciting lark of the lot, filled with adventure and untold promise. I couldn't conceive of the darker realities of course, not then. I interpreted everything that happened as if everything was just for fun and nothing could ever harm you.

Eventually my father must have said something which alerted my mother to what he was doing – or maybe I even said something to her, who knows? But I recall one evening during *Sunday Night at the London Palladium* there was a row between them which finished up with her in tears screaming at him. My father scarcely reacted to the whole outburst; I remember there was a look of indifference on his face. The argument came down to money – as every argument between them did. I remember him saying he had to do things the way he did because he could earn more that way.

So he kept working the way he'd always worked – except that if ever I was around and he was repairing a machine which was switched on he'd give me a knowing, conspiratorial wink as if to seal my lips forever. But of course, by then my lips *were* sealed forever, even to myself. The fun had gone out of this game, you see. I'd begun to suspect that it was being played for much higher stakes than I could understand.

He nearly got his comeuppance. A few years after this, one of the hundreds of barbed needles that lay at the core of the Comets caught a gold signet ring he was wearing and nearly succeeded in stitching him up the length of his arm. He managed to wrench himself free in the nick of time and save the limb, not to mention his life. He never worked on an active machine again after that as far as I know. He never wore the ring either and he gave it to me soon afterwards. I'm wearing it now, as a matter of fact.

The men of that period had skills which to my mind seem so much more real than those we have today. This isn't to undermine contemporary expertise, for I'm sure I could never design and build a computer microcircuit, let alone write a programme that might utilise one. Nevertheless, everything today seems less *tangible* than the metal-bashing accomplishments of our recent past. And less commonplace too, for when I was a kid there were people like my dad all around me – engineers, mechanics, toolmakers – people who could work machines that made socks and shoes, knitwear and lace; people who could build diesel trains like they did at Brush in Loughborough, or construct cranes like they did at Herbert Morris next door.

No, we just don't play Premier League any more in this country as far as manufacturing goes; it's no use kidding ourselves that we do, or that we ever could do again. Times have changed inexorably and what we did best no one wants any more. Or they don't want it at the price we charge for it. Nowadays we do computer games and pop music, audio visual and a bit of prestige architecture; we can do fine art, design and fashion; and good movie effects. We can even turn a deal or two in the City when the conditions are right. And of course we can pull in tourists by the coachload, flogging them a carefully cultivated image of our past.

But this isn't anywhere near the tabernacle in today's church, and in our heart of hearts we know it, despite all the pap the politicians feed us about being at the sharp end of the future. The problem isn't that those old greasy craft skills are a thing of the past, but that they're a thing of the wrong sort of past. A past that's unmarketable. A past that you simply can't sell to anyone except enthusiasts and no-hope sentimentalists like me.

And anyway, inside a generation, so much of the expertise which made us what we are will have died out completely. Today even getting basic skilled work done is a major operation. Forget the cutting edge of new technology, have you tried getting a burst pipe repaired recently? Or a room decorated? In some parts of the country the only people who have any proficiency in these things are like top international opera stars and booked for years ahead. They charge the same sort of rates as opera stars too. The best that most of us can hope for is someone from Eastern Europe. Or the sort of fly-by-night cowboy who thinks he's doing you a favour by deigning to turn up at your house within a couple of days of agreeing to be there.

There didn't seem to be much in the way of traditional skills in evidence at the garage where I'd left the Debsmobile. When I went back to pick it up I found I'd accrued an enormously high bill for a new main cylinder in the clutch. Yet after I'd paid and driven away, the car began to play up again in a way entirely consistent with needing a new main cylinder in the clutch. So I turned round and drove straight back to the garage, only to discover that an instruction that was so express it might have been the 9.03 out of Euston had somehow managed to get garbled in translation.

'I thought we'd agreed you were going to replace the main cylinder in the clutch,' I said in such a reasonable tone I surprised even myself.

'Ah, I must have got the wrong end of the stick,' said the boss who – give him his due – sounded as if he was an expert in dealing with this sort of thing. By which I mean an expert in dealing with angry customers on the verge of ripping out his throat with their bare hands, the better to suck his blood.

He smiled at me. I smiled back at him.

I said: 'Strange that you should have misunderstood because if you look at your bill here' – I took it out – 'you'll see that you have charged me the equivalent of a couple of useful limbs for what you describe as – how do you put it? – "A replacement main cylinder on the clutch." Puzzling this, wouldn't you say?'

He pursed his lips. This was probably not the worst customer relations problem that he'd ever been called upon to resolve. All the same it was a tricky one.

'You see, you may think me old-fashioned,' I went on, 'but I'm left wondering, if you haven't replaced the clutch, and yet you've billed me for it, what exactly is it that you *have* done to the car? Am I, for instance, to expect it suddenly to surge forward with a new intensity as a result of some turbocharger you've inadvertently installed? Or maybe, unbeknownst to me, hidden in the bowels of this modest machine is a new in-car entertainment system complete with digital television and 360-degree surround-sound...'

Of course, I didn't say anything of the sort, every word of which – if you haven't guessed already – is complete fiction, like most of this book.

Instead I did what we English *always* do in these sorts of situations. I took the car back to the garage somewhat contritely, mumbling about there still being a bit of a problem and, if they could possibly find time, I'd appreciate it *very* much if they could look at it again...

The bloke in charge was, of course, totally unmoved by the fact that I'd already paid an enormous bill to have the car repaired. 'I'll try to get someone to have a look at it later this week,' he said, 'but I can't promise…' For which read: another sad sucker of a customer come for another dose of the same. I suppose this time I better at least get it half right.

And half right's about right too, for when I eventually came to pick up the Debsmobile – not later that week, or even the week following that, but the week afterwards when the garage finally got around to doing some work on it – I found that though they'd successfully repaired the clutch this time, for some reason they'd felt the need to drain the radiator to do it. And they hadn't bothered filling it up again.

The car began overheating so badly the thermostat showed temperatures high enough to roast a Sunday dinner. I had to stop at a house along the way to beg for water.

Lucky I noticed. Another few minutes and the engine would have seized up entirely.

Leaving Banbury on the canal you pass the Alcan aluminium factory north of the town and then go under a railway bridge and through a lock. Finally the canal swings under the M40 which – mercifully – now veers off in a totally different direction, the last you see of it, so that you can begin to enjoy the Oxfordshire countryside in the couple of miles or so before you reach the small village of Cropredy.

I was pleased to be travelling again and pleased to be away from the town and back in the countryside. Even after such a short absence it seemed somehow sweeter and fresher than it had before, somehow more luxurious and verdant. It was bucketing down as I left Banbury that morning but soon it eased up and the rain turned into a mist so fine it seemed to hang in the air, clinging to the hedgerows and the overhanging boughs of trees. Later, when the summer sun finally condescended to appear, everything around me began to glisten as if caught in the grip of a winter's frost.

Even *Justice* seemed pleased to be on the move once more and before long her engine settled into its regular soporific rhythm, like the slow and steady beat of a heart. At times like this she seems to be totally at one with the environment, her bow cutting through the water so gracefully she scarcely creates a ripple on the surface.

At Cropredy the canal passes under the main village road and almost immediately afterwards it enters the shallow cutting that leads to Cropredy Lock where there's a tiny humpback bridge at the bottom of a narrow street of thatched stone cottages facing the village church. For some reason I've never understood, the churchyard is at a higher level than the street. I can never pass it without the grotesque thought that one day it might give way and spill the bones of the village dead over the pavement.

Cropredy used to be a farming village but farms and villages don't go together nowadays. Residents complain about traffic congestion as soon as anyone takes a tractor on to the road, and however long a farm has been around there'll still be those who'll grumble about the smell and the noise it creates. Crazy, isn't it? In Oxfordshire this has led to the paradoxical situation where farms have actually been moving *out* of villages, relocating to purpose-built premises on the fringes as one did in Cropredy just a few years ago. Meanwhile, the old farmhouses and their outbuildings and barns are converted to what are euphemistically termed 'executive homes', that is, overpriced houses that cost a bomb and are out of reach to anyone with a normal job.

For some time I was uncertain how to respond to this process. Part of me felt instinctively that I didn't like it, but this was the part that lives in London and has a Londoner's metrocentric view of the countryside as a place where you go for long walks to get away from the rat race. This bit of me felt that the process was destroying the country village and everything it stood for. But I was born in the country and brought up in one of these villages, and I know as well as anyone that these rural communities are living, organic places which are constantly changing, and always have changed, and need to change again in the future if they're to survive in any real sense rather than just as fossilised fragments of the heritage industry.

Cropredy's a good example of the positive way it's possible for villages to develop. A casual visitor passing on the canal might dismiss it cynically as just another rural rest home for the retired on the fringes of the Cotswolds, or at best a commuter town for London and Banbury. But nothing could be further from the truth. In fact, Cropredy's a place with real soul.

And not just soul either: it's got two pubs, a small supermarket that doubles as a post office, a saddler, a signwriter, a craft shop and cafe, a welder, a bronze-casting foundry, a classic car renovation garage, an arts centre and a small music studio, a ceramics workshop – and God knows how many electricians, plumbers and builders, not to mention painters of so many different sorts that you'd be as well to be cautious employing one for fear you find yourself with a landscape on your living room wall when all you were after was a coat of magnolia.

Most important of all for the future, Cropredy's got a school of 120 kids, and an environment safe enough for them to grow up in. And I'll tell you one other thing: when these kids get older they won't all be as desperate as I was to get away from the countryside, because villages like Cropredy offer real opportunity to young people. Not just as pleasant places to live – because what youngster in their right mind is looking for *that* in their teens? – but as engaging places to live, places where things happen, and where a night out doesn't have to mean just kicking around the bus shelter, which was about the only option open to me at that age.

It's got a sense of fun about it, Cropredy, and once a year over one weekend in August it puts this part of itself on display when it hosts a folk-rock festival organised by the band Fairport Convention. Over the two days as many as 20,000 people pile into the village with a resultant colourful clash of cultures as young, dreadlocked New Agers, barefoot hippies and face-painted eco-warriors rub shoulders with the type of Miss Marple characters you find in Cropredy as you find them in every other English village.

These days if you visit Cropredy by canal for the festival weekend you need to plan well ahead. The towpath gets packed with boats, and moorings are at a premium. In the past you could turn up on spec on the Friday night and find somewhere to stay as Em and I did one year when we cruised up from Banbury with another boat owned by a friend who at the time was working as a restorer of historic wooden craft.

We arrived about seven o'clock on what was a balmy Arcadian evening, and with the music already filtering down from the stage, we moored as quickly as possible next to an old houseboat from Oxford which was up for the festival like us. It was the early hours when we got back and the scene that confronted us was dreadful. The boat we'd moored next to was now listing at an alarming angle. It was apparent it wouldn't be afloat much longer. Standing on top of it was a young guy almost in tears with panic, screaming for help.

He wasn't in danger; canals aren't particularly deep. But it was his home which was disappearing under him. Between bouts of hysteria he kept disappearing into the cabin and dragging as much as he could onto the roof, which by now was beginning to resemble the scene of a bomb explosion with bedding, lamps and clothes strewn over it.

Our friend surveyed the scene for a second or two, and while Em and I were aimlessly running about hither and thither, bumping into each other and tripping over our feet like characters in a Buster Keaton movie, he went back to his boat to retrieve a pail of that vile concoction called 'charlie', made of tar and horse dung which wooden boat builders have traditionally used to caulk the timbers of their craft.

Half an hour later the stricken boat was repaired and floating again, and the distraught owner had calmed down enough to start taking his possessions below deck once more.

Well, lucky or what? To have your wooden boat sink next to a man who repairs wooden boats for a living and who just happened to have some charlie on board because he'd been using it himself that day? I wonder what the odds against that were at a time when there probably weren't more than two or three people in the whole country capable of repairing a wooden boat.

But that's life, isn't it? Random, arbitrary and a bitch if you're not born lucky.

Which I was beginning to realise I wasn't.

I got a call from Em. Some other pipe somewhere in the viscera of the Crumbling Pile had burst asunder and no more than a month after sorting out one crisis it seemed there was another requiring my attention.

ELEVEN

Beyond Cropredy the Oxford Canal continues its gentle rise from the Thames valley by way of a series of isolated locks which nestle among rich and fertile fields. It was two weeks later and high summer by the time I got back from London – a considerably poorer man as a result of yet another wad I'd had to hand out to some dodgy builder for services rendered to the Crumbling Pile. The trees were now in full leaf, so as I cruised through what was still a season of incessant and unremitting rain, it was against the background of sound like a gently steaming kettle; a soothing monotonous sonata caused by myriad raindrops falling softly on the countryside.

The hedges were high and lush, threaded with dog roses and lined with thick bands of cow parsley; and along the remorselessly green towpaths were sudden vivid patches of yellow or purple where clumps of vetch had strayed from the meadows and now sat uncomfortably isolated, reaching upwards towards the sky for company, their curled tendrils twisted tortuously upon themselves. Cropredy Lock is followed by Broadmoor Lock, and after that Varney's and Elkington's come in quick succession until very soon you arrive at the foot of the short flight of six locks at Claydon which take the canal to its summit level.

There's something perpetually evocative about the names associated with canals, rooted as they are in folk memory. Many of the designations are predictable enough, and it doesn't take an archivist to work out why a bridge carrying the towpath from one side of the canal to the other might be called Crossover Bridge, or why the locks passing close to some village should unsurprisingly be named after that village. But many canal-related names are more reluctant to be deciphered, and they hint at a mysterious and lost past peopled by characters who established themselves in their own world sufficiently to be esteemed by it, but whose memory has eroded with time, and whose existence nowadays is only marked by this trivial nomenclature which has survived the years.

Who on earth was this guy Varney, and what manner of man or woman was Elkington? And was Broadmoor a real moor once?

You somehow feel that locked into English place names is a coded chronicle of the English past which could tell you so much if only you could crack it. But the same could be said about the landscape too, especially in the heart of these Midlands shires where the ridge and furrow patterns of old strip farming are still indented on the fields, and where the ghosts of a thousand and more abandoned villages lie just below the surface of the soil.

At Fenny Compton you pass through a straight cutting of almost half a mile which is all that remains of what once used to be a tunnel until they took the top off it in 1868. Nowadays, travelling north, it's the last straight of any kind that you experience, for you are at the high point of the canal and for the next eleven miles the Oxford winds around on itself and back on itself, arcing in a series of agonisingly tight bends so that steering a narrowboat you no sooner extend the tiller in one direction to turn one way, than you have to heave it in the opposite direction to go the other. The reason for these convolutions – as for so much else on the canal system – was the need to save money. Twisting and turning in this way, following the level contour of the land, the canal engineers avoided the cost of expensive locks to carry the waterway up or downhill.

The effect of travelling along a canal of this sort can be most peculiar, for it engenders a strange sensation of unreality. Early on misty mornings, or late in the evening when the onset of night blurs your perceptions, any sense of direction you have seems to dissipate and you can become hopelessly confused as to the way you're going. You pass a radio mast at one point, and this seems positioned to confound you, since when you first catch sight of it, it's ahead of you on your left-hand side; but then it disappears behind a copse, only to appear again behind you on your right. No sooner have you adjusted to this unusual configuration of the natural world than the damned thing moves again – and suddenly appears in front of you once more. This time you work out that it should be on your left. Except it remains resolutely and irrationally to your right. This is baffling, and so counter-intuitive that it's weird. So you promise yourself that you won't take your eye off it to ensure that it doesn't get up to any more of its tricks; but this becomes increasingly difficult as the canal swings around in ever tighter arcs until, strangely, what seems to be moving now is not you on the boat, but the radio mast itself, gliding gracefully across the fields…

Spooky or what?

Believe me, it *can* be on vaporous mornings when the mists swirl in wreaths above the water, playing around your bow like some malign miasma from the nether world. Or on those high summer's evenings after nine o'clock when the sun has set and when the onset of darkness seems halted in that uncertain lacuna between day and night so that the world appears to fracture and distort, and every small movement in the hedgerows becomes a threat, every screech of a bird or rustle in the trees a malicious affront to reason.

The corkscrewing of the Oxford Canal summit reaches its culmination in the journey around the 400-foot-high Wormleighton Hill where, if it's speed you're after, you'd be better quitting your boat and walking, since a five-minute stroll across the fields will take you to a spot you'd need three-quarters of an hour to get to by water. But it's worth leaving the canal at this point anyhow to visit nearby Wormleighton village, which the guidebooks recommend for its church and the remains of its old manor house, but which I think is much more valuable for the take it gives you on the contemporary world.

Now this may come as a surprise to anyone who's visited the village, for it seems about as far away from the contemporary world as it's possible to get. It's got neither a shop nor a pub, nor much in the way of a population; but instead sits resplendently severed from everywhere, a perfectly proportioned English village resting soporifically, apparently abandoned in a sea of Warwickshire pastureland.

But it wasn't always like this. In the thirteenth century in the time of King John its thatched manor house was the focus of a nearby community of forty or so homesteads which supported a population of several hundred people. It was an affluent place then, big for its time, and it bustled with the industriousness of labour, its fields busy at the quietest of periods, but almost frenetic during the harvest season when everyone who could walk would have been lending a hand with the crops and when the surrounding lanes must have been full of horses returning from the fields with heaving cartloads of produce for the barns.

Two hundred years afterwards though, everything had changed completely. By then hardly anyone lived in Wormleighton. This was because there'd been a boom in the price of wool and the manor had been bought by one of that new breed of entrepreneur who would inherit, if not the earth, then at least that bit of it in the rich and fertile Midlands plain where they could get rid of the tenants without much opposition and enclose the land for sheep pasture.

'So what happens?' explains Thomas More in *Utopia*. 'Each greedy individual preys on his native land like a malignant growth, absorbing field after field, and enclosing thousands of acres with a single fence. Result – hundreds of farmers are evicted. They're either cheated or bullied into giving up their property, or systematically ill-treated until they're finally forced to sell. Whichever way it's done, out the poor creatures have to go: men and women, husbands and wives, widows and orphans, mothers and tiny children.'

This enclosure movement seems such a distant issue for us today, a thing of such dry irrelevance that it's barely possible for us to conceive the suffering it must have caused as families who had no other means of earning a living were cast off the land which had been their birthright, forced to beg or steal, or throw themselves on the parish and the new Poor Laws which had been introduced to deal with the crisis. It marked the beginning of the end of that medieval social contract by which the wealthy, in return for their privileges, recognised their obligations to the common good.

And so John Spencer, farmer, who had bought the Wormleighton estate became a land rustler in the name of progress, and so grew rich on his profits and became Sir John. And 500 years later one of his descendants, Diana, married the Prince of Wales and a few years afterwards gave birth to the child who will eventually become our king, and to whom, if we love our country, we must all pay deference, honouring this sordid past as a legitimate justification for the present.

*

My meanderings through the countryside had by now developed their own routine. I'd stay a day or two in the same location and move off in the mornings, cruising until mid-afternoon at the very latest, never longer. Then I'd cycle back to wherever I'd left the Debsmobile, load the bike and drive back to the boat. The Triumph Herald is a small car, and the only way of getting a bike into it is by taking down the hood and jamming it behind the front seats. This makes it impossible to get the roof up again, and since there is nothing so designed to invite rain than someone in an open convertible car, I regularly got soaked to the skin.

Food became a high point of my day. I'd determined from the outset of my journey to eat well and avoid the ever-present temptations of canalside pubs and their consistent, if suspicious, menus of cow in various forms, whether cheap steaks, pies or casseroles. I'd got interested in Thai food and realised that as long as I kept a few basic ingredients on the boat, it could be cooked almost effortlessly.

Gui Paht Meht Mamuang Himapahn is a genuine Thai dish from the central part of the country: it's delicious and quick, and can be thrown together in a wok so there's not much in the way of washing up for anyone cooking in a limited space. The genuine version I give here is made with chicken, but in the past I've used pork just as successfully; and fish-lovers could just as easily use prawns, which I've done too, and which I can warrant is just as delicious.

Another Recipe

Cut a small chicken breast or small pork steak into strips and fry it with one or two chopped garlic cloves until it's cooked through. Towards the end of the cooking process crumble one or two dried red chillies into the pan along with a small onion cut into quarters. The onion needs to be crunchy when you eat it, so don't worry about cooking it thoroughly, though it does need to colour on the outside so as to rid it of the worst of its raw taste. When this begins to happen, add a handful of cashew nuts to the pan along with a teaspoonful of sugar. Brown the nuts gently and toss everything around a bit until it's heated. Finally, sprinkle a tablespoon of fish sauce and half a tablespoon of soy sauce over the mixture and stir well. Serve with plain boiled rice.

The drawback to this meal is that it's a bit short of vegetables to be bowel-friendly, so if you're not too wedded to the idea of total culinary authenticity, do what I do and add a few frozen peas to the rice, or maybe throw a few Chinese leaves into the pan after you've added the sauces. Or perhaps some green beans cut into strips, or even a sliced fennel bulb. Actually, you can add any vegetable that's available…

The Oxford Canal summit ends at Marston Doles where a peculiar warehouse with a couple of outside walls built at the angle of an arrowhead marks the beginning of the picture-perfect flight of nine locks. This takes the canal past the foot of the hill after which Napton-on-the-Hill is named. From the top where a windmill dominates the countryside there's a wonderful view of the surrounding Warwickshire Plain, and usually I find it hard to pass the place without stopping and having a walk around. Napton is one of those unassertively comfortable English villages which fit the English way of life perfectly. It's pretty, but it's not prissy-pretty; and the old houses sprinkled around its narrow streets and village green are mixed with a significant amount of honest new building, so that you get a sense of the place – as you do in Cropredy – as a working village, living without the threat of the conservation order and the kiss of aspic death that can so often result from it.

I have good memories of Napton. Em and I spent Christmas afloat here one year. On another occasion, walking up the hill in the early evening, we watched enthralled for almost an hour as a family of badgers rooted around for food – the only time in our lives that either of us has seen such a thing.

However, on this occasion I had to pass through without stopping. The problem was that after a decade of fighting every bit of brickwork on the system, *Justice* was beginning to show her age and she was scheduled to go into a boatyard at Braunston eight miles further on where she was to be pulled out of the water the next day for her hull to be repainted. I had no choice but to press on and it was dark when I passed under the elegant double-arched cast iron bridge that marks the approach to the village.

There's a paradox about Braunston which is immediately apparent the first time you visit. On the one hand it's generally accepted as the capital of Britain's inland waterways system, but on the other it's actually a tiny place – not much more than a single street stretched along the escarpment of a low hill and bounded on one side by an imposing parish church and on the other by a poky council estate. The canal winds along the bottom of the hill, where years ago were a series of commercial boatyards which have adapted for the new canal age and now cater for the leisure boater with repairs, chandlers and repainting.

Braunston's significance to the canal system comes about because of a historical accident of development which left it, if not the Spaghetti Junction of the canal world, then about the nearest thing you're ever going to get to it on water. In other words, it's the junction of various different routes where you have to be alert to the possibility of taking a wrong turning. This is very unusual on canals, almost unique in fact. With the exception of Birmingham where the remains of old loops and arms can still make getting about a bit tricky, canal boating in England isn't likely to tax your map-reading skills. Or putting it another way, among the canon of oft-quoted inland waterways axioms, 'I'm lost' does not exactly figure highly.

Essentially, what canal navigation comes down to is ensuring that you're not going south when you should be going north. Or vice versa. This is not exactly an intellectually demanding challenge since the northerly direction generally takes you to cities like Leeds, Liverpool and Manchester, whereas travelling south you generally end up in London. On rivers it's even easier. There, if you get confused, there's even a clue to which direction you're heading. Going upstream the flow of the water will generally be against you; going in the opposite direction it's more often than not in your favour.

Braunston, however, can be a challenge for crews who arrive after having journeyed at 3 or 4 mph for up to weeks on end with nothing more sustaining than enormous quantities of beer to facilitate their passage. It lies, you see, along the central arm of the H-shaped junction of the Oxford Canal with the Grand Union, so that boats have the unprecedented choice of routes available to them. True, one is the route they've already travelled, and another involves negotiating a flight of locks and a tunnel more than a mile long. Even so you'd be surprised at the number of intelligent people, many of them with university degrees, who find themselves going to Coventry when they thought they were travelling to London, or discover they are heading to Leicester when they were certain they were on their way to Oxford.

Its geographical location ensured that Braunston became an important canal centre. In the past when the canals were haulage arteries it was convenient for getting to places; nowadays, situated in the centre of the country close to motorways, it's just as convenient to get *to* by car. So it's become a popular place for people to keep their boats.

And they do. In their thousands.

As a result, it seems that not a week passes without a move to dig up another local field as a marina, presumably with the ultimate intention that this bit of Northamptonshire should become a sort of inland lake where boaters who are attracted to the canals can moor their floating cottages without the inconvenience of actually having to go anywhere in them in order to enjoy the authentic waterways experience.

Parts of Braunston are already like a vast caravan site on water, and such is the ethos that pervades the place that on some weekends in summer it can be like walking through suburbia for all the crowds of people waxing their paintwork and buffing up their already gleaming brasswork to ever greater levels of lustrous shine. Sometimes you can't help but think that there's a game being played out here whereby you establish a sort of social dominance over your neighbour by the luminescence of your boat.

What's been clear to me for a long time is that in the caste system which has become modern canalling, *Justice* lies some way down the pecking order. Even putting aside the question of her battered hull, the sad state of her brasswork alone is enough to guarantee her social ostracism in Braunston. It's not that boats in Braunston have to be absolutely pristine, more that they can only be scruffy within set parameters. So it's OK if you're thought of as a 'working boat' or can otherwise claim connection – however far removed – to the days of canal carrying. Then you can fill your hold with scrap metal and cover your cabin in engine oil, for a bit of rubbish and a patina of grime will be thought to add to your authenticity.

But show up in a modern boat which could do with a lick of paint and you'd think you'd farted in church for all the raised eyebrows and averted glances you get from the towpath traditionalists.

Much store, you see, is set by the authentic in Braunston – or at least the authentic looking, which is a totally different thing. There is much in the way of the application of washers to the hulls of boats so they appear to be rivets, for instance; and much grooving of steel to make it look like planks of wood. There is also a lot of talk about the 'right' way of doing things on a boat, whether it's the 'right' way to go through a lock or the 'right' way to turn at a bend. One of the things it is most definitely *wrong* to do – in fact, it's a heinous crime by canal standards – is to carry your stern rope coiled over your tiller, and there are many arguments advanced by the traditionalists as to why this should be the case, each of them studiously designed to avoid the glaringly obvious fact that it's far and away the most convenient place to keep it.

I *always* keep my rope over my tiller on *Justice*.

I do it mainly to annoy them. I do it because I can't see the use of maintaining sterile tradition just for the sake of it, especially when it runs contrary to common sense.

Like *Raymond*, for instance, a boat which generally sits at Braunston after a long and expensive 'renovation'. For many years *Raymond* was home to Arthur Bray, one of that extinct breed of boatmen known as 'Number Ones' who actually owned their own craft rather than having worked on boats owned by carrying companies. After his death there was a move to conserve the boat to commemorate the life of a man who was a link to a past canal age, and who in his final years had become something of a living monument in Braunston, moored as he used to be in one of the most prominent positions in the place, and the sort of bloke who when you were passing always had time for a chat about the old days.

So they started work on the boat, trying to preserve what had survived the ravages of time, and replacing what hadn't. Only it soon became apparent that very little actually *had* survived. Certainly they couldn't salvage any wood from *Raymond* and this presented the renovation team with a thorny problem. You see, *Raymond* was a wooden boat…

Which is why today when you see her, though she's an exceptionally beautiful craft – one of the few built recently to the design of a traditional wooden working boat – she's hardly what you'd call original. Indeed, the only parts of her that are genuine are the iron brackets or 'knees' used to fix the sides to the bottom – and a single cupboard door in the back cabin.

I think Arthur would have seen the funny side of all this, though I'm not sure he would have seen the purpose of it, given how much it cost.

★

I was pulled out of the water the next morning, a process that involved manoeuvring *Justice* over a rickety trolley which was then hauled onto the bank up a track like a tram line. It all happened so quickly. One moment I was wondering whether you could trust a boat to this Heath-Robinson contraption and worrying about whether I should have informed my insurance company about what I was doing; and the next the boat was up the bank in a single cloud of exhaust from a Land Rover.

Out of the water *Justice* was awkward and ungainly. She towered above me, her hull scarred and stained by her long cruising, and so high that after I'd climbed onto her by a precarious ladder I could, for the first time in my life, look down my nose at Braunston.

Which at least made a change from it looking down its nose at me.

TWELVE

*A*s meetings between great men go it wasn't exactly in the Stanley and Livingstone league, though you can't help but think that the effete literary agent and his wife on a day-trip from London must have felt they were in deepest Africa. After all, they lived in the heart of Bloomsbury, one of London's more fashionable areas, and in order to get to what must have seemed to them a god-forsaken spot they'd taken a train to Bromsgrove in the West Midlands and walked for more than a mile using a map to navigate.

They must have made an odd sight as they climbed the steep towpath by the side of the near-derelict locks: she with her bright violet-blue eyes and he short-sighted and deceptively boyish in his heavily framed glasses, the pair of them like a couple of fish out of water away from the city.

It was August 1945, a clear and sunny day, and only a few months after the end of the war in Europe. The place was a flight of locks at Tardebigge, just outside of Birmingham, and the literary London pair were Robert Aickman and his wife Ray, both of them only just in their thirties. They'd come to meet the author of a book they'd read recently which had impressed them greatly.

The author was Tom Rolt; the book *Narrow Boat*.

The Tom Rolt of Tardebigge – this Tom Rolt – was a totally different man from the one who'd left Banbury five years earlier. A lot had happened in the interim – so much that Rolt himself must surely have been pinching himself, wondering how it was that when everyone else's life had been torn apart by war, everything he'd planned for himself had fallen so neatly into place. He was still living on *Cressy* with Angela but the despairing and depressed engineer who'd left Rolls-Royce for a new job all those years ago had now become a successful writer, and that 'design for living' he and Angela had fantasised about for so long had become a reality.

How on earth had it all happened? And how had it happened so apparently painlessly?

The future certainly hadn't looked so bright after they'd left Banbury for Hungerford and Tom had started the new job at the foundry. It involved reconditioning agricultural equipment and although he liked the work well enough, the pay was bad and he and Angela were often left depending for survival on the small allowance that Angela's father still paid her. In the beginning Tom wasn't any more successful with his writing either and despite his attempts to get the book about the honeymoon trip on *Cressy* published no one would touch it. One company wanted him to print it at his own expense, another tempted him with an offer to buy it outright; but most of the major publishing houses just sent it back with the mandatory rejection slip. The final straw came when he sent it to a literary agent who unceremoniously refused to have anything to do with it. After that the manuscript was dispatched to a proverbial bottom drawer – though the reality on *Cressy*, where space was at a premium, was that it finished up in a suitcase under the bed.

'Poverty, like the toothache,' Rolt wrote, 'can play havoc with philosophers.' Eventually a meeting with an old friend led to the offer of another job and the Rolts moved back to the Midlands where, despite Tom's distaste for bureaucrats and bureaucracy, he took up a position with the Ministry of Supply. It was a bit of a sell-out for a man of his mettle – and he knew it. But at least it was a sell-out at a good price: his new salary was three times what he'd been earning.

Another bonus of the move was that it allowed him to continue writing, for though his new position as an 'Isolated Technical Assistant' in the dusty-sounding Department TT3 was important enough as war work went, it wasn't a high-pressure job. The department was responsible for the manufacture of vehicle spares for the services, and his work involved travelling around Birmingham liaising with factories. After he returned from his site visits he'd write up his reports at his desk on *Cressy* and then, working under the light of a paraffin lamp, he'd turn his attention to a new project he'd started: a second book, this one a philosophical treatise in which he was trying to marshal some of his ideas on the way that modern technology was destroying the ecological fabric of the earth.

This was a deliriously happy period of his life, and it was a creative one too. As well as the new book he'd started writing articles for small-circulation magazines. His main obsession was still what he called 'the tyranny of the machine' which he believed was altering the old relationship of people to the work they did and destroying the last vestiges of traditional craftsmanship in the process. But he was gradually beginning to write about other topics too – anything from surrealism to stage design. In short, he was becoming a professional writer and as such he was starting to come into contact with other writers of the same bent. One of them was the rural author H. J. Massingham.

Harold Massingham has been given a bad press since his death fifty years ago. Most recently Jeremy Paxman had a pop at him in his book *The English*, describing him as 'a townie who'd escaped to the Chilterns' and criticising him for producing 'book after book telling the English people that the Industrial Revolution "had destroyed the true England"'. Well, yes, Harry *was* alarmingly prolific, it's true: more than forty books in his lifetime and countless articles everywhere from the *Listener* to the *Times Literary Supplement* – not to mention a body of correspondence that would put most of us to shame, despite the way we make such a fetish of our emails.

It's true too that Harry's political perception of the world wasn't particularly penetrating, being what one critic described as 'profoundly reactionary' and based on 'an unusually bitter detestation of modern, industrialised, urbanised civilisation'. Or as someone else put it more bluntly, 'He was a crypto-fascist.'

This shouldn't be any great surprise; there were a lot of them around at the time. Despite everything we're told at school about the UK's plucky resistance to German fascism, the home-grown variety was always simmering under the surface on the 1930s. It may be a bit of a shameful secret nowadays – the sort of thing we don't talk about much in company – but its existence played a part in creating the conditions out of which the horrors of Nazi Germany were to spring.

Not that I'm laying all this on Harry Massingham. I'm sure he visited his mum regularly and was kind to his cat. Revisionist romanticism was par for the course at this time and not every idealist looking to the countryside for a vision of a lost England kept a pair of jackboots in the cupboard. Indeed, during the inter-war period the mythic past became alluring to intellectuals of far greater weight than him.

And it's not hard to see why. After the First World War ended, the remnants of those who'd survived the blood and the mud of Flanders and the Somme were forced to confront the whole purpose of their existence in a way that is scarcely conceivable to us today. A whole generation had been wiped out. Those left needed to be able to justify their place in the world and come to terms with the carnage. Yet what did they see around them except a country becoming increasingly despoiled as 60,000 acres a year were being eaten up by uncontrolled housing development, and miles of roads which were being laid to feed the voracious appetite of the increasingly popular motor car.

The fact was, they could see that something had been lost – and it wasn't necessarily all materialistic. God had been lost; and the certainties of the Victorian age had been lost, so that when in 1922 the poet T. S. Eliot came to assemble his cultural inventory of the period in 'The Waste Land' all he found was an arid catalogue of spiritual despair. The future didn't seem to offer anything more encouraging either and as the dictatorships began to rise across Europe, and the world was yet again plunged into the slaughter of war, it seemed a stark choice between Huxley's 1932 nightmare of a *Brave New World* where babies were fertilised in bottles, or Orwell's 1948 vision of *1984* in which every facet of our lives would be monitored and controlled by the political-industrial machine.

If I should die think only this of me:
That there's some corner of a foreign field
That is for ever England…

Rupert Brooke's evocation of the soul of England felt tangible enough to a soldier seeking reassurance in nationhood as he faced the incalculable prospect of death. But what about those who were left behind afterwards? Those who survived the trenches and later the horrors of the second war where some of the worst atrocities weren't committed on the battlefield, but in places with silly foreign names like Auschwitz and Belsen where death itself became an industrial process?

What price little old England then?

At least there was some certainty in the past. At least there was comfort.

At times Massingham's evocation of England sticks in the craw. It's sweet and nauseating like that mead they used to drink in the Middle Ages – a period he viewed as a golden epoch. But even though he was forever looking backwards, he wasn't necessarily always walking in that direction. Years before anyone had ever heard of Greenpeace or Friends of the Earth, he was warning of the threat to the natural balance of the world posed by chemical fertilisers and pesticides. A long time before the future of the Brazilian rainforests had become an international issue, and before British birdlife had been decimated by modern farming methods, he'd written about the likely effects of deforestation and the indiscriminate destruction of hedgerows. Years before anyone was willing to listen, he'd cautioned about the effects of pollution on rivers and streams.

And he wasn't just playing the Jeremiah either. In books he started writing towards the end of the war he began to outline a series of positive strategies for the revival of sound agricultural practice. Way before Fritz Schumacher argued for decentralised, small-scale technology in *Small is Beautiful*, and years before traditional methods of organic farming began to be reintroduced as a response to the health risks of modern corporate farming, Massingham was warning about the dangers of rural monoculture and advocating a return to smaller, more controllable mixed farms based on more traditional methods of husbandry.

I know what Harold Massingham was getting at. *Anyone* who spends time on the canals knows what he's getting at.

Once, not so long ago, Em and I were cruising in Shropshire when we filled our water tank at a tap in the middle of the countryside provided for the purpose. It was at a place near enough to a company selling bottled mineral water for us to feel that we were onto a good thing since ours was free and theirs was 80p a litre. Only that there was a warning posted nearby cautioning people not to let children drink it because of the high concentration of poisonous organophosphates leeching from the overfertilised land.

I didn't fancy it after that.

The bottled water, presumably, is drawn from some naturally occurring spring that flows thousands of feet below the water table and is filtered for trillions of years by the geology of the natural landscape. Or something like that.

All the same, I wouldn't fancy that either.

Neither do I like cruising through the countryside when they're spraying crops, for regardless of how often I'm told that this is perfectly safe, I can't forget that the chemicals they use were developed from the poisonous gases employed on the Western Front during the First World War. Of course, I may be missing some sophisticated bit of science here, but sometimes it's as well to go with your instincts. And as far as modern agricultural practice is concerned, I saw the way things were going twenty years ago at the height of the BSE crisis when I saw a government minister on TV forcing a hamburger down the throat of his 4-year-old daughter in order to reassure us about the safety of beef. All my instincts told me then there was something fundamentally wrong with beef production in this country.

And boy, was I right.

Some basic natural balance seems to have been disturbed, some disjuncture seems to have occurred in the natural world, and cruising the canals you notice it more than from a car because at canal speeds you've got time to observe the detail of the world around you. The waterways are a back door to England. They take you into the heart of the countryside and force you to look at the countryside.

Try as I might, I still can't get used to cruising in the winter through fields of growing wheat. There seems to me something freakish about these crops that buck the ebb and flow of the seasons, green when everything around them is brown, blooming when everything else around is dead. And I still can't get used to these rural prairies which seem to go on forever, especially the bright yellow fields of rape which may seem pretty enough flashing by on a motorway, but which can have you heaving with the smell of it after half an hour on a boat.

*

So, united by the common features of their separate philosophies, Tom Rolt and Harry Massingham began writing to each other in a correspondence that was to last for years and which would become more intimate as time went on. It was in the course of this that Massingham asked whether Rolt had ever considered writing anything about the waterways. You can imagine the anticipation Rolt must have felt as he salvaged the manuscript of his book from the suitcase under the bed where it had lay neglected for almost four years. He must have realised that with Massingham's backing the manuscript might finally get into print. Which is how it turned out, for Massingham recommended it to the publishers Eyre & Spottiswood who immediately accepted it for publication.

This was September 1943. The book finally went on sale in early December the following year in an edition produced to war economy standards, priced 12/6d – just over sixty-two pence in today's money. It carried an introduction by Massingham and a frontispiece which contained two stanzas of Rupert Brooke's anguished lament to lost love, 'The Chilterns':

I shall desire and I shall find
The best of my desires,
The autumn Road, the mellow wind
That sooths the darkening shires.
And laughter and inn-fires.

White mist about the black hedgerows,
The slumbering Midland plain,
The silence where the clover goes,
And the dead leaves in the lane,
Certainly, these remain.

In his autobiography Rolt describes the jubilation he felt at getting the book published after having pretty well given up all hope for it. 'I read through the contract over and over again to assure myself that it was really true,' he wrote. 'And yes, there was my name at the top (hereinafter called The Author) and, believe it or not, the Publishers did "undertake to produce and publish (the) work…"'

But getting a book published is one thing; getting people to buy it and read it is something entirely different, and even Rolt himself admitted that he was astonished by the reception *Narrow Boat* received. Not only did it get a series of long and favourable reviews in the newspapers but the book sold well too. Afterwards he was overwhelmed with fan mail, confirming (if he needed confirmation) that his ideas had touched a chord in the national psyche.

One of these letters was from a young literary agent living in Bloomsbury in London. It raised the possibility of founding an organisation to campaign for the preservation of canals. This wasn't an original idea: there'd been a National Inland Navigation League in 1919, and an Inland Cruising Association in Cheshire in the 1930s, but neither had survived, let alone had any significant long-term effect in safeguarding the waterways. Until the publication of *Narrow Boat*, Rolt wouldn't have thought such an idea feasible, but the letters he'd received made him think there might be something in the proposal.

He wrote back immediately, inviting the young man to visit him at Tardebigge where he was living on *Cressy*...

*

My time in Braunston was mostly spent with my sleeves rolled up painting the hull of the boat with the thick, black bitumastic we inland waterways types slap on anything vaguely metallic. In the evenings I'd take the Debsmobile into the deepest countryside, searching for the perfect English pub – a job which I saw as part of my research for this book, for where else is the English soul rooted, but in the traditional English pub?

I can hardly claim that this was an onerous task. All the same, I wasn't expecting it would be all holiday either. Being a pessimist, I was anticipating that most decent country pubs – like a lot of the best pubs in towns – would have been destroyed long ago in the name of progress, and that I'd be condemned to spend a succession of miserable nights in the middle of nowhere relying for entertainment on my ability to engage bilious rustics in conversation about turnip yields or ploughing techniques.

Urban prejudice or what?

In village after village I kept finding a succession of remarkably unspoilt places, some of them untouched, and most of the others restored with a sensitivity to taste and tradition far beyond anything I'd expected. The people I met were exceptionally friendly, quick to engage me in conversation and interested in what I was doing. They were certainly more affable than in London pubs where sullen detachment often seems an intrinsic part of the drinking experience. If I did meet any initial reluctance to talk to me as a I travelled around, it was only because the sight of a battle-worn traditionalist from a canal boat driving a 30-year-old Triumph Herald was anathema to authentic country people whose natural inclination is more towards top-of-the-range BMWs or huge items of farm machinery with more horsepower than a Newmarket stables.

The beer was good too – a lot better than you'd have got years ago at the height of the 'Red Revolution' when the ubiquitous Watneys Red Barrel was being sold at a strength only a little higher than might legally have been given to children as a soft drink. In those far-off days when messing about on the canals marked you out as a radical as much as long hair did, enthusiasts used to navigate the system less by maps than the pathetically slim *Real Ale Guide to the Waterways*. This at least ensured that at the end of the day you met up with similarly hirsute people who would almost certainly share one of your preoccupations, whether hard drinking, soft drugs or the primitive traditional music we listened to which was played on acoustic guitars and was such a painful experience that even those who sang it had to stick their fingers in their ears to avoid the full consequences of their actions.

But my, those real ale places were few and far between. And sometimes even when you sought them out after walking for miles across fields and along no-hope country lanes, all you'd find was a pub like any other aside from the fact that stuck away at the far end of the bar was a single dusty hand pump that had rusted up for lack of use. So you'd be forced anyhow to have a pint of tasteless pasteurised keg, and you'd thank your lucky stars for it, since the licensing hours were so restricted that to arrive at a pub in that critical window when it was actually selling beer required planning of military precision.

Of course, there *were* good pubs then, and some outstanding ones. The Anchor on the Shropshire Union, for instance: a traditional unspoilt canal inn where once the old boatmen used to stable their horses overnight. Or the Bird in Hand on the Macclesfield Canal just outside Kidsgrove which was like a country kitchen with just a single scrubbed wooden table in the middle of a small room and no sign of a bar because they'd fetch up beer from barrels in the cellar in a chipped enamel jug. And the Black Lion at Consall Forge in Staffordshire on the Caldon Canal where I've spent many happy hours, since at one time you couldn't conveniently get to the place except by water, which meant that closing time could be – how shall we put this so as not to offend anyone? – sensibly flexible – will that do?

Sadly the Bird in Hand is closed now, the elderly lady who ran it for years – said to be an old music hall star – long since dead. And they've built a road to the Black Lion which has altered its character fundamentally. The Anchor has altered as well, though perhaps not so much in its fabric as in the clientele it attracts, since what is antiquated and decrepit and once thought folksy has nowadays become such a commonplace of contemporary style that the place is filled with mid-management marketing types who've copied it in their homes.

So don't let's get sentimental about English pubs of yesteryear: this lot was the best of the bunch. Going for a drink in those days could be a grim experience. It's easy to forget that the reason the breweries were so keen on serving us pasteurised beer was that there were so many pub landlords who were incapable of looking after the decent stuff. Ordering a pint then was a lottery in which if you were lucky you might get something bright, sharp and flavoursome, but where you'd an equal chance of getting a glass of something that tasted of tooth suckings and looked as if it had been bucketed from the Tyne.

And believe me, some of the people that you used to find in those places were like characters out of *The X-Files*. And I'm not talking Mulder and Scully here, either.

I speak with authority on this topic, for in the determined pursuit of alcoholic oblivion I have been constrained to spend countless dispiriting hours amongst the sad and disinherited of Mother England, many of whom still appear in my nightmares smelling of beer slops and wreathed in misty clouds of stale cigarette smoke. The difficulty is remembering them all, for the merely unusual ones have faded from memory and it's only the totally grotesque that I recollect with any clarity.

Like the guy in one pub near Stoke-on-Trent who waited until I'd sat down and then drew up a chair directly opposite me at my table. He had eyes like the comedian Marty Feldman and as I began to sip at my beer he fixed me as best he could with the only one he could keep stable. Then, while the other went for a wander around the bar, he watched attentively until I'd drained every last drop from my glass. Eventually, in a lugubrious voice that might have been out of central casting for *Hammer House of Horror*, he said, 'Nice that was, was it? It is nice to drink a pint of beer when you've a thirst on you, isn't it? Perhaps I could be allowed to get you another one, could I?'

If it hadn't been that it was daylight and there were one or two other people around, I think I'd have run screaming for the door in search of a crucifix and wooden stakes.

At another pub I visited near the Welsh border I stood for what seemed like hours before the landlord so much as deigned to look up from a group of people he was with. They were all bunched around a fruit machine in the corner and it seemed that whenever I was close to getting served, the machine would suddenly burst into life, shrieking and flashing like a fairground carousel while they kept frenziedly feeding it with whatever spare coins they could dig from their pockets.

I suppose you have to expect to be ignored in pubs close to the Welsh border. In fact, it's part of the preparation for actually going to Wales where as an Englishman they make a point of ignoring you all the time. But enough is enough. The landlord finally did notice me, but just as I was beginning to get excited that I might actually get a drink, he turned away… and walked off… straight out of the pub…

Don't ask me – I never found out what it was all about either. And I never got my drink. All I know is, you just couldn't get away with it running a pub nowadays when your customers are paying a small fortune for their pint and expect a bit more for their money than to be treated as if their presence is somehow an imposition on the routine of the place.

Nowadays the problem is the opposite. Nowadays as a customer you get *too much* attention from bar staff. They're always insisting on giving you a clean glass every time you ask for your old one to be filled up. They're forever wiping down your table and clearing away your crisp bags as if you were some patient in a nursing home. Nowadays it's impossible to have a quiet drink in a pub. If the staff aren't fussing around you like so many clucking hens, they're pestering you for details of your private life with the sort of doggedness that would be considered rude anywhere else.

'Come far, have we, sir? Going anywhere in particular? Staying long? Had oral sex recently?'

We English seem to have lost our natural tact. It seems like only yesterday we were world renowned for our discretion on personal matters. Your house might have burnt down, your loved ones been killed in a car crash. Even so, if anyone asked you how you were you'd have been thought hysterical if you'd replied any more demonstratively than saying that you 'mustn't grumble'. In those days it was a maxim of life that everything could only get a good deal worse than it was. Most people just kept their heads down for fear of tempting fate to take a crack at them in the shooting gallery of life.

Today though, it seems you only have to break a fingernail to be openly emoting and in need of therapy. This is another area where pub landlords are a pain. They're either offering you counselling with their beer, trying to draw you about the state of your marriage or your job, or they're expecting you to listen to them while they bang on about some problem that *they* have.

I came across a publican like this in one of the small villages around Braunston where I finished up one afternoon on one of my excursions in the Herald. The pub was empty but the landlord fixed on me and insisted on buying me a drink. Eventually he led me off to a discreet corner where, without so much as a by-your-leave, he regaled me with all manner of details about his personal life.

I didn't know where to look. I'd only just met him, and here he was confiding intimate things about himself I wouldn't even tell my best friend. At length I offered the opinion that perhaps the root of his problems might be stress and overwork. After all, it was a tough job running a pub which was open every afternoon and evening.

'Oh, but I don't open afternoons,' he said brightly. 'Well, not in the week anyway. I just left the door open today for you.'

'For me?' I said. 'But how did you know I was…?'

But I didn't finish. I didn't need to. There was the sound of pennies dropping. Then a silence fell between us which you could have cut with a knife.

He turned a deep shade of scarlet. 'You mean… you're not the bloke Colin arranged for me to see?

THIRTEEN

I stood on the grass verge by the church in the tiny village of Lower Shuckborough near Daventry, watching a small pool of oil form on the road surface. It was coming from my engine. The engine of my Triumph Herald, that is. The Triumph Herald which I'd been happily driving only moments before until I'd been brought to an abrupt halt by an emergency warning light on the dashboard. I lifted up the bonnet which as any aficionado of the Herald will know opens out the whole front of the car so that the complete engine becomes totally and instantly accessible. The reason for the leak was all too clear: a small drain screw in the base of the sump had corroded and worked loose.

This was no big deal. It's the sort of thing that happens every day of the week driving a classic car. It was an inconvenience, yes. And a pretty irritating inconvenience too since, unusually, it was a gorgeous afternoon and I had the roof down, basking in the warmth of a mysterious orange star that had inexplicably appeared in the sky where normally there would be thick cloud cover. But I could deal with it easily enough. I could use a bit of old anything to plug the sump and then all I had to do was top up the car with oil.

Except, of course – and isn't this the way life goes? – I hadn't got any oil.

Now precisely *why* I hadn't got any oil, I couldn't say. I'd got spare petrol with me, and spare filters and fan belts too. I'd got spare spark plugs and a spare set of points, and spare condensers and spare wiper blades. I'd even got a spare petrol-tank cap, not to mention a breathtaking variety of other bits of bodywork of all shapes and sizes. In fact, I'd got so many bits of car in the boot I could probably have built myself a new one from scratch if I'd wanted. But of oil, I had not one drop, not anywhere, not even a renegade teaspoonful sitting in the bottom of a can awaiting this moment for its hour of glory. And yet… and yet I had this recollection that I'd only just bought oil – what? – a couple of weeks before? I'd put it in the boot. I clearly remembered putting it there. I even remembered *where* in the boot I'd put it. Damn it, I even remembered *how* I'd put it in the boot. But however many times I went back to the boot, desperately trying to convince myself that I'd somehow missed it, or overlooked it, or misplaced it, I couldn't for the life of me see any sign of it.

It was Em's fault. Obviously it was. It had to be her fault. No one had broken into the car and stolen the oil. Even so, the oil had gone, and since I hadn't taken it, there was only one other person who could have done. It was probably her idea of a joke. I went back to the boot again to check once more, but I still couldn't find what I was looking for. I slammed the blasted thing shut, convinced beyond persuasion that Em was to blame for all this. She must have taken it the last time she'd visited. She'd done it to… well, she'd done it just to annoy me, why else? I took the opportunity of checking the boot one last time. There was still no oil. Now I was absolutely convinced. This was definitely Em's responsibility. There was absolutely no doubt about it.

Luckily I remembered passing a garage not long before and so, swearing death, damnation and divorce, I grabbed my coat and started on what I knew would be a long and unpleasant trek. At that moment, as if to confirm my pessimism, the sky darkened and a whole regiment of cumulonimbi gathered on the horizon like a cosmic football crowd looking for a urinal at half-time. Before I'd walked more than a hundred yards the rain had started falling on me with that provocatively fine drizzle that mocks you by appearing not to be rain at all, even though it takes but moments to permeate through to your Y-fronts.

An hour later I got back to the car with a gallon can of oil. By then I was soaked to the skin, and my mood was so thunderous the weather paled by comparison. It was at that point, throwing my sodden coat onto the back seat, that I noticed – tucked away behind the passenger seat where I immediately remembered leaving it – a gallon can of oil…

Even though I was outside a church my behaviour wasn't exactly ecclesiastical. Nor was my language. It attracted attention from inside, and I became aware of someone I took to be a clergyman pressing his nose against the car window close to my face. He'd heard me screaming. He probably thought I'd had an accident and needed the last rites instantly. He was, I remember, waving around a large set of garden shears. With his face distorted by the rain, and the shears making him look like Edward Scissorhands, I thought I'd got locked into *The Twilight Zone*. He probably thought the same thing, confronted by this shrieking idiot dementedly battering his head with the palms of his hands.

Afterwards I felt the least I could do was visit the church – which was fortuitous since I'd probably have missed it otherwise. It's a little treasure, a textbook example of Victorian Gothic characterised by a twee little spire set on top of an ornate six-sided tower. Once I'd got my bearings, I realised that I recognised the building and had passed it many times before, for you can see the back of it from the canal.

It's much more impressive from the front, though. From this elevation you see it in its full splendour across a small green where the village stocks used to be. Beyond that, leading to the church door, is a path bordered by an unusual avenue of yew trees shaped like great teardrops. The man I had taken to be a clergyman was actually the verger, and he'd been pruning them until he'd been disturbed by the rain and then me.

Inside, the church is just as remarkable, especially the vaulted roof of the tower which is decorated with star-spangled tiles that seem bizarre in this setting. The author of a book on churches around Daventry comments that the first impression they give is of a Hindu temple, and this was exactly my reaction. This is odd for any English church but it was odder here, for the more I looked at the verger, who was now acting as my guide, the more it seemed to me that there was something of the Indian about him too.

Part of it was his colour, for his face had a weather-beaten tan about it which gave him the complexion of someone more used to the climate of Rajasthan than Rugby. But most of it was his bone structure. Though he was into his seventies he was a strikingly handsome man, fit and lean, with a head of hair like a 20-year-old and high cheekbones which gave him a proud, aristocratic bearing.

He showed me a spot in the church where the floor had given way, disclosing an unknown crypt which, he said, he'd had the devil's own job getting any expert from Warwick to come and investigate since as far as they were concerned they'd surveyed the church once fifty years ago and found everything that was worth finding then. As I was leaving he pointed out another structural failing – this time a massive indentation in the path where only a few months before a piece of stonework had dislodged from the tower and come crashing down.

'The place is falling to bits,' he said. 'There's not the interest in these old buildings the way there used to be, you see. They cost too much to maintain and nowadays people just aren't willing to…' he trailed off, shaking his head sadly. 'I don't know what's going to happen to it when I go,' he said.

He'd been involved with the church in some capacity for most of his life, I learned. 'My father too,' he said, proudly, 'and my grandfather before him – after he'd got back to England.

'He was in the army,' he explained, seeing the curiosity on my face. 'India. My grandmother was Indian, in fact. He married her and brought her back here to the village. I can still remember her in her sari telling me stories when I was a child.'

Even after so long he remembered these stories with clarity. The world she described to him – her world – was a strange and faraway land of gleaming marble palaces and thick jungles where man-eating tigers stalked. It touched his imagination deeply. She talked to him of dusty villages too, where wild-haired holy men sat, their bodies smeared with strange red dyes; and of towns with great markets full of exotic fruits; and of snake-charmers, and elephants, of great wide rivers and expansive deserts; and most of all the constant burning heat which caused the world to become richly aromatic, and the air to shimmer as if in constant anticipation of the future.

Listening to him it was obvious that these stories were a precious part of his childhood. It was clear that his biggest disappointment was that his own family didn't embrace anything of this personal history; in fact, he gave me the impression that they were intimidated by it, fearful that when a child was born to any of them, it might somehow turn out 'coloured' and a throwback to what they seemed to consider a shameful family episode.

Eventually something of this sort seems to have happened. One of his grandchildren was born with a dark patch of skin across his back which caused some concern until the doctor reassured the family that it wasn't anything to worry about and that it would fade with time. Actually I got the feeling that he wouldn't have been too upset if the mark had been permanent so that there might have been some tangible reminder of the past; but perhaps I'm investing him with my own romantic nostalgia. This is a dangerous thing for anyone to do. It is especially dangerous for people on narrowboats who drive around the countryside in old convertible cars and who are particularly susceptible to romantic nostalgia.

But you can understand it, can't you? Nursing romantic nostalgia, I mean. Things seem to alter with extraordinary suddenness nowadays, and the past seems to offer a security. Yet change is often an illusion in England where attitudes are more deeply entrenched than we realise, and where things alter much more slowly than we think they do. Especially in the English countryside where people need longer to come to terms with the present.

Just how deeply these attitudes are entrenched was brought home to me when I dropped into the Blue Bell not so very long ago with my old mate Dave. This is a pub in the village where I was brought up, and where the two of us squandered a large part of our youth on the basis that since drink was the equivalent of 10p a pint and would never be as cheap again in our lifetime, we were justified in the name of thrift getting as much of it down our throats as we could. The Blue Bell in those days was a posh pub. You could always tell posh pubs because they had a carpet on the floor, served you bitter in dimpled glass jugs with handles, and took exception to you throwing up in the toilet. It hadn't altered much – in fact, if anything, it had got even posher and had spawned a restaurant where you could enjoy a selection of pies of various types topped with towering crusts of puff pastry.

In all other respects though, the village had changed totally.

In my day it was a dour place with a grey council estate built of pre-fabricated concrete, and an equally dismal primary school where I got bullied for breaking the first rule of the playground and learning how to read. It was a utilitarian place with a lot of utilitarian terraced housing, a few small utilitarian factories and a row of utilitarian shops grouped around the war memorial on a utilitarian village green.

Not any more, though.

Little did I know as a youngster, but lurking underneath all this, like a butterfly waiting to emerge from its chrysalis, was a modern English village. All the terraced houses have now metamorphosed into cottages with Quality Street-style bijou bay windows, and the ubiquitous geranium is as much in evidence here as anywhere. The school still just about survives but all the factories have gone, knocked down to be rebuilt as 'executive' housing. Even the council estate's rocketed upmarket because, of course, the houses are now in private hands; and though you can't altogether hide the aura of post-war municipalism with which it's imbued, you can do a great deal to conceal it by the judicious planting of climbers from the local garden centre.

Even the fish and chip shop on the green has changed beyond recognition. It's now got tables inside where they'll let you drink wine. Wine? With fish and chips? When I was a kid, wine was something you drank once a year with your Christmas dinner. And then it was sweet Sauternes.

It was early evening in the Blue Bell and the pub was empty but for a scattering of locals standing around the bar. One of them stood on his own, a little removed from the others. I'd been aware of him watching me but now he turned in my direction and I realised with an unpleasant frisson of recognition that I knew him from nearly forty years before. I hadn't liked him then either. We nodded at each other stiffly and though we didn't speak it was clear that the next time I went to the bar I wasn't going to be able to avoid saying something to him.

But exactly what could I say? I toyed with the idea of '*It's been a long time,*' but a period of four decades is self-evidently a long time, and I thought that it might be a shade unimaginative. '*Fancy running into you, then,*' I dismissed too, since my memory of him all those years ago was that he spent more time in the Blue Bell than Dave and I did – and I guessed since then, not exactly being the pioneering sort, he'd probably never wandered far from it.

Something anodyne like '*You OK, then?*' risked hitting the wrong note too, for as far as I knew he could have been suffering from some affliction like constipation or athlete's foot which he might have been compelled to talk about at great length. Eventually I fixed on a straightforward '*Hello,*' which, while not exactly eloquent, did at least have the advantage of being short, pithy and uncontroversial.

In fact I needn't have worried for he got in first. No sooner was I within earshot than he said something that left me speechless.

Remember, this is a man who has never lived outside the parish boundaries but who has doubtless enjoyed a full and contented life, believing not just that this village was the centre of *his* universe, but that it was centre of *the* universe – a place from which no one with any sense would ever wish to venture far.

He said simply, with the conviction of one who had never doubted that I would, 'You've come back, then.'

*

They dropped *Justice* back into the water after three days, her hull now pristine and even her livery looking sprucer than it had for ages thanks to a pot of touch-up paint and a coat or two of wax polish I'd found time to apply. I started the engine and edged off the precarious trolley on which she'd been balanced, carefully manoeuvring away from the slipway and navigating towards the centre channel so as not to risk damaging her glossy new finish against any moored boat.

When I met oncoming craft I steered as far away from them as I could to avoid the slightest risk of collision; and passing through the narrow bridges leading out of Braunston I slowed almost to a stop to avoid scuffing her hull against the edging stones.

Justice was a proud queen, dressed for a coronation. I was determined to ensure that she stayed that way.

I steered her like no other boat had ever been steered before. I steered her with a consummate, unparalleled precision. I steered her with care and rigour. I steered her with complete concentration and meticulous attention to detail.

Then at the first lock I came to I steered her into the wall and gouged a scratch down her side half the length of a car.

But by that stage Braunston was far behind me, and somehow I didn't care any more.

FOURTEEN

There comes a time in life when you have to take stock. A time when you need a sense of purpose and a goal, a time when you have to be clear about your ambitions and aspirations.

It's the same with boating.

Like life, it's invaluable to have some idea of where you're going. It's useful too to have a vague notion of how to get there. Otherwise, in the same way that you can finish up in some office shuffling papers when you thought you were going to be a brain surgeon, you can arrive in Braunston when you were actually going to Bristol.

You may recall that going to Bristol was my original plan for this trip, and that the only reason I'd gone north was because I'd left Oxford in a fit of pique and an avalanche of dog shit after being delayed so long from getting on the Thames by the rain. But in going north I'd taken a route that was in an entirely different direction to Bristol – which somewhat ruled out Bristol as a destination for the trip, and ensured that this whole confused mess was turning into a far better metaphor for existence than it was a journey.

However, the question still remained: where on earth *was* I going?

'Stratford,' said Em with some conviction.

'Stratford?'

'Stratford-upon-Avon – birthplace of the Bard, the home of the Royal Shakespeare Theatre and a town...' she faltered.

'A town built on the River Avon, maybe?' I suggested.

'Something like that.' She glowered at me. 'What do you think, Mum?'

'Mum' was Chris, Em's mother, who had joined us for a holiday cruise. She was an eighty-something – a small, alert woman with meticulously kept pure white hair and sharp eyes which darted about constantly like a bird's.

She said: 'I don't really care where I go; I'm determined to have a good time whatever.' And with that she poured us all a glass of the very good malt whisky she'd brought with her as a gift.

The two of them had arrived on the boat that morning in high spirits, looking forward to a break from London, but as if on cue the rain which had been in brief respite started hammering down, playing out such a rhythm on the top of the boat that you couldn't sit in it long without feeling you were trapped inside a drum. The noise was about the only incentive we had to go anywhere. Only we hadn't been able to work out *where* it was we wanted to go.

Now, with the mention of Stratford-upon-Avon, we were all galvanised into action. Suddenly a new energy infected us. Now we all wanted to go to Stratford.

'Stratford it is then,' said Em. 'Let's get going this very moment. I'll put my coat on.'

'And I'll clear up the glasses,' said Chris.

It could have been the elation at finally making a decision. It could have been the promise of the freedom ahead, the prospect of the miles of sylvan canals in front of us; the anticipation of endless days of lazy cruising and nights of conviviality. It could have been *joie de vivre* and nothing else…

Then again, it could have been the whisky.

One way or another, we were all fired up, so I went and fired the engine up too. It was nice to have some company on my travels for a change.

★

Going west from Braunston the architecture changes radically. Gone now are the narrow seven-foot-wide locks of the Oxford Canal which accommodate a boat like *Justice* with just a couple of inches to spare on either side. Gone too is that sense of Georgian twee, with warehouses and cottages built to the scale of dolls' houses. As you turn onto the Grand Union Canal the waterway widens and straightens and everything becomes so much bigger and more industrial. One immediate change is the banking, and from now on brutal concrete edging stones installed in the 1930s line the canal with instructions set into them for the dredging depths required to accommodate the commercial traffic that was still plying its trade then.

There's still significant haulage trade on Britain's rivers and canals, but the investment in the Grand Union between London and Birmingham in the years leading up to the Second World War was the last time that money was spent with any real hope that water transport might take its place with roads as part of an integrated system of moving freight. Even then, it was a pretty forlorn hope. The improvements were too little, too late, and in the long run the main beneficiary of them would turn out to be the leisure traffic that began to expand in the

1950s in the wake of *Narrow Boat* and the foundation of the Inland Waterways Association (IWA).

You can see the change clearly at the three locks at Calcutt, the first you meet after the turn. You're going downhill now, dropping into the valley of the River Avon, and they look huge as you approach. Each of their gates is as wide as a small lock and each has an immense, delicately balanced beam like the pointing finger of a great dark fist. The scale of the thing is different to the Oxford Canal locks, and there's a different system of paddles to manipulate the water flow too. In place of the rudimentary cogs and ratchets of the narrow canals is a hydraulic system necessary to release the 250-ton weight of the 56,000 gallons of water that each lock holds.

Chris was quite taken with this system because although it all looks a bit macho and rufty-tufty, the paddles are pussy cats when you start to play with them. It's not brute force they need, just the persistence to keep winding a lock key, or windlass, for long enough – something easily within her capacity. We were soon past Calcutt and after a couple of miles we arrived at the first of the eight locks that compose the Stockton flight. By now we were into the swing of things, back into a routine of locking which we've done so many times over the years that the technique we use hardly seems like a technique at all, so second nature is it. In what seemed no time we'd negotiated the flight and were cruising through the empty countryside that carries the canal towards Warwick.

That night we moored just outside Leamington Spa in the bosky basin below the lock at Radford Semele, between the humpback bridge which carries the village road from Offchurch and the high-level railway viaduct on which the long-since abandoned line to Rugby once ran. It's adjacent to the River Leam which runs parallel at this point; and it's so thick with trees that despite being close to the town, and despite the occasional noise of a passing car, the kingfishers feed undisturbed, nesting around the crumbling chamber of the adjacent narrow lock which was replaced and abandoned as part of the 1930s improvements.

It's a beguiling place, but all the same there's an unmistakable melancholic feel about it. Before *Justice*, Em and I had another boat which we kept for a long time in Leamington in those heady years of the 1970s when we'd cruise up to Radford with friends at least once a month on searches for hallucinogenic mushrooms, or for weekend parties when we'd have the kingfishers cowering between night-long bouts of Pink Floyd or the Rolling Stones. My memories of Radford are tied up with that time, and the memory of friends, some who have drifted out of our lives the way people do, and some who are sadly no longer with us. So there's an eerie but pleasurable poignancy I always feel mooring here, especially when the evening closes in and the light begins to play tricks with the world, so that you can almost see the past playing out before you as if in a half-formed dream where you almost expect to glimpse long-lost faces emerging from the shadows to greet you again.

We were moored at Radford many years ago when our friend Malcolm took us to a party in Warwick and we borrowed his car to get home after he decided on the spur of the moment to stay on. It was the early hours before we arrived back and we decided to have a nightcap before turning in. Somehow the conversation turned to talk of the bizarre and the supernatural, the way it sometimes can on the canal when you're in the middle of nowhere and the fire's flickering behind the stove glass, and when there's a wind gently rocking the boat and outside there's the creaking of a branch or some other inexplicable noise that makes you feel uneasy.

We had a guest with us that night. She'd just finished telling us the chilling tale which was doing the rounds then about the couple whose car broke down in the middle of the woods the night a notorious psychopath escaped from a local asylum. You remember the story? Surely you must. He was responsible for a dozen or more vile killings, and the couple realised that they were in grave danger, so when the man decided to take a risk and go for help he gave his girlfriend strict instructions that she should lock the car doors behind him and under no circumstances open them to anyone.

An hour went by but he didn't return. Two hours passed and still he didn't reappear. By now she was beginning to panic. At one stage, desperate to believe he was safe, she thought he *had* come back, for she could have sworn she felt the car move slightly, as if he'd tried the door handle and found it locked... But it was nothing, just a trick of the wind. Only that soon afterwards she became aware with horror of a faint scuffling on the roof just above her head. Eventually a gently rhythmic banging began – Bang! Bang! Bang! – and it became louder and louder, and louder yet, a persistent terrifying hammering on the roof so that she felt it could only be moments before it gave way under the pounding, and whoever – or *what*ever – was causing it finally got to her. She would have screamed except her lungs had constricted in icy terror. She would have bolted except that her boyfriend's last words to her still rang in her ears.

'Don't – under any circumstances – *any* circumstances at all – leave the car. The car is your only hope of safety.'

Suddenly, like a curious nightmare in which events are out of kilter with the natural world, the whole forest lit up, bursting into harsh white light. Once her eyes had adjusted to the blinding brightness she could make out the blurred core of arc lights positioned all around her, on every side, as if this were a film set and she were the star of the scene. She could make out figures crouched beneath the trees, figures kneeling and – strange this, she thought – looking as if they were carrying rifles tucked into their shoulders and trained in her direction.

A megaphone burst into life with the voice of a policeman. She knew it was a policeman even before she could make out his uniform through her squinting eyes.

'Leave the car,' he said. 'Leave the car NOW. Walk towards me slowly. Do not panic and do not look back. Under no circumstances look back.'

She was in a daze now, so bewildered that she was in no position to exercise any will of her own. So drugged with fear that when she rested her hand on the catch of the car door, it wasn't her hand which pressed it down, or her strength which pushed the door open or even her body which hauled itself from the car…

'Just walk towards me,' the voice kept saying through the megaphone. 'Walk slowly. Do not look back. Under no circumstances look back.'

But how could she avoid looking back? How could she resist, even at the moment of her greatest terror, that appalling curiosity which impels us all to probe the deep and dark recesses of our soul?

So she glanced behind her, and that was enough, for in that passing instant she saw an image that would be burnt forever into her memory, an image so horrifying that in future years when it returned to her in odd unguarded moments it would still have the power to paralyse her with terror at the remembrance of it. It was the image of the psychopath sitting on top of the car, cross-legged like a recalcitrant child in a nursery school, banging a broken toy on the roof.

Except this was no broken toy he was banging. It was the severed head of her boyfriend, the ghastly gap of his mouth frozen in the rictus of his last bemused smile.

It was at that very point, as the three of us sat in the boat at Radford Semele in the early hours of the morning, frightening ourselves with this story – at that precise moment after the story had finished, but before we'd had time for the gratifying chill of it to wear off – we each of us clearly heard a bang on the top of the boat roof.

We all turned to ice. Then we looked at each other, puzzled whether our senses were deceiving us. Hoping that one of us would come up with some rational explanation of what was happening, some interpretation that we could all happily accept as the truth so that we could laugh at ourselves for thinking it so menacing. Maybe a broken fragment of a branch had fallen on us? Possibly some pine cone had dropped from a height? Or maybe one of us was just playing a trick on the others?

But then it happened again: a regular banging now, gentle at first as it was in the story, but then becoming louder, and louder yet. I remember looking at the other two wondering whether my face had turned as white as theirs. Or if their mouths could be as dry as mine.

When you're frightened like this – especially frightened after telling stories – there's a curious half-stage which is neither one thing nor the other, neither fact nor fiction, but between the two; and it was into this lacuna we were plunged that night on the boat at Radford as we all sat visibly blanching while the knocking slowly began to move up the length of the boat towards us. We knew that what was happening to us was real enough, but it was so divorced from what we expected of the natural world that we couldn't *believe* it was real and so felt – strangely – that we must somehow have become trapped inside the story.

Eventually, of course, Malcolm, in a half-whisper, said, 'Hello. Anyone awake in there? Hello… hello…'

When I opened the door to him, he realised straightaway how much he'd terrified us and he couldn't stop apologising for what had happened as if it had been some schoolboy jape that had gone horribly wrong. 'I got a lift, you see,' he kept explaining. 'I thought I'd save myself the walk tomorrow to collect the car…'

So it all ended happily – or if not happily, then at least rationally. Which is more than can be said for another experience Em and I had one autumn in Wales a few years back. Even recalling it now makes my flesh creep.

We'd been for a drink in a pub in the small village of Froncysyllte on the Llangollen Canal near Thomas Telford's famous aqueduct which carries the canal across the valley of the River Dee. It's a staggering structure even by today's standards, yet it's just a narrow iron trough the width of a boat which rests crudely on nineteen stone piers. These tower more than 100 feet high but they taper towards the top, imbuing the whole edifice with a surprising delicacy and grace. It was built in 1805, the year of the Battle of Trafalgar, and it's still carrying thousands of people across the valley each year, for not only is the Llangollen the most heavily cruised canal on the whole system, attracting boats from all over the country, but the aqueduct's become a tourist attraction in its own right and draws sightseers from all over the world.

Our moorings that night were at Trevor, so we had to walk over the aqueduct to get to the pub. It was late when we set out and we weren't there long, and we certainly weren't drunk or anything like it when we left. It was after closing time though, and with little or no moon, dark enough to need the torch we'd brought with us. In fact, we could have done with more than one torch. The towpath was more overgrown than today and awkward for two people to walk side by side comfortably so we were forced to walk in Indian file. I was at the front using the torch to see ahead before swinging it behind me in an arc to allow Em to see where she was going.

We eventually arrived at the beginning of the aqueduct where a path running up the side of the valley joins the towpath. There a young man appeared from the gloom and began to walk in front of us – though neither Em nor I thought this particularly remarkable since it's probably a popular local short cut across the valley. He was – what? – maybe ten or twenty yards ahead, certainly no more.

As it crosses the aqueduct the towpath at night is a good deal less daunting than during the day, especially for someone like me who suffers from vertigo on the top deck of a bus. During the day you've a clear view for miles across the Welsh hills, and there's simply no avoiding that 1) you're very high up and 2) the only thing that prevents you plummeting the sheer drop to the river and immediate death is a frail-looking waist-high fence forged of cast iron. At least at night, when you can't see, you've no conception of how high up you are. The worst you think you risk is tripping up and falling into the canal.

Mind you, on a chilly night, that's hardly a prospect to be relished. We were both walking carefully, still in Indian file, me ahead carrying the torch, and Em following on. I'd take two or three paces and swing the torch forward, allowing me to see where I was going. At the highest point of the arc I'd briefly catch sight of the young guy walking in front. Then I'd swing the torch back towards Em, lighting her world and darkening mine for the time it took for me to take another two or three paces when – once again – I'd swing the torch forward until it once more illuminated the figure in front.

Three paces of light and a glimpse of the man ahead, then three paces of darkness. Three paces of light and a glimpse of the man ahead, then another three paces of darkness. Three paces of light and a glimpse of the man ahead, then – inexplicably – he wasn't there any more. He'd vanished.

Disappeared.

At this point we were towards the middle of the aqueduct and both of us stopped dead. I trained the torch forward so that it illuminated the whole of the path ahead. But there was no sign of him, and I could feel my blood beginning to curdle. Em, I remember, was clutching my arm so hard that it hurt.

'He's gone,' was all I could think to say before grabbing her hand and running. My only aim at this stage was to get us both off the aqueduct and back to the safety of the boat as quickly as possible.

Later that night we compared notes on what had happened, trying to make sense of it. At least we agreed on what we'd seen, for as I'd swung the torch forward, Em had been watching the beam of light too, and she, like me, had been aware of the figure ahead. She'd been conscious of him disappearing at the same moment too though neither of us could come up with any rational explanation for it.

'Could he have just run off fast?' Em suggested.

'No way! Not in the brief second or two of me swinging the torch. Not even if he'd been an Olympic sprinter.'

'Well, he couldn't have fallen in the water,' she said. 'We'd have heard him splashing about.'

'Or fallen over the edge,' I added. 'We're too high up. With a drop of that distance, he'd have cried out involuntarily even if he'd been committing suicide…'

We looked at each other blankly. Barring a local practical joke of tortuous complexity designed to terrify tourists, there didn't seem to be any satisfactory way in which we could account for what had happened.

Or at least one that wasn't supernatural.

'What was your impression of his clothes?' I asked, reluctant to concede that possibility.

'Modern, light-coloured, white – nothing special. Nothing to make him stand out.'

'And nothing special about the style of his hair either,' I said. 'Or his shoes. In fact, nothing special about him in any way.'

There was, however, one detail we could recall that we both thought was unusual – though to call it that rather exaggerates matters. Even so, the two of us had been struck by the fact that when he'd first appeared on the towpath he hadn't so much as glanced in our direction so that neither of us ever saw his face.

'I think if I'd been coming out onto a dark towpath on my own at night and seen a couple of people walking behind me, I'd have at least *looked* at them,' Em said. 'You never know, do you? They might be robbers or murderers…'

'Or even ghosts, perhaps?' I said.

*

There must be an intrinsic link between the waterways and the supernatural, for it sometimes seems as if every mile of the canals is associated with some spectral happening. Every self-respecting cutting or tunnel has its own ghost and so our experience on Telford's aqueduct was in keeping with the best elements of canal tradition, though this paranormal stuff goes over your head most of the time. Cruising on a canal boat you spend a lot of time in the middle of nowhere, more often than not mooring deep in the countryside at night. If you're the sort who gets terrified every time you hear some small, furry mammal scrabbling around in a hedgerow, then it's unlikely you'll find boating up your street.

Perhaps it's because we're so generally resistant to these things that we canal types need a more imaginative diet to get our blood moving, and it's remarkable how many people associated with the waterways have written ghost stories. Tom Rolt, among his other work, produced a book of them set largely on the canals. And Robert Aickman, the other founder of the Inland Waterways Association, was so obsessed with the occult that as a young man he slept overnight at the infamous Borely Rectory, a place said to be the most haunted spot in England. Afterwards he went on to publish seven books of what he called 'strange stories', as well as editing a further eight anthologies of ghost stories by other people.

In later life, and without any training whatsoever, he even set himself up as an amateur therapist counselling those 'disturbed by psychic experiences'.

But that was Robert Aickman all over: a man who without the slightest cause for it was endowed with such overwhelming self-confidence that there was nothing he believed he couldn't do. Once he'd met Tom Rolt at Tardebigge and got his blessing for the idea of an inland waterways association, there was no stopping him. His wife Ray was conscripted to the cause and their Bloomsbury flat completely given over to an office from which in no time at all he was firing off letters and arranging meetings with anyone prestigious enough to further the cause. He worked with a frenetic, almost manic, energy; and at such a prodigious rate that those close to him couldn't help but find him intimidating.

You wonder what his secretaries must have thought. He had a knack for dictation and used to reel off letters and reports by the page, picking up his train of thought effortlessly whenever he was disturbed by the telephone. But Aickman wasn't a likeable man. He lived in a distorted world of his own, at one and the same time bereft of self-doubt and yet paradoxically plagued by it. You feel that the perspective of his vision must often have made him resistant to other people's ideas. It certainly made him pompous about his own.

One secretary couldn't stand the pace and the fussy meticulousness of his working methods and resigned after just a couple of weeks. Later Aickman enlisted the services of a 24-year-old who was desperate for work after having only just upped sticks and walked out on her husband and 4-year-old daughter. Her name was Elizabeth Jane Howard, a woman eventually destined to become a writer, perhaps one of the most underrated English writers of the century. She was halfway through her first novel at the time, and was paid £2-10 (£2.50) for a couple of days work a week.

If, as Milton maintains, beauty is 'Nature's coinage', then at this point in her life Jane (as she was generally known) was rich indeed. She was drop-dead gorgeous, with delicate yet powerful features, high cheek bones and a mass of fair hair which tumbled down her back and which in later years earned her the nickname 'Wog' because of its similarity to the tangled tresses of a golliwog.

Unfortunately her attractiveness would always be a destructive force in her life: it made people of both genders desire her for her appearance, not for what she was. And it made her too vulnerable to the sort of men who were dangerous for her.

Of course, it wasn't long before she and Aickman finished up in bed.

FIFTEEN

Life on *Justice* had become much more complicated since Braunston when Em and her mother had arrived hotfoot from London in the household's Mighty Metro. This was yet another vehicle to add to the growing convoy which was moving inexorably westward across the countryside towards Stratford-upon-Avon like some twenty-first-century wagon train.

Theoretically the Metro should have made things easier. Before its arrival I'd used the bike to get back from wherever I'd taken the boat to wherever I'd left the Debsmobile. This involved a substantial amount of cycling which was not exactly easy-peasy stuff for a 50-year-old whose last experience of unmotorised two-wheel locomotion had been around the time of puberty. But it did at least have the advantage of simplicity. Once I'd cycled to the car it was a straightforward task to fold down the roof, wedge the bike behind the seat and drive back to the boat.

With the Mighty Metro it *should* have been even easier. With two cars we *should* have been able to ferry ourselves around at will, taking the cars to wherever we planned to moor that night, leaving one there and driving back in the other. With two cars, once we'd got to our evening mooring, we *should* have been able to drive back in one of them to pick up the other. This *should* have been relatively uncomplicated stuff. Not exactly rocket science. Except, of course, life is never that straightforward. It's a mistake to think you can plan for it.

For a start, with a crew to help me, I was travelling further now. On my own I'd been pottering along, cruising for no more than a couple of hours a day and staying for weeks on end in the same place. Now, with Em and Chris on board, we were moving upwards of seven or eight hours a day, which even at a rate of three miles an hour still meant we were shifting considerable distances.

So in order to effect the strategy with the cars we found ourselves driving for hours on end. In the morning we took them to where we thought we were going to be that night. This could sometimes be up to 30 miles away, a total travelling distance for two cars of 60 miles. We'd leave one car and drive back to the boat in the other which put another 30 miles onto the clock. Total mileage for the morning: 90 miles. And then we had to drive the same distance again in the evening to get the cars back together again. Total mileage for the day: 180 miles.

It was madness. It was bad enough on country lanes but once you got anywhere near a town – as we did around Leamington Spa and Warwick – the hassle factor was further exacerbated by rush-hour traffic jams and incomprehensible systems of inner ring roads.

OK, so Warwick may not exactly be up there with the big boys in terms of the irrationality of its road planners. It isn't exactly a Reading or a Milton Keynes, I grant you that. But it can still spring enough surprises for me to have come close to believing one evening, having passed its castle four times in as many minutes, that there was more than one of them in the town.

Then there was the problem of what we did if we couldn't get to our planned destination. Or if we got to it too early and wanted to go on a bit longer that day. Canal travel, as anyone who's done it will testify, is an entirely unpredictable method of getting around. You only need a dodgy lock or a plastic bag around your propeller, and your plans go to pot.

Why on earth did we do it? What could possibly have been in our minds? OK, having a car available theoretically meant that we could get out and about more, though apart from shifting cars we didn't get out and about at all. Why would we? We were on a boating holiday. We were perfectly happy on the canals, thank you very much. I suppose a car did give us the advantage of not needing to worry about food since we could always get to a supermarket. But the gloss of that attraction soon wore thin after the first transition from the tranquil peace of the towpath to the frenetic trolley-rage of the canned vegetable aisle. After that I'd have been happy enough to exist on a diet of dry bread and water just to avoid the coronary stress of shopping.

Eventually we threw in the towel and did the sensible thing. We decided not to bother about cars. From now on we would be free. Well, free after a fashion, for the Debsmobile had gone on the blink again and I spent a frustrating afternoon high on the smell of petrol fumes driving around attempting to find a replacement for a diaphragm which had split in the carburettor. It wasn't easy but eventually a helpful garage traced one for me from a mail order parts catalogue in Kazakhstan or somewhere. It only cost £3.46, including postage. Mind you, the garage charged me thirty quid to park in their forecourt until it arrived.

You can see why they were helpful.

*

That night we moored at Cape Locks on the northern outskirts of Warwick and the following morning we cast off early for the endurance test which is Hatton Locks – the 'twenty-one steps to heaven' as the old working boatmen used to call them.

Hatton isn't the longest flight on the British canal system, that being Tardebigge on the Worcester and Birmingham Canal where a total of thirty locks (thirty-six if you count Stoke Locks, which are practically part of the same flight) lift the canal from the River Severn to the hill on which Britain's second city is built. They're not the most difficult locks on the system either, that cussed title belonging in my opinion to the twenty-one double locks at Wigan where the chambers are uneven and where each paddle has to be inconveniently unlocked with a special key because of the oiks who regularly open them and flood the town. Which is, I suppose, one way of passing time when you're bored.

Even so, arriving at the bottom of Hatton is an awesome experience. Once you've got yourself into the swing of things by cantering through the first three or four locks (phew – difficult? *Pour moi*?) you round a bend to be confronted by the next dozen or so sweeping intimidatingly up the hill, their gates like colossal steps to… well, to heaven, I suppose (gulp!). Even with a well-drilled, disciplined crew up for the job, you're looking at a minimum two or three hours of hard graft to get to the top. And 'well-drilled' and 'disciplined' were not precisely the adjectives that sprang to mind when I cast my eye appraisingly over the crew of *Justice*.

Up for it? Downcast by it might be a more accurate way of putting things.

For a start there was me, who for the last two months had been ditch-crawling from Oxford at a rate of knots so slow that to have gone slower would have meant going backwards. Then there was Em, whose idea of exercise is occasionally walking down the escalators on the Underground and who thinks she's Sporty Spice if she gets to the bottom without falling over. Chris is the most naturally athletic of us all but even she seemed daunted by the prospect of the flight and played the age card, deciding that there were far more interesting things to do than locks on a summer's day, even a summer's day which was turning out to be overcast and drizzly.

Luckily we met another boat crewed by an energetic young couple and we travelled with them which meant we could share locks and cut our workload. Pete and Sarah – I won't give their real names – had just bought their boat, and it was in that glossy, just-painted state which to a cynical eye like mine suggests they paid five grand over the odds for it. Because of this Pete was inordinately worried about scratching his hull and, with Em steering *Justice*, he insisted that she go into locks first so that she wouldn't hit him.

Instead he set about hitting her. At their first lock together he caught her stern-on and at the second he took her out broadside. By the third he'd developed an amusing little variation on their *pas de deux* whereby he could hit her both stern-on *and* broadside in the same move. Eventually all this became too embarrassing even for him and he handed over to Sarah who, because she knew she couldn't steer, was altogether more careful about doing it. By the time they got to the top, she and Em were moving together as elegantly as anything you'd see on *Strictly Come Dancing*. It was a joy to behold.

Well, a joy for everyone except Pete, that is. He was still nursing his wounded pride.

'She seems to have tightened up a bit, your missus,' he commented at one lock while we waited for the boats to enter.

'Tightened up?'

'Her steering, I mean. It was all over the place before, wasn't it? She seems to have got the hang of it now...'

★

Our mooring that night was beyond Shrewley Tunnel at an extraordinarily beautiful spot where the canal perches on the high embankment which overlooks the fields and the small village of Rowington. About five in the morning I woke and lay fitfully tossing and turning until it became clear that I was beyond sleep now and that out of fairness to Em I might as well get up.

I dressed and stepped out onto the deck where in the dark the mist was lying impenetrably thick over the water as it often does in summer. I watched it swirling enigmatically in the calm windless morning, and gradually it began to lift, melting away gently like a soft fall of snow in the warmth of sunshine. Suddenly, and without warning, the sky became luminous with a deep reflected purple as the rays of the sun, not yet risen, began to touch the underside of the blanket of cloud which was lying across the sky. I was totally entranced. The cloud cover shifted and fractured until there appeared behind it a sharp splinter of perfect enamel blue; and after that, resplendent in its sharp outline – so clear I swear you could see flames leaping from its surface – a most magnificent, spectacular, breathtaking sunrise.

I stood hypnotised for as long as it took daylight to break upon the world – fifteen minutes, maybe twenty. As I did the birds began to stir, at first a cautious wood pigeon in the trees nearby, then another calling to it, and then another so that in no time at all it seemed there was a choir around me, welcoming the morning. At length, a remote cockerel crowed, and a second soon answered it from far-off across the fields. Then thrushes and blackbirds and a whole cacophony of birds and creatures seemed to wake, hopping about the trees and scratching in the hedgerows with a presence that was palpable.

The new day, it seems, had begun. But in a way I'd never experienced before.

Which I thought was odd – since though I've been oblivious to it, it's happened much like this every single day of my life.

★

Robert Aickman had a difficult childhood. There was an age disparity of more than thirty years between his father William and his mother who was twenty-three at the time of their wedding and apparently so naive that she seems to have been unaware of what it involved physically. Robert joked later he'd been conceived as a result of his parents' one and only coupling and this could well have been the truth. It was a loveless marriage, arranged by Robert's grandfather who had met William in the unprepossessing location of a lavatory in a south coast hotel; and who afterwards seems to have manipulated matters to get his daughter off his hands as quickly as possible.

After their wedding Robert's parents settled in the countryside near Stanmore, north of London, in a five-bedroom house called Langton Lodge, which was large, cold and draughty. His father was a loud and dominant man with the sort of idiosyncratic personality that suggests mental imbalance, and his son lived in dread of him. He seems to have had no concept of time, and would turn up for work in the afternoon, or at theatres during the second act of a play. This sort of behaviour didn't help attracting clients to the architectural practice he ran, and the family was always short of money which conspired to prevent Aickman from completing his education and from making friends – two factors that turned him into the loner he was to remain for the rest of his life.

He was an isolated and naturally narcissistic man and it was strange that he should ever marry. But it was a strange marriage with a strange woman whose background was even less happy than his own. Ray Gregorson was from a wealthy family but her upbringing had been blighted when her parents had separated and her mother – with an absurd sense of farce – had run off with the chauffeur. Less amusingly, that relationship ended in a suicide pact which must have had a deep and enduring effect on Ray, making her in her own way as emotionally unstable as Aickman.

The two of them met through a mutual friend called Audrey Linley, a rich and pretty 19-year-old student at the Royal College of Music who Aickman had been courting. As was his way, he'd become hopelessly infatuated with her. The feeling wasn't reciprocated so that when Aickman invited her to go to the opera with him, she suggested instead that he take Ray, a childhood friend.

The affair with Ray, you feel, developed more out of their shared sense of insecurity than as a result of any affection between them. Indeed, after their wedding in 1941 – they were both 27 at the time – Aickman wrote to his new bride making it clear with startling insensitivity that he'd married her not for love but out of sympathy. But this was typical of Aickman too. He frequently acted in ways which allowed him to believe that what he did was selfless whereas the truth was frequently the opposite.

One way or another, the arrangement between them that passed as marriage was hardly an emotionally charged liaison, let alone the sort of meeting of minds on which long and enduring relationships are built. By the time Elizabeth Jane Howard appeared on the scene you can't help but feel that their 5-year-old union was already on the rocks and that the Aickmans were both in their own way ready for an injection of passion.

In Elizabeth Jane Howard they both found it.

★

Jane Howard was born in 1923 into a family that would have instinctively attracted a man like Aickman, being wealthy and intellectual and tailor-made to appeal to his worst pretensions. One of her grandfathers was a successful timber merchant; the other the distinguished composer and musician Sir Arthur Somervell.

From the outset she had a passport into a rarefied social circle and in Easter 1940, in the early months of the Second World War, she found herself a guest at a house near Great Yarmouth where an old family friend, Kathleen Young, had invited her to stay as company for her son who was down from Stowe School for the holiday. The house – actually a bungalow – was set among the woods overlooking a lake; and there at the same time on sick leave from the navy was Kathleen's older son Peter, from her previous marriage to the explorer Robert Falcon Scott – the famous Scott of the Antarctic who died in 1912 trying to reach the South Pole.

Jane was just seventeen and flattered to the point of being overwhelmed when the 31-year-old began to pay her attention. They soon became lovers, though the relationship was a difficult one, constantly blighted by the spectre of Kathleen who exerted considerable (some might say unhealthy) influence over her son until the day she died.

Kathleen was a formidable personality and in an era when women could barely leave home unchaperoned, she'd studied at the Slade and afterwards earned for herself an international reputation as a sculptor. She had worked on the Left Bank in Paris and knew Auguste Rodin. The young Picasso was a friend too, as was the dancer Isadora Duncan whose first illegitimate child she had helped deliver. Later in London, her studio, on the site of what is now Victoria Coach Station, attracted a glittering procession of the rich, famous and powerful of her time.

Kathleen had strong views on how a child of hers should be brought up. Indeed, her choice of husband had been determined by the sole criterion that he should be a man worthy of fathering her son. When she got pregnant she took to sleeping on a beach in Devon, living on a diet of nuts and wild fruits; and after Peter was born she brought him up after the fashion of a Spartan, starting his day with a cold bath, and making him wear bizarre short-sleeved tunics she had designed for him.

A relationship with someone who had a mother as single-minded as this was always going to be a problem for a woman like Jane Howard, stubborn and self-willed. So from the outset there was a bitter but quietly fought head-to-head between the two women. Kathleen thought the flighty young thing who had attached herself to her son was 'rather pretty' and 'sweet' but a bit of a 'flibbertigibbet' – an 'airhead' I think we might say now. Mind you, at this stage Jane was little more than a child.

Peter by comparison was not only older but a glamorous icon of his age. He was an officer in the Royal Navy; a graduate of Trinity, Cambridge; an Olympic bronze medallist at sailing; the author of a bestselling book; and a successful wildlife painter who'd exhibited in both London and New York.

Paradoxically though, in their letters it is Peter – named after Peter Pan, the boy who never grew up – who emerges as the younger and more indecisive of the two. Jane is uncertain, yes; but she knows her own mind and where she's going. Peter admits he's 'scared' of her. There's so much inside her waiting to burst out, he says. You also get the sense that notwithstanding her patina of vulnerability, Jane's clear sense of purpose and her emotional intensity threatened him too.

Peter Scott responded to Jane's intelligence by doing as men often do when faced with women they care for but who unsettle them: he patronised her. This irritated her tremendously. 'Please *darling* Peter pretend I'm not twelve,' she pleaded in one letter to him, 'if you don't I shall come in plaits and… you'll have to keep giving me ice creams even though it's snowing.'

The two were married in April 1942 in London, a reception for 300 being held afterwards in Claridges. There is a wedding picture which shows them coming out of the church, he in his naval uniform looking tired at the whole business; she, as tall, in a broderie anglaise dress, tight at the bodice and waist, with broad, padded shoulders that wouldn't be out of place in a City boardroom today. Their daughter Nicola was born within the year; the birth was excruciatingly painful. But then nothing associated with this marriage was without pain. By now Peter's naval career was taking off and as the war progressed they were drifting apart as he was sent away increasingly often on active service.

It would have been difficult for any woman alone in wartime London with a young child and history unfolding around her, but it must have been harder for Jane Howard whose insecurities throughout her life have always led her to rely overly on men as a means of confirming her own worth. Inevitably she had an affair. Unfortunately she had it with Peter's brother and worse, the two of them insisted on confessing their forbidden love. Afterwards Jane got involved with another man, maybe more, for there was a period of twelve years in her life when she had so many affairs she admits she was a 'tart for affection'.

'I had very, very brief affairs with people I never want to see again,' she once said, 'but I always hoped they were going to be much more serious that that. Several times I thought I was very much in love with them... but actually it wasn't true.'

Jane and Peter attempted to patch things up but they were unsuccessful. In the summer of 1947, with only £10 in her pocket and carrying only a suitcase of clothes and her half-finished first novel, Jane bolted, leaving Nicola behind. 'Bolting' is the word she uses herself for the way in which she leaves relationships that she can't handle. She did it with her next two husbands and she eventually did it with Aickman too.

It's difficult to understand what Jane saw in Aickman. She was exceptionally good-looking while he was nerdish, fresh-faced and serious, with lips tending towards the thickish and a nose too delicate for the heavy-framed round glasses he was obliged to wear for his severe short-sightedness. He was, however, a powerful personality – though this didn't count for much where she was concerned. She so entranced him by her beauty that he once claimed 'little in the way of completely normal business was possible... when she was in the room'. Perhaps it gratified her that she obsessed him so much. That she could so subvert his confident decisiveness and natural authority.

They had a lot in common. Aickman never went to university, a chip on his shoulder he carried his whole life. Jane had even less formal education and had only been to school for a couple of terms during which she'd been so badly bullied she was farmed out to a governess. Both were from problematic families too, and if Aickman's lacked affection from his father, so too did Jane from her mother. She'd lost a child – another girl – the year before Jane was born; and whether she believed

ONE MAN AND A NARROWBOAT

her surviving daughter somehow responsible for this, or resented her for being a reminder of it, Jane came to believe that her mother never really wanted her so that she was always searching for maternal love which she never felt she received.

'There are certain experiences you need to have had by a certain age; and if you don't have them, you're stuck in a time warp either waiting or experimenting or reacting the wrong way,' she once said. 'One basic one is feeling quite sure your mother loves you.'

It was their ambition to become writers, however, which bound them together most. Aickman maintained that he'd deferred his writing career to become chairman of the Inland Waterways Association and whatever the truth of this, it is the case that he always thought of himself as a writer and knew that sooner or later writing was what he would do for a living. While he and Jane were working together they collaborated on a series of ghost stories, *We Are for the Dark*, which was her first book and for a long time his only published work.

Odd then that in a relationship that could be so creative there was such inherent potential for destruction too. So much so that their affair would almost ruin the nascent Inland Waterways Association.

SIXTEEN

For a change, it was raining.

The same as it had rained as we'd come through Leamington and Warwick. The same as it had when we'd left Braunston, and before that, when I'd been travelling on my own when it had rained every blasted, god-damned day I'd been on the boat from the moment I'd first arrived in Oxford. In fact, further back than that, for it seemed to me it had been raining non-stop since my adolescence – before that even, from when I was a kid at school – and maybe even earlier than that as well. Indeed, the more I thought about it, the more it seemed to me that it had been raining from the very moment of my birth; for as I sat in the boat listening to it hammer on the roof, it seemed to provoke some deep primeval memory which might have been of the rain hammering on the hood of my pram, or even of my pregnant mother sheltering under an umbrella.

The weather records were falling as fast as world records at a drug-fuelled Olympics. At first it was the wettest spring of the century, then the wettest since 18-something-or-other and then the wettest summer since records began... Every day, it seemed, the forecasters were struggling for new levels of hyperbole until I came to believe that I was living through the wettest period in British history – the wettest ever – since the very dawn of man when the first hominids crawled upon this, our island home.

At least all this was positive in one respect, since when it gets as wet as this you stop caring about being wet at all. Wet becomes the nature of your universe. Being constantly saturated becomes as natural to you as being surrounded by air. When it's *that* wet you forget about ever being dry. You stop worrying about falling into the canal as well – and that's unusual, since even though no one likes to admits it, the prospect of tumbling into the water is a niggling concern for anyone who spends any length of time on a boat. Regardless of how experienced you are, or how careful, it's always there in the back of your mind, one of those things you know is going to happen sooner or later. And generally when you least expect it.

There you are, sitting on the deck quietly reading, or contentedly leaning against something sipping a cup of tea in the sunshine when – glug! – suddenly you've been deposited as if by sorcery into some cold netherworld of frondy plantlife and strange creatures with fins.

At Kingswood Junction, about five miles from the top of Hatton, the Grand Union links with the Stratford Canal at a tricky little junction which connects through a short spur and brings you out in the middle of the Lapworth flight of locks. You're back on a narrow canal again now, a waterway like the Oxford Canal and one which is equally as pretty. It's characterised by little cantilevered split bridges built of cast iron, designed to allow the tow ropes of horse-drawn boats to pass through a gap in the middle without having to unharness; and there are also a series of bijou cottages with barrel-shaped roofs said to be constructed from the wooden scaffolding which was used to build the canal's distinctive humpback bridges.

The Stratford Canal has been a disaster area for Em over the years in terms of falling in. We were cruising along it once engaged in a heated discussion about divorce or something when I looked away from steering only to find that she'd disappeared from the deck. She'd just vanished. Gone. Instead – for reasons that are even now not entirely clear to me – she was floundering around in the water at a point the boat had been a few moments before. She was shouting a lot, I seem to recall. More precisely, she was shouting at me. And shouting with a note of profanity which I don't think was entirely justified by the context of our conversation.

Another summer we stopped at one of the locks to buy a window box from an adjacent cottage which had a lucrative seasonal sideline selling to boats. It advertised itself by covering the whole of its frontage with flowers, trailing them around its doors and windows and hanging them in baskets from its brickwork so that it was a riotous blaze of colour. We bought a mixture of the most glorious blood-red geraniums, great garish pink petunias and clumps of ice-blue lobelia. Em put them on the bow of the boat and took a pace or two backwards to admire them.

And stepped straight into the water.

I've fallen in myself too from time to time. Judged on theatrical spectacle alone my best was at Hawkesbury Junction at the northern end of the Oxford Canal, not far from Coventry. Sutton's Stop, as it's also known, is a busy place: there's one pub on the waterside and another nearby. It can sometimes get hectic – especially on warm summer evenings when the boisterous crowds at closing time congregate in groups around the basin, reluctant to admit it's time to get off home to their beds.

Em and I had been in the pub all night and when it was time to go it didn't occur to me for one moment that cruising at night with large quantities of beer swilling around my gut might not exactly be a sensible thing to do. I pushed the boat off from the bank without really thinking about it. It moved almost imperceptibly at first the way heavy things do in water. Then it began to accelerate faster than I was ready for in the state I was. Soon I was suspended over the water, my feet on dry land and the balance of my weight on the boat as I clung to it. Things go into slow motion at times like this. You get a sort of out-of-body experience which allows you to see yourself as others see you. There was really only one way this could end.

I wouldn't have minded so much if I'd been on my own. But I wasn't on my own. Far from it. The crowds turning out from the pub had seen what was going to happen long before I had.

And as I disappeared under the surface they burst into rousing applause.

★

When Em and I first cruised the Stratford Canal it was owned and administered as a totally separate waterway from the rest of the system by the National Trust, an organisation which is doubtless unsurpassed when it comes to the appreciation of the finer detail of eighteenth-century English country houses, but which isn't exactly up there with the world's best when it comes to its expertise in canal management. Indeed, so little did the Trust know about running waterways that it took years for it to grasp some of the basic principles of the process.

Like the fact that in order to move a boat on water you first need water.

In those days the canal was so poorly dredged that there was barely enough of the stuff to float a toy boat, let alone a real one. The locks were in dreadful disrepair too, with lock gates leaking badly and some falling off their hinges. This wouldn't have been so bad, except that to cruise the Stratford Canal then you had to buy a separate National Trust licence which was a prohibitively expensive business for young people like us who were struggling to afford the basic British Waterways' one.

However, for all its failings, this route to the River Avon wouldn't exist today without the National Trust; for when the canal was threatened with closure in the late 1950s they took responsibility and restored it on a shoestring using any labour they could get hold of, from volunteers to serving prisoners. At a time when canal restoration is the flavour of the month and newly renovated waterways are opened so regularly they don't even make the news, it's as well to remember the importance of the Stratford Canal which was the first to be completed and the pattern for many that would follow.

Saving a waterway in those days wasn't exactly a piece of cake. The Stratford Canal was only brought back into use by confronting Warwickshire Council who threatened to close it rather than spend a few thousand pounds repairing a bridge at Wilmcote. Stratford Council wasn't any more enthusiastic either, and at one stage it had plans to fill in Bancroft Basin – the terminus of the canal and the junction with the Avon where today thousands of visitors to the town gather around the gardens to enjoy the boats.

They wanted the land to extend the bus station. Like the council did in Banbury.

Thankfully common sense prevailed and restoration went ahead. It was completed in the astonishingly short time of just three years, with the opening taking place in 1964 to coincide with the four hundredth anniversary of Shakespeare's birth. The project was a personal triumph for Robert Aickman who had encouraged and inspired the project; but it was an archetypal English victory for the muddled forces of amateurish enthusiasm too, and as such it was a close-run thing. Or as David Hutchings, the man mainly responsible for it, said in words that have inspired the waterways restoration movement ever since, 'None of us were experts, or we should have known it was impossible.'

*

To make ourselves comfortable as we travelled down the canal in the driving rain, we'd turned on the central heating and lit the cast-iron coal stove in the back cabin. This is set at the level of your feet, just below where you stand to steer, and it generates such an immense heat there can be an Arctic storm raging outside and you'll still be cosy.

These back-cabin stoves were what the original boatmen depended on for their livelihood. They not only provided the source of warmth which meant they could keep going in extreme conditions, but they were little cookers too – small Agas – which ensured there was always a hot meal at the end of the day. In Dorothy Hartley's classic *Food in England* she gives a traditional recipe for what she calls a Bargee's Pail – a meal cooked in a galvanised bucket which is used like a medieval cauldron, with soup, main course and dessert all simmering away on the stove in the same pot.

If it's genuine it must date from the early days of the industrial revolution when the job paid well enough for boatmen to afford to keep a separate home for their families, and when they had to fend for themselves while they were working. In later years as the rates for the job dropped, their wives and children were compelled to join them on the water as crew; the women taking over the responsibility for cooking, preparing meals at the same time as they steered the 'butties' – the second of the two boats which were worked together as a pair, one towing the other.

The women were also responsible for looking after the kids. And doing the washing. And the cleaning. And helping with the locks. And unloading cargo too, which meant them rolling up their sleeves and shovelling out coal from the hold.

It wasn't an easy life for anyone then working on the water – men, women or children. But it was particularly hard for the women.

Even so, I suspect that when they were on board the food would have been more imaginative and creative, if for no other reason than for the sake of economy. I imagine the women would have made more use of available ingredients, whether seasonal vegetables they could have grubbed from the fields, or the sort of fruits like sloes and crab apples, or herbs like thyme and chervil, that you can still find growing wild around towpaths. This recipe for Shin of Beef in Ale below has absolutely no historical provenance that I can attest to, though for some reason I always think of it as a traditional dish, possibly because until relatively recently shin was one of the cheaper cuts of beef and within the reach of poorer folk; and possibly because I always think of it in the terms I've described it, the meat cooked in traditional 'ale' rather than modern 'beer'.

Or then again, maybe it's because I imagine the recipe to be one of those dishes the boat people in Victorian times might have cooked as they were moored in London at Limehouse or

East India Dock, close to where ocean-going ships would have berthed to unload their cargoes of spice and demerara sugar from the Caribbean, and where there was always the possibility of something finding its way out of the hold, no questions asked.

Whatever its background, it tastes just as good in an ordinary oven as it does cooked in a saucepan on the top of a stove; but there's no doubt in my mind that it tastes even better cooked in a coal-fired oven, and best of all in a back-cabin stove on a narrowboat on a wet day in Warwickshire with the rain driving horizontally, blown by a sharp wind. That way, when it's cold and inhospitable, you can get it simmering first thing in the morning and have it bubbling away gently all day, tempting you with its rich and delectable smell whenever your spirits are low.

The Third Recipe

Though these days the price differential between shin and other steak may be less than it used to be, don't be tempted to cook this with anything except shin since you won't get the taste. Besides, any better quality meat will break up to an unappetising mush during the long cooking the recipe requires. Shin of beef is sinewy, but so packed with flavour and goodness that it's what they used to make beef tea for invalids in the past. It lends itself to this sort of dish.

For four people you need about 1–2 lb of meat – though my inclination would be to go for less and buy organic. You can eat it with rice or potatoes, and any green vegetable in season, so there's no danger you'll go hungry. Dice it into largish chunks and sear it quickly in a small amount of lard until it goes brown on the outside. Better still, if you're on a boat and want to avoid washing up, sear it in the fat left in the frying pan from the breakfast bacon. When all else fails use vegetable oil which, yes, I know is healthier, but which just doesn't taste anywhere near as good.

Transfer the meat to a casserole dish and fry a large, roughly chopped onion in the remaining fat until it begins to brown at the edges. Put that into the casserole too, along with three or four thickly sliced carrots, a stick or two of diced celery, and a handful of the chopped celery leaves. Then – the magic of cooking this – add two teaspoons of demerara sugar, and a heaped teaspoon of mixed spice. That's right – the same mixed spice that you use in cake recipes. Mix all of these ingredients together in the casserole along with a tablespoon of flour, a teaspoon of mustard powder and a generous sprinkling of black pepper. Then cover the contents with beer.

Now, if you want to impress your guests, you could at this stage be very particular about the beer. You could use only Legless and Hangover's 9 per cent Special Rotgut Easter brew. Or Stagger and Fallover's malt-based Throw-Up bitter, brewed at the Old Cobblers Brewery using only the finest 100-year-old Wiltshire gusset yeast. You could do this – and then try to convince your guests that this is what makes this dish taste as good as it does.

Actually the truth is, it doesn't make a heap of difference what beer you use. I've cooked it with best Shepherd and Neame bottled bitter at more than two quid a throw, and with cheapo French lager at 10p a gallon. I have made it with live Worthington Shield India Pale Ale, including the sediment from the bottom and – when it was the only thing available – with Guinness past its sell-by date. I have even made it with the salvagings from a rather good party the night before, including fag ash from the bottom of old cans for all I know. All I can say is, it tastes good every which way.

Cook it in an oven at a lowish heat, or on the top of the stove at a slow simmer. Either way, ensure that you keep it topped up with beer (and maybe a little beef stock if you have it) so that it doesn't dry out. It will be ready to eat in about two to two and a half hours, though in a damped-down back-cabin stove it can cook for twice that time and longer without spoiling.

Our first night on the Stratford Canal we spent at the small village of Wootten Wawen, which straddles the A34. We moored up a few yards short of one of three aqueducts on the canal which are as characteristic of it as its bridges and cottages. They are no more than cast iron troughs and they're unusual in that the towpath drops down adjacent to them. This means that pedestrians walk at the level of the canal bed with the trough of the aqueduct (and all the water behind it) to one side of them and with their eyes at the same level as the water.

It's a strange experience, but it was a strange evening all round. After the awful weather we'd had there was an unmistakable sense of change in the air, but change for the worse – as if the rain that we'd been suffering was really just the beginning, the harbinger of something much darker and more threatening. Great purple clouds made stately procession across the sky and the atmosphere felt heavy and ponderous. Even though it was cold, there was a damp clamminess in the air of the sort you occasionally experience in the tropics.

I thought it was building up to a storm. I thought it was going to be the mother of all storms.

Funny how wrong you can be sometimes. Overnight there was a meteorological miracle and when we woke up the sun was so fierce that before ten o'clock the thermometer was touching ninety degrees.

Summer, it seemed, had finally arrived on the waterways.

SEVENTEEN

The diaphragm had arrived for the broken-down Debsmobile, and I went off to the garage early next morning to collect it. Installing it in the carburettor took a few minutes. With the car on the road again, I felt inordinately pleased with myself and driving back that morning in the warm sunshine I began musing on matters of design – a train of thought triggered by the fact that so many of our contemporary views on style originated in the car industry where, for better or worse, the Triumph Herald played such a critical part in getting us to the point we're at today where the car you drive says more about you than a DNA profile.

To be blunt, the Herald represents a triumph of style over substance. It's an OK car. It looks good. But it's not a *great* car. Mechanically its engine was antiquated when it was built, and the bodywork wasn't made to last more than a few years.

But what else could the company have done? In the 1950s it was saddled with a series of outdated models powered by engines and gearboxes in which it had invested so heavily that it hadn't got the resources to go back to the drawing board and start again from scratch. It had no option but to design around what it already had, even though this effectively meant putting a new body on top of old parts.

It was at this critical point that Giovanni Michelotti entered the company's history. Michelotti is recognised now as one of the most prolific sports car designers of the twentieth century, but at the time he was a freelance who had only just set up his own studio after working for the famous Italian company Vignale. He was introduced to Standard Triumph by someone who had worked with him at Ford, and he agreed to take over the styling of the troubled Zobo project which the company was ambitiously hoping to complete in time for the 1958 Motor Show.

It was a tough assignment. For a start the styling work which had already been done on the car didn't help Michelotti. In fact, it handicapped him, impairing his natural creativity. The prototype was shipped over to him in Turin and he agonised over it while virtually every weekend the company's chief engineer Harry Webster drove to Italy to monitor progress. This in itself was no mean feat in the days when there were few motorways and when cars were far less reliable and powerful than today.

Michelotti worked from a small penthouse studio on the tenth floor of an anonymous office block and it was there in the summer of 1957 that matters came to a head. If the company was to have sufficient time to meet its deadline on the new car, then decisions on styling needed to be taken by August at the latest. Yet by then the designs for the project were no further progressed than when Michelotti had come on board.

As it happened, Harry Webster was holidaying in Sorrento that year with his wife and daughter and on his way back to England he decided to pop in to see how Michelotti was getting on. He wasn't anticipating much in the way of progress and he didn't expect the visit to be long, so he left his wife and daughter waiting for him in the car outside.

'Nothing! It was hopeless,' Webster recalled later. 'I said, "We are wasting our bloody time! Look! Suppose you could start again from scratch, here in Turin, to begin with a clean sheet of paper, what would it look like?"'

Michelotti was a hyperactive, headstrong man; an impulsive, energetic genius who would eventually kill himself with overwork. There's a picture of him taken outside the corrugated-iron walls of a factory somewhere, and you can almost feel his irritability at being taken away from his work for the sake of such a time-wasting irrelevance. He's clutching his hands together as if to constrain them into inactivity and what at first sight seems to be a weak smile on his angular face, on closer examination turns out to be an impatient grimace. There are a row of three pens in the breast pocket of his natty suit. You feel he can't wait to take one out and start drawing something.

To a man like him, what Webster said was a challenge. Within a few minutes the Italian had sketched out the outline of a new car. It was a design similar in almost every detail to the Triumph Herald we know today. He immediately started transferring the drawing to a full-scale draft on the wall and with Webster alongside him and the creative juices flowing, the two men worked on solidly for the next nine hours until around midnight Webster suddenly remembered with a shock that he'd left his wife and daughter outside.

He found them both curled up in the car fast asleep.

Michelotti worked overnight to complete his drawings but back in Coventry there was still a good deal of scepticism that he'd ever be able to deliver a physical prototype of his plans on time. As the clock ticked closer towards Christmas, the next relentless deadline in the production schedule, tension in the company mounted. In those days, when we had industry in England, it was the custom for most major manufacturers to close down their operations over the main holidays to save on the costs of overheads, and it wasn't until 24 December – the very day of the shut-down – that to everyone's great relief an Italian truck finally rolled up at the factory gates.

Inside was a completed prototype of the Herald coupé in black and gold. Webster and Alick Dick wasted no time in having it transferred to a turntable in the styling studio where everyone who saw it agreed it was a magnificent design. And even today fifty years later when you look at its low wheelbase and its sleek narrow lines, it's impossible not to be struck by the aesthetic beauty of Michelotti's creation.

★

Once we'd got the boat moored in Stratford we went off for a drink. We deserved it. After the change in the weather, it had been a long and sweltering day, so blisteringly hot that in the couple of hours it took us to work our way through the flight of locks that lowers the canal down to the level of the River Avon, Chris managed to get herself badly sunburned. She dropped off to sleep in a chair on the front deck, shaded by the overhang of the cabin; but as we'd moved she caught the full force of the sun so that with her white hair and her eyes protected by her sunglasses, she finished up looking like an albino panda.

The first critical decision you have to make when approaching Stratford by boat is where to moor. There are two alternatives. The first, Bancroft Basin, is the town's equivalent of Piccadilly Circus, except that where the London tourist magnet is grubby and squalid, the basin is exactly the opposite, overlooked as it is by the Royal Shakespeare Theatre and surrounded by meticulously tended flowerbeds and neatly manicured lawns. But it's just as busy as Piccadilly Circus. In the height of summer it's always crowded. Even assuming you can find a place to moor, you often have to disturb people picnicking on the grass to tie up.

If you are fortunate enough to find space, Bancroft Basin is the last word in convenience. Paradoxically, it's so convenient it's *in*convenient. It's so close to the town centre that some boats in the basin are shops themselves and it's not unknown for crews mooring here to be disturbed at night by tourists who've mistaken them for a hamburger stall.

Privacy? Forget it. In the high season you can't leave a curtain in your boat open for people shamelessly peering in at you; and I've known tourists to clamber unselfconsciously onto boats in order to get a closer view, as if boats were just another visitor attraction.

Which, thinking about it, is what they've become.

The alternative is to tie up on the river. The best mooring sites are directly facing the theatre, so close that if you go to a play you can check out your boat from the balcony of the bar while you're having drinks in the interval. You're only the width of the river away from the town but you leave the tourists behind, for visitors to Stratford are creatures of the herd and the overwhelming majority of them never venture over Tramway Bridge, despite the fine recreation ground and splendid river walk there.

Mind you, don't go running away with the idea that just because you're further from the tourists you're completely insulated from the crowds. You may leave humankind behind but wildfowl have traditionally inhabited Stratford's river and there are hundreds of noisy birds there – avian combatants in an internecine war which has been raging on the waterways for more than fifteen years. Nowhere better encapsulates the tensions at the heart of hostilities than this reach of the Avon.

The conflict has its roots in the eighteenth century when county landowners dug ornamental lakes on their estates and began to stock them with exotic birds. One favourite was the pale Atlantic-coast version of the North American wild goose, the largest of the species and absolutely unmistakable with its black neck, white face patch and mottled feather pattern. It's called the Canada Goose and as recently as 1953 a survey found just 1,500 pairs in the whole of Britain. Today, on a summer's afternoon, you'd find that many in Stratford between the bridge and the bandstand, and there'll be as many again on the bank opposite jostling for bread from tourists, not to mention another predatory flock twice as large cruising the river looking for trouble.

They're rather beautiful creatures; and with their deep-black, pleading eyes they're somehow able to hypnotise you into feeding them. They seem to have hypnotised our indigenous white farmyard goose too. Today around Stratford-upon-Avon the two species have mixed and mated with disregard to the outcome, each imparting to the other its worst characteristics. To say the indigenous English goose was never a particularly friendly bird is a bit like pointing out that Attila the Hun never signed the Geneva Convention. English geese were always bad-tempered, aggressive creatures, despite their Goosy Gander nursery image. But they did at least have the good grace to keep themselves to themselves – as opposed to the gregarious Canadian breed which think nothing of moving in on you with the strength of Panzer divisions if they suspect you of harbouring anything remotely edible.

Unfortunately many of the hybrids populating Stratford's waterside are aggressive *and* gregarious. They not only come looking for food but they're capable of taking off your arm if they don't get it.

Meanwhile, all this has left the graceful Stratford swan – the traditional monarch of these waters – on its webbed back foot. OK, swans haven't exactly been restrained in their breeding habits either. Nevertheless, I sense in these parts that their elegant, gliding progress through the water is sometimes less confident than it may appear on the surface. I worry that despite their showy style many of them are subconsciously traumatised by the fear of suddenly getting mugged by their North American cousins.

And violence happens, I can testify. When the tourists have finished for the day, their supply of stale Hovis and Mothers Pride exhausted, the Avon reverts to what passes for normality; and any boater who casually throws anything into the water, even a discarded cigarette, is in danger of precipitating a major ornithological incident with so much squawking and flapping and irritable pecking of feathers that you wish you were back in Bancroft Basin for a bit of peace and quiet.

We finally decided to moor on the river – but either place would have done. They're both wonderful locations, places you couldn't pay to stay, simply because there isn't anywhere except a boat where you *could* stay. In this respect Stratford is similar to many places on the waterways where there are moorings at unique sites over which you claim a short but intense ownership. It's one of the delights of cruising.

Where else apart from on water would you be able to sleep under the city walls at Chester, or adjacent to Henley Bridge on the Thames? Or deep in the hills on the very Pennine Way where hikers trek? Or in Bath facing Poultney Bridge which is like the Ponte Vecchio in Florence with shops along its length?

★

We went to the theatre that night and saw a dreadful production of *Romeo and Juliet*, the quality of which you could judge by the numbers of tourists who leapt to their feet in thunderous applause the moment the curtain fell as if to congratulate themselves at having got through it without dying of boredom. It served us right. All the tickets for the performance that night were sold out. I'd only managed to get hold of some by calling in a favour with a friend who knew an actor in the company. Would that all string-pulling like this could end in such disappointment. The world would be a better place for it.

To be fair though, our response to the play was as much to do with us as the production. We were downbeat because the next day we were going home. Em and Chris's holiday was over, and I needed to go back to London to clear up the latest problem plaguing the Crumbling Pile.

After the performance we walked across Tramway Bridge for the last time. The lights of the town were reflected on the rippling river and through the uncurtained windows of the theatre you could see the staff as they busied themselves cleaning the bleak bars and restaurants, now emptied of the crowds that had earlier been milling around inside so cheerfully. It was a sultry evening, and a lone busker stood on the bridge strumming out some melancholy ballad which we could make out echoing across the water when we got back to the boat, and which we could still hear tucked up in our beds as sleep came upon us.

EIGHTEEN

*J*ane Howard has never understood the power of her looks or the effect they have on men. It's something which has made her feel uncomfortable about herself, and so she's professed never to believe that she was beautiful, and to deny that beauty itself has value. 'I realise now that a lot of people took up with me because of what I looked like and didn't know anything else about me at all, or want to know,' she admits now. 'It was a kind of awful trap because I never liked my appearance very much.'

Her striking demeanour has been the cause of problems in her relationships with men. Robert Aickman saw her as Zuleika Dobson, the heroine of Max Beerbohm's 1911 novel whose exquisiteness led the young men of Oxford to queue up to drown themselves in the Isis out of love for her. 'Jane's presence,' he said, in his typically flamboyant way, 'had the effect of making everything else in life seem worthless and absurd beside her radiant identity. By merely existing, she promoted loves and hates which, through no fault of her own, left some who felt them fevered and wasted.'

He was obsessed with her and the three mornings a week they worked together must have been charged with intensity for them both, especially since for most of the period they knew each other, the Inland Waterways Association used as its office the living room of Aickman's small London flat where he still lived with his wife Ray and where she worked running their literary agency.

Ray seems to have been indifferent to their affair; indeed, in some ways she welcomed it. She told Jane that Robert was depressed and that it would do him good. When they were away, she looked after the office; when they were around, she cooked for them. She once remarked that she didn't mind Robert and Jane having a relationship – she just drew the line at having to take them breakfast in bed. 'He exploited Ray frightfully,' Jane has said of this period, in a way that seems to deny that she herself might have had any part in events. 'He recognised in Ray that there was somebody who would type his letters, wash his clothes, do the housework and cooking, be a sort of First Lieutenant which she certainly was.'

The claustrophobic incestuousness of life in this Bloomsbury bohemia wasn't helped by the fact that Jane's estranged husband Peter Scott was also implicated in it. He was in the process of setting up the Severn Wildfowl Trust (subsequently the Wildfowl and Wetlands Trust) at Slimbridge in Gloucestershire, on a site a half mile or so from the Gloucester and Sharpness Canal where he kept a narrowboat called *Beatrice*. This was modelled on Rolt's *Cressy* and was used as overflow accommodation for guests.

Robert Aickman was attracted by celebrity and he was attracted by Scott who among his many other achievements had shortly before commentated for the BBC at the wedding of the young Princess Elizabeth and Philip Mountbatten. This had made him a nationally famous figure and Aickman soon identified him as a useful contact. Before long – the affair with Jane notwithstanding – Aickman struck up a personal relationship, and Scott became a vice chairman of the IWA. To complete the circle, Scott subsequently employed Ray on *his* staff as his organising secretary.

As anyone who has experience knows, romance in a work environment, however well managed, causes nothing but distress to those involved and upset to the organisation concerned. Jane Howard and Robert Aickman's affair was no different and it began to cause problems after they took a boating holiday on the Thames. Ill-advisedly, they went during work time. And without Aickman saying anything to Tom Rolt, who was not just the IWA honorary secretary and joint boss of the organisation, but an instinctive traditionalist who Aickman must have known would have strong views about this sort of behaviour.

Until this point Rolt and Aickman had been close, not just as personal friends but as part of two couples whose wives were friends with each other as well. The Rolts had often been guests of the Aickmans at their London home and the Aickmans guests of the Rolts on *Cressy*. The four of them had holidayed together, and partly because the Rolts lived on a boat and hadn't got a phone, and partly because they were a generation – the last one – for which it was commonplace, there was a period they corresponded with each other regularly.

Aickman's romance with Jane Howard was the catalyst for a clash between the two men, though you can't help but feel that there'd been a lot else festering under the surface between them for some time beforehand. Rolt fired the first shot by writing to Aickman complaining that while Jane had been cruising the Thames, he'd been 'deliberately misled' into thinking she was in the office. There's little doubt that what he was feeling cut a good deal deeper than this though, for he added disingenuously – almost as an afterthought – that, of course, he 'could not care less' how Jane had spent her holiday and *who* she'd spent it with…

Really? So if he cared so little, why mention it at all? And if *this* wasn't bothering him, then what *was*? Jane being out of the office for a few days when she'd not taken a holiday in a year? The marginal inconvenience to the IWA that this might have caused? The trivial drain on the funds of the organisation?

Clearly there was more than Jane's absence at issue here, and Aickman focused on this when he replied to the criticism. He admitted he'd known Angela and Tom wouldn't be happy about what he'd done but he argued that Jane had been working for the Inland Waterways Association for a long time without ever having been on the waterways. As if this somehow justified him taking her away. As if it somehow vindicated what had happened, which was that the two of them were having a passionate affair and had decided to go away together without telling anyone.

Rolt wasn't satisfied. 'I do not think that this was right,' he said bluntly, 'and, as I said before, it damages the feeling of mutual confidence without which a concern like [the] IWA cannot carry on, at least not happily.'

This had become a moral question now, a matter of right and wrong; but people's perspective on right and wrong can be distorted, consciously or unconsciously, by other factors. Did Rolt find the liaison distasteful as a matter of principle? Or was there something more subliminal in his response? Was he, for instance, somehow attracted to Jane Howard himself? Or did Aickman think he was?

Perhaps underlying Rolt's response was a sort of jealousy, for around this time Aickman had started a flirtatious relationship with Angela which didn't go down well with anyone, and which may have tempted Tom to take liberties with Jane in a way that wasn't completely natural to him. There's an intriguing incident that takes place a little after these events when all of them had patched things up and gone away together on another boat trip – this one arranged legitimately as part of the IWA's campaigning activities. Rolt for some reason had plaited Jane a boatman's belt out of long grass which she is reported to have 'swung provocatively around her hips, infuriating Robert'.

What on earth was all this about then? Was the provocation an overtly sexual one? Or was the real affront Rolt's? Was his gift of the belt made knowing Jane well enough to predict how she would respond to it? And was it made anticipating how Aickman would respond to *her*? Either way, why *did* Aickman react so angrily? Was this covert sexual jealousy or something even more complicated, something rooted in Aickman's own muddled morality which allowed him to bed women with impunity while at the same time expecting them to act like prim Victorian virgins?

Correspondence between the two men continued, with Aickman becoming increasingly defensive about Jane in a way that took the form of a growing aggressiveness towards Tom and Angela as a couple. It was as if the gloves were suddenly off between them. Soon Angela pitched into the fray. 'I *do not hate* Jane,' she wrote bitterly. 'Indeed, I admire her brain and her beauty immensely but, from the day we all four went to the opera together, Jane has never spoken a civil word to me… Apart from one conversation with Ray (which I now regret) I have never discussed Jane with anyone… Why you should think that Tom and I want to interfere in your affairs, God only knows…'

So they 'all four' had gone to the opera together? Two couples as they had always been, except that instead of Ray Aickman there was now Jane Howard. It is not hard to imagine how uncomfortable this outing must have been for the Rolts, especially for the emotionally voluble Angela who always found it difficult to hide what she was feeling. It's not hard either to imagine why, out of loyalty if nothing else, she might have felt obliged to speak to Ray about it later. Or why, knowing this, the insecure yet self-willed Jane Howard would have reacted the way she did to Angela.

The affair ensured Aickman and Rolt would never again be able to work together with the same degree of trust they'd shared when they'd first set up the IWA and when they were united by their passionate zeal and enthusiasm for the waterways. In those days they'd bonded in common purpose but from now on the relationship between them would be prickly; and although Rolt always professed himself a deep admirer of Aickman's organisational abilities, from this point he seems never to be able to resist bickering with him about something or other, whether the state of the IWA's bookkeeping or the way he believed Aickman was using the organisation for his own self-aggrandisement.

You can't help but wonder if the way things were developing didn't suit Angela's purposes too, for just as Robert Aickman's relationship with Ray was rocky at this time, so her own marriage to Tom was coming under strain as their 'design for living' increasingly became subsumed by the burden of Tom's IWA responsibilities. Eventually they began to think of themselves as tools of the Gower Street office.

Which was another way of saying tools of Robert Aickman.

A couple of weeks later, I returned to Stratford and met my brother Jay who was to join me on the next leg of my journey.

He had a few days' holiday owing, and because his time was limited we set off as soon as we could. It was late, evening already starting to set in. As soon as we cast off and she was released to the river, *Justice* surged forward with the downstream current, her propeller responding to the depth of the water beneath her. In this, as in so many other ways, navigating a river is a totally different experience to being on a canal. A river is nature's creation, a live creature with a will of its own and its own moods and foibles. And it's much more dangerous than still water, especially at times like this when there's been a lot of rain and it's 'running fresh' as us boaty-types say.

Weirs rush powerfully and the river can build up alarmingly behind the narrow archways of bridges. It can get unpredictable too as the accumulation of water leads to confusing cross-currents that buffet you in all directions. When the water's high and you're travelling downstream, the best thing is to go with the flow, working in a sort of partnership with the elements, albeit sometimes a rather uneasy one.

All this is a totally different experience to steering on canals, which are human constructions. Compared with a river, canal water is inactive and lifeless – like a block of plastic to a plank of wood. You're not so much travelling on it, as moving through it – ploughing your course with a sort of dogged perseverance.

Speed is the one thing you notice most in open water. Released from the drag factor of canals, a moving narrowboat sits differently in a river. It drops at the stern and rises at the bow so that it slips through the water with less resistance, reaching 7 or 8 mph, or even more. Now I grant you, speeds like this wouldn't impress on your local by-pass, let alone at Hockenheim or Silverstone. But on a racetrack you're not steering a vehicle sixty feet long or more which can weigh anything up to twenty tons. And when you're driving at least you have things called brakes, which are useful if you need to stop quickly.

The best you've got on a boat is reverse gear.

Try using that on a fast-flowing river when you're in danger of smashing into another boat, or being swept into some dark threatening place where the water's gurgling and eternity beckons with its ominous finger. At the very best, making your propeller go backwards might bring you to a halt in twenty or thirty feet, but that sort of stopping distance hardly inspires confidence. Which is why – like death and the prospect of relegation if your team's having a bad season – it's best not to lose too much sleep contemplating things in life you can't control.

Like the weather, for instance…

Predictably, after a few consecutive days of sunshine, the British summer had drawn to a close; and the British, having thrown aside whatever items of clothing they decently could in an attempt to work up a good melanoma, had reverted to a more traditional summer garb of shell suits and light sweaters, the better to flaunt their peeling noses and flame-red complexions. Not that in our climate this sort of clothing is much use at any time when the priority should always be keeping dry. But we don't wear it to keep dry. We wear it to proclaim our nationality. It is a badge of chauvinistic pride.

You could tell the overseas tourists easily enough in Stratford. The tourists were the ones prepared for the rain. The English were the ones walking around like drowned rats.

My younger brother Jay is a seasoned canal traveller who's done many trips with me over the years but who seems to attract extreme weather conditions whenever he does. Years ago as a schoolboy he joined Em and me and a few friends on a hire boat through Shropshire. No sooner had we started than we were caught in the eye of a storm so fierce that we literally couldn't see where we were going and had to stop in the middle of the channel to wait for conditions to improve. On another occasion near Nuneaton it began pelting hailstones so dangerously large that we had to abandon the boat again in the middle of the canal.

True to form, as soon as we cast off from Stratford it began raining in a way that you just knew was going to turn nasty. It started with a light drizzle which we endured for half an hour or so; but then it got windy too, and the rain blew up more furiously until it was coming down like stair rods, making the boat lurch around unnervingly in the swell. At this we decided to throw in the towel and stop at the next lock where there were decent moorings. These I suppose would have afforded a pleasant outlook on the water had you been able to see the water through the unpleasant murkiness which had fallen on the river.

Of course, no sooner had we tied up and abandoned any hope of going further that night than His Honour Lord Justice Sod decided to lay down the law. The weather cleared immediately and it became, if not exactly the end of a flaming June day, then at least the beginning of a half-decent summer's evening.

So we decided to go hunting for rabbits.

Now, the concept of killing bunnies is something which may shock the more urban-minded of my readers for whom a run past the chilled-meat counter at Sainsbury's is the nearest they ever get to a blood sport. In mitigation I have to confess that my shooting skills are so poor they threaten little beyond my own pathetic view of myself as a hunter-provider who in a better world would be spending more time banging on drums in the woods with his mates. In ten years my total tally with the air rifle I keep on the boat has been a few Coke cans bobbing around in the water and a pigeon that I left traumatised outside

Whitchurch in Shropshire one year after I'd pulverised the crab apple it had been unenthusiastically pecking.

And Jay isn't even as good as this.

However, in the past our appearance at local farms requesting permission to shoot has given us instant countryside credibility. You can understand it. In some places rabbits are a scourge on the land, a real pest. But they're a rather tasty pest. Which can't be said of foxes.

Before long we were nestled in the fold of a nearby meadow taking turns at blasting off at a drove of rabbits that had assembled in such numbers I can only think there must have been some special event taking place – maybe the appearance of some furry celebrity, a sort of Zoë Ball with long ears, there to open some new warren or another. Certainly our presence didn't cause much of a stir for though we peppered the air with pellets, it was clear they weren't getting close enough to their target to make us even objects of curiosity, let alone threats to health. Eventually one rather tatty and bruised old beast did fix us in his gaze, rising provocatively on his hind legs in such a way that to have attracted our attention more he'd have had to pull on a sweater decorated with bullseye markings.

He was so obvious a passing dog ran at him, which sent the whole colony scurrying for cover and left us looking pretty stupid lying there aiming at buttercups in the gathering gloom.

'Disturb you, did he?' the owner of the dog asked somewhat unnecessarily. He waved his arm towards another field nearby which, he said, backed onto a large modern bungalow. 'You'll find twice as many of the things there. All around the pasture and running wild in the garden. The lady living there used to feed them. But she was from London, she was,' he said, as if this explained such eccentricity. Which, of course, it did.

'She's dead now, though – died just last month,' he added, giving us the sort of look that communicated precisely how fitting he thought this fate was for anyone from the capital, regardless or not of whether they had a penchant for cuddly creatures.

Jay and I went to the place he suggested and sure enough we found an even larger assembly of rabbits. There must have been several hundred of them, if not more. There were rabbits all over the place: rabbits hopping about aimlessly, rabbits playing with each other, rabbits doing... well, doing what rabbits do. Some of them were spilling from the field through a hedge and into the bungalow garden where they were gorging themselves on the thick, uncut grass of the lawn. Not that this helped us much. However many rabbits had been around that evening, it felt like we'd never hit one even if they'd had been tied to the barrel of our gun making rude faces at us. After another half an hour we were ready to pack up for the night.

Then Jay had a lucky hit. It *must* have been lucky since by this point it was almost dark and he couldn't have known where he was aiming. A young buck which had been grazing close to the hedge with a group of others suddenly stopped in its tracks and double somersaulted straight out of the field and into the middle of the bungalow lawn where it dropped like a stone.

At the same time – spooky, this – a light went on in the bungalow kitchen, illuminating the lawn outside. A figure appeared – a man – and we watched nervously as he glanced towards the lawn. Finally, to our relief, he turned away and began preparing a meal.

At this stage in the evening a surreal note crept into proceedings for a Scotsman walked by in full regalia. There was no reason for a Scotsman walking by in that state, but there he was – kilt, dirk and bagpipes, the full monty.

'Good evening,' he said. 'Bit drier now, isn't it?'

'Er, yes,' Jay replied. 'Much nicer.'

We heard the strains of 'Amazing Grace' echoing from the direction of the river. Then we heard 'Mull of Kintyre' which was even worse.

'What the hell are we going to do now?' asked Jay.

'Just grit your teeth, it'll end soon,' I said.

'I didn't mean the music – I meant the rabbit.'

Ah. The rabbit? Yes. The rabbit. The rabbit was a trickier problem. We'd shot it, we couldn't leave it. But then again we could hardly walk across the lawn of the bungalow to retrieve it. Not in full view of the owner. Not when it was probably his dead wife's pet.

After some discussion, we agreed that it was best to avoid drawing unnecessary attention to ourselves, and that carrying a gun around at night probably counted as that. I suggested Jay should take the gun back to the boat while I hung about and retrieved the quarry as soon as I got the opportunity. I'd already earmarked it for tomorrow's dinner.

Jay wasn't comfortable with this. Perhaps the rabbit was beginning to play on his conscience. The evening had almost turned into night by now. Suddenly my young brother didn't seem as cocky as he normally does. Perhaps he expected his victim to rise up and haunt him, pointing at him accusingly with a bloodstained paw in the manner of Jacob Marley confronting Scrooge. He was not a happy bunny himself, you might say.

'Maybe I'll wait for you,' he mumbled.

'No you won't!' I said. 'Just bugger off. If we get clocked, it'll be cheese sandwiches tomorrow.'

Jay set off down the path back to the river where, as I learnt later, he immediately ran into the Scotsman who was engaged every night to play for American tourists on a boat as it turned back towards Stratford at this, the furthest point of its journey.

'Any luck?' the Scotsman asked, seeing Jay with the gun.

I can imagine Jay jumping out of his skin at this. With blood on his hands and a professional Scot showing an unhealthy interest in his activities, he wasn't going to admit anything which might subsequently prove incriminating. After all, what if he was a friend of the bloke in the house? What if he were an animal liberationist?

So Jay denied we'd been shooting at all.

Which put me in a very difficult position as I passed the Scotsman on the same path just a short while afterwards. He was on his way home, swinging his bagpipes in his hand. I was on my way back to the boat, swinging the rabbit which I'd managed to retrieve after a breathless dash across the lawn.

He gave it – and me – a very strange look as we passed. But he didn't say a word.

He probably thought I was a shifty bit of work. But I suppose when you walk around in a skirt with a sheep's stomach slung across your back and an offensive weapon in your sock, you get used to keeping your own counsel about the peculiarities of other people.

*

It's easy to prepare a rabbit, and if you hang it by its back feet and rip its skin off downwards, then its fur will peel over its head making its decapitation a more agreeably anonymous business. Gutting it is not difficult either since the weight of a rabbit's entrails virtually strips them itself once you've split the thin membrane which holds them in. Cleaning up can be messy, true; however if you're doing this outside in the countryside then it's hardly worthwhile bothering since the foxes will almost certainly do the job for you if the crows don't. There's a balance to all this which I like, a naturalness. The rabbit becomes a food to nourish different species and nothing of it gets wasted.

This sort of thing bothers a lot of people I know, but being brought up in the country I learned early on that there was a connection between the animals around me and the food on my plate; and so even now I find it difficult to account for the squeamishness of those who eat meat regularly and yet somehow deceive themselves about what it actually is and what's involved in its production and preparation. Certainly I have less moral scruple taking out a rabbit which has lived its life freely and organically than I do eating a slice of bacon from a processed pig that I know will almost certainly have suffered a diet of daily indignity and antibiotics along with its putrefying swill.

In that sense killing is part of the food preparation process. Or as every medieval recipe for rabbit always started, 'First catche yr rabbit.' Here's the recipe for how I cooked this one; it was made up on the spur of the moment from what happened to be in the galley.

The Fourth Recipe

First catche yr rabbit. Cut it in half, carefully jointing and reserving the thick hind legs and the back or 'saddle'. Marinade these in red wine, black pepper and thyme and leave them overnight. Meanwhile simmer the sparse front portions in a large pot with an onion, some dried mixed herbs – or whatever fresh you can muster – a couple of carrots and a litre of water to make a pint or so of light stock. Always be careful when jointing rabbit since their bones are like needles and can be dangerous.

The next day cut up two or three rashers of smoked streaky bacon or similar, and fry them slowly so as to sweat out the fat. Be careful not to burn them. Dry off the marinated pieces of rabbit with a kitchen towel, dust them lightly with flour and brown them in the bacon fat. Afterwards put them into a pot with the bacon pieces, another coarsely chopped onion, a large roughly sliced carrot, some more thyme, black pepper, the wine marinade and the stock, all of which should comfortably cover the rabbit. If not, make up the volume with water. Bring this all to a steady simmer and add a can of chopped tomatoes or, if you have them, three or four roughly chopped fresh ones that have gone past their best. Simmer all this, without covering the pot, for about an hour or so or until the rabbit has become tender. But be careful. Once rabbit has cooked, it disintegrates very quickly and falls off the bone in a sort of textureless mush that tastes OK but looks unattractive.

At this stage if the cooking liquid has formed a rich and thick sauce, the dish may be ready for eating – in which case season and sprinkle it with coarsely chopped parsley. However, if it's too liquidy remove the rabbit pieces carefully and reduce the cooking stock. Similarly, if your simmer hasn't been gentle enough you may need to add more water to the pan. Don't worry about this. And don't worry either if the cooking time is longer than indicated since you may get an older, tougher rabbit which many maintain tastes better, but which may need more time in the pot. For this reason, since you can only accurately estimate the cooking time by the individual rabbit, this is a good dish to cook and serve heated through the following day when it seems to improve in taste.

NINETEEN

Y_{ou} don't get much for free in the world today – which is why mooring on canals is such a good deal. Apart from in locks and at water points, you can pretty much stop where you want anywhere on the towpath. Today, sadly, more and more restrictions are being applied to how long you can stay in any one place. Even so, mooring is still about as easy-going a process as you find anywhere in this increasingly regulated society of ours.

Not on rivers though.

In most places on a river you couldn't moor if you wanted to because the banks are too high and overgrown. But even if it *were* possible, you wouldn't be allowed to anyway. Rivers are very much older arteries of transport than canals, and the riparian rights have been jealously guarded and squabbled over since time immemorial. Even if you saw a good place to pull up for the night, you'd probably find the only people allowed there were the fair-haired second sons of parish cobblers who'd been granted some charter or other by Henry II or whoever.

The only alternative is to stump up an exorbitant sum to a farmer to stay on their land – a source of income which on some reaches of the Thames is every bit as lucrative as their EU subsidies. Otherwise you have to compete with other boats to get one of the rare public moorings provided by local councils, and which nowadays, nine times out of ten, you'll probably find yourself paying for anyhow.

The Avon isn't too bad by the standards of other rivers and there are generally enough free spaces to be had, even in towns like Evesham where the night after the rabbit hunting Jay and I moored a little away from the town centre, opposite what I suppose you have to call the lock-keeper's 'cottage' – though that's a poor word for what is such an unusual structure. It's built on a contemporary A-frame design, bridging the chamber of an old lock and a weir stream that once used to feed a mill here; and it looks a little like an Alpine ski chalet which is the more intriguing for being so totally out of character in a place which in other respects is a traditional English market town built in the classic Georgian style and brimming with English soul. Evesham marks the traditional boundary of the Upper and the Lower Avon, a distinction which is not just academic since until recently both were administered separately, and even now both are separate from British Waterways which runs most of the rest of the system. This means you have to pay an additional licence fee to cruise them.

This division of the river goes back centuries. The Upper Avon – the section we had just cruised from Stratford – was once owned by the Great Western Railway, which in the 1860s stopped charging boats tolls for passage. This wasn't altruism but a callous commercial strategy. By doing it the company avoided all its maintenance obligations. Within a decade the river was unnavigable, thus leaving the way clear for the Great

Western's new-fangled steam engine thingy to pick up lots of lucrative freight business – which, of course, had been the intention all along. For the next hundred years the river steadily went into decline until by the 1960s many of the weirs had completely collapsed and most of the locks were derelict.

However, with the foundation of the Inland Waterways Association, restoration was on the agenda. There was soon pressure to open the river to navigation again – not just for its own sake but as an important link to the Severn, from which other canals connect to the rest of the network. In 1950 a trust was set up with the aim of renovating the Lower Avon; and with the backing of Robert Aickman and the IWA, remedial work started using voluntary labour. By 1962 it was possible for the first time in years to take a boat from the Severn *up* the Avon to Evesham.

But it still wasn't possible to do what Jay and I had just done and take a boat the opposite direction *down* the newly opened Stratford canal and *into* Evesham. For that, enthusiasts would have to wait until 1974 when a second charitable trust finally succeeded in completing work on the river, opening it in its entirety for the first time in more than a century. This effectively laid the foundation for the national restoration movement which would explode into activity over subsequent years as more people became aware of the economic and leisure potential of the waterways.

*

The small town of Pershore is about ten miles from Evesham and because there's a reliable bus service to Stratford where Jay had left his car, we decided to make it our goal for the remainder of his short trip. There are about a dozen or so moorings here which lie dappled by willow trees adjacent to a park and only a step or two away from the town centre, famed for its pubs. This alone would make it an attractive enough proposition as a place to stay for a night or two, even if it weren't for the fact that – like the Evesham moorings – the ones at Pershore are free too.

They get crowded though, and so to avoid disappointment we thought it would be wise to stake a claim as early as possible. The journey from Evesham is a short one and we planned to arrive at Pershore before four o'clock which we were confident would give us the pick of the best spots. So certain of this were we that at the lock near the intriguingly named Wyre Piddle, not far from our destination, we were happy enough to let a cruiser overtake us – even knowing that like us he was heading for Pershore and that this would give him priority mooring. It didn't seem to matter: the rain the previous day had cleared the air and though it wasn't warm, and the wind was blustery, it was at least dry and bright and we were feeling good about the world and our place in it.

Except that Rule One of rivers is never to count your moorings before you're actually in them. When we arrived every single available space was occupied. Well, all of them except one – and that was about to be taken by the cruiser we'd allowed to overtake us which at that very moment was manoeuvring snugly and smugly into position.

There was much cursing on *Justice*. There was much fraternal recrimination as to whose lousy idea it was in the first place to let the bloody cruiser overtake us… Then we spotted another mooring space. It was at the end of the line in what would have been an ideal position, except that it was about twenty feet too short for us and stopping there meant us tying up with our stern poking into the river like some badly parked four-wheel drive taking up two bays in a municipal multi-storey.

Still, beggars can't be choosers. With no other option available, I nudged the bow of *Justice* forward until I remembered Rule Two of river cruising which is never to believe when you see a patch of water that it will necessarily be deep enough for you to manoeuvre a boat. *This* patch of water certainly wasn't. In fact, strictly speaking, it wasn't water at all, more a sort of sludgy mudbank in which we soon found ourselves inextricably stuck. All my attempts to reverse off made matters worse. The river current caught us and we started corkscrewing. In no time at all we'd done a 360-degree pirouette and we were facing upstream in the direction from which we'd come.

All this cavorting about, accompanied by much revving of the engine and much black smoke from the exhaust pipe, soon attracted the attention of other craft moored along the bank, thus confirming Rule Three of the river and every other waterway too. This states that you shall never make a balls-up without there being an audience of at least a dozen people to witness you making a complete prat of yourself.

Again there was much bickering and recrimination on *Justice*. Fortunately, before things could get out of hand, we found ourselves drifting off the mud, inexplicably pulled by the river. At the same time – as if on cue – another narrowboat which had been moored immediately in front of us glided into midstream, giving us easy access to a perfect spot into which we fitted without any problem whatsoever. It was the best mooring on the bank. The place we'd have chosen ourselves if we'd had first pick.

As if to make us feel even better about how things turned out, we discovered that the space taken by the cruiser which had passed us wasn't anything like as good as it seemed from the water. The reason it was the last mooring to be taken was that it straddled the concrete mouth of a small weir draining from a brook in the park. It wasn't a very pleasant place at all.

Looking back, I suppose Pershore was an example of the perverse way that life can sometimes pan out when it's not being a complete bitch. Sometimes things don't happen in the way you want them to – but all the same they happen for the best. It was the same later that day when Jay and I sat in the beautifully tended garden of one of Pershore's fine pubs nursing a couple of pints of home-brewed bitter. We had kissed and made up and were talking about my plans for the following day after he'd left. I'd brought along some maps which I'd spread out on the pub table and we were looking at some of the options for where I might go. I suppose at this stage I was thinking that once I'd reached the confluence of the Avon with the Severn, I'd maybe head upstream towards Worcester and from there perhaps swing around towards Birmingham…

'But you said you were heading for Bristol, didn't you?' Jay said. 'Why have you given up on that idea?'

For a second or two I looked at him blankly. It wasn't that I didn't understand what he was saying, it was just that what he was saying seemed unaccountably stupid. 'That was a plan I had when I was in Oxford. That was months ago and a million miles away. That was when I was thinking about going down the Thames and on to the Kennet and Avon Canal… I can't do that now. I can't go back to where I started.'

'So what's wrong with the back way then?' he asked.

Once again I looked at him blankly. As far as I knew there wasn't a back way to Bristol. The only way to Bristol was down the Thames and along the Kennet and Avon.

Jay pulled a map towards him and pushed it in my direction. 'So what's that then?' he said, jabbing his finger onto the sheet. 'Scotch bloody mist?

'If you go *down* the Severn, onto that canal – there – what's it called? – the Gloucester and Sharpness – then you'd come out here. That'd get you to Bristol, wouldn't it?'

I looked at where he was pointing and took a long swig of my beer. It was as much as I could do to avoid openly sniggering. But how could he be expected to know better? He's got no experience of waterways.

'That,' I said, speaking slowly so that there could be no misunderstanding between us, 'is the Severn Estuary. It is the trickiest and the most dangerous estuary in England. It has a savage set of complex and dangerous currents, a constantly changing weather pattern and a tide range of forty-five feet, which is the very highest in the world and which strikes fear into the hearts of round-the-world yachtsmen, let alone people like me cruising in a boat which is little more than a sophisticated steel box.'

Jay looked at me for a moment or two.

'So? You chicken, or what?' he said.

*

The next day, alone for the first time in many weeks, I wandered around Pershore aimlessly until I finished up in the abbey which dates from the seventh century when Ethelred, King of the Mercians, donated land to establish a monastery on the site. It's a terrific building, once part of a much larger religious foundation of mainly Norman design which over the years survived fire, gales and flood until the Reformation finally did for it and Henry VIII's commissioners pulled most of it down. They would have razed the rest too except that to their credit the people of Pershore clubbed together and bought it off them for £400 so they could use what survived as their parish church. The bit they got was the Monk's Choir, a great vaulted space which is the size of a cathedral and is worth an hour or two of anyone's life if you're in the area. The roof is spectacular, soaring above you in a breathtaking 'ploughshare' design.

The Monk's Choir, in case you were wondering, got its name because… well, because the monks used to sing there. And the vaulted 'ploughshare' design is so-called because the vaults resemble… erm, how about the blades of ploughshares? A funny thing all this, but it does demonstrate how easy it is to get your head around the bullshit of medieval architecture if only you don't panic.

I couldn't concentrate on it though. I kept thinking about the conversation I'd had with Jay the night before. I kept thinking about Bristol and the Severn Estuary. I kept thinking about the bizarre implications of getting to a place I'd intended going by a route I didn't know existed. Most of all, I kept thinking about some article I'd read in a magazine years before about cruising the Severn Estuary. I remembered from that it was possible to hire professional pilots for the trip, making it – if not exactly risk-free – then at least not so foolhardy it was reckless.

That night, with some trepidation, I telephoned Em to run the idea past her. She had some holiday owing, and she'd been planning to join me again later in the summer.

'Right!' she said straight off, without even thinking about it. 'Why not? Sounds fun. It could be a great adventure.'

'But aren't you worried about the currents? The tide fall? The weather? It can be dangerous, you know.'

The line went silent. When she spoke again I don't think I was mistaken in detecting a hint of disdain in her voice.

'So? You chicken, or what?'

*

I set off the next day down the river. It was one of those mornings when the barometer which hangs in the boat was showing fair when outside it's clearly *not* fair, and when you didn't need a degree in meteorology to see it. So unusual was this disparity that it was mentioned on the weather forecast on Radio 4's *Today* programme, so it was no surprise that after half an hour's cruising the sky darkened and it began to pour down with an exceptional intensity. The rain was warm and heavy. It plummeted to earth like so many tiny explosive charges which burst in crystal shards on top of the boat, pitting the surface of the river around me into a thousand craters.

Considering how much it rains in England and how rich is our language, it's surprising we don't have more terms for it. There are only about half a dozen and one of them is 'precipitation' which sounds more like a coy sexual sweat than the good rutting downpour I endured that day. At first the deluge hit me head-on in a frontal attack, not so much stinging my face as bruising it with remorseless force. Then great peals of thunder broke out, and nature mounted an additional attack on my flanks with raindrops the size of saucers drumming an exuberant fortissimo on my coat. Soon I was raked by a bitterly cold wind and the dark sky was seared with lightning. The heavens which had opened long before, now seemed as if they must be available for immediate occupation, if not general colonisation.

This wasn't rain as we know it. It was a combination of war and Wagnerian opera. This was the 'Ride of the Valkyries' as conceived by Francis Ford Coppola. It was the apocalypse and it was very much happening now.

Then all of a sudden the whole show stopped. One moment it was detonating like a percussion orchestra, and the next everything was completely calm. A celestial millpond. No wind. No rain. No nothing except for the first glintings of sun reflecting off the water as the river arched around in the gentle series of wide, gracious sweeps which take it towards Nafford Lock. I was soaked to the skin though it didn't seem to matter at this point. In fact, nothing seemed of much consequence. The storm had acted as a reminder of the raw force of nature and thrown life itself into perspective; and it wasn't just me, but the countryside itself which counted itself fortunate to have come through unscathed.

Just at that moment, as if to drive home the point, I was regaled by the cacophony of what seemed like a dozen flocks of birds noisily celebrating this part of the morning with the same ebullience they normally welcome the dawn.

★

Nafford Lock is a fearsome sight for a boat coming downstream when the river's a bit lively. For a start, it's difficult to work out where you're supposed to go since the river appears blocked by a set of massive iron gates. Once you've worked out that these are part of some mechanism of water management, you've so little time to react that it's easy to miss the sharp right turn needed to avoid them. Immediately afterwards, just when you think you're over the worst and can relax, you have to swing a sharp left to get you into the channel for the lock itself. This is so short it hardly gives you the opportunity to decelerate before you hit the gates.

As if to remind me that I was supposed to be a seasoned boater, accomplished enough to be considering navigating the

Severn Estuary to Bristol, fate dealt me an added challenge as I approached the lock. A hire boat happened to be emerging at the same time and as he saw me bearing down on him he lost his head completely, panicked, and went careering across my path. To avoid what could have been a nasty collision, I swung into the only clear water available which was the channel of Nafford's ferocious weir. Only the expedient of running myself up the bank prevented me going over the top and making a somewhat quicker descent to the lower river than would have been safe.

Cruising got no easier afterwards. The intricacies of Nafford were at least marked on my map, even if – like the barometer earlier in the day – it didn't bear much relationship to reality. After Nafford the river transforms completely, though you wouldn't know it from the map which continues to mark the river as a gentle blue line elegantly curving across the page.

The real thing wasn't like this at all. The wide, graceful sweeps that had characterised the river to this point had gone, replaced at first by a series of arching swans' necks and afterwards by a progression of tight meanderings similar to the summit of the Oxford Canal, only that instead of the Oxford's radio mast to confound me, I now had the pinnacle of Bredon Hill looming above me on the horizon. At first it seemed to be to my right, then to my left, and finally behind me, so that I finished up so utterly confused that I ran the boat up the bank for the second time that day.

The irrational wanderings of any waterway can leave you disoriented, but it's much worse on a river than a canal. For a start the bank of one river is much like the bank of any other, which is to say – since you can't see over the top – that they consist of the edge of fields and incessant lines of willow trees. Take my word for it, even for an enthusiast like me there is a limit to the level of passion I can muster for a willow tree. There aren't as many bridges on rivers either, so unlike canals where you're lucky to go more than ten minutes without passing under one, there's nothing on a river against which you can gauge your progress. Travelling along one becomes hypnotic, particularly when you're on your own and especially when the river starts to straighten out as the Avon does as it moves towards the Severn.

I completely lost track of where I was. I was constantly arriving at places hours before I thought I'd reach them or sometimes – when impatience set in – hours after I thought I should have passed them.

I vaguely recall going under Eckington Bridge, a fiery-red sandstone structure etched with the ancient patterns of two hundred winters or more. Then there were one or two railway bridges, and then the M5 motorway, until finally – eventually – there were no bridges at all any more, and I seemed to be drifting in the insensate lacuna between earth and sky where nothing but the gentle feathering of the water from my bow provided any connection with the moment.

The river got wider, and wider yet. It got straighter and flatter and windier until I could have been cruising the Fens, or maybe the level wastes of the Low Countries where the land has been clawed from the sea. In truth my mind was so abstracted from the present I could have been anywhere or nowhere, until the appearance of a flotilla of sailboats and a line of plastic coastal cruisers three-storeys high signalled that at last I had arrived somewhere.

It was Tewkesbury where I was to join the Severn.

TWENTY

The festival was Tom Rolt's idea.

In the 1930s after he'd finished his apprenticeship, long before he'd written *Narrow Boat* and years before he became involved in getting the Inland Waterways Association off the ground, he'd gone through a tough period in which he'd been kicking his heels, picking up work here and there as best he could. These were the Depression years and any sort of job was hard to come by. Eventually he'd borrowed money from his father and gone into partnership with a friend running a garage in Hartley Wintney in Hampshire. This was a natural move for him since he'd always been interested in cars – old cars especially – and he'd had a succession of them himself, including a rare 12/50 Alvis two-seater which he bought in the early 1920s and had for most of his life.

Next door to the garage was a pub called The Phoenix whose landlord was, fortuitously, another motor enthusiast. Before long the two of them cooked up the idea of a club for classic sports cars – an idea that benefited them both since the pub became its unofficial headquarters and members provided work for the garage. The Vintage Sports Car Club still exists today; and though Rolt's old garage has become a self-service petrol station indistinguishable from thousands of others across the country, The Phoenix remains relatively unchanged and car buffs still meet there regularly for a chat and a pint as they've done for decades.

The club's grown a bit over the years though. Today it's got more than 7,000 members worldwide and it employs a full-time staff of seven, most involved in organising a calendar of thirty or so events which it holds every year. One of the biggest is an annual hill climb in Prescott in Gloucestershire which Rolt created. It's an uphill time trial which has been running since 1938 and which today attracts many thousands of spectators. For a long time the club used to organise rallies for its members too, awarding prizes not just for place positions but under different categories such as the best turned-out vehicle, or the best maintained engine.

Tom Rolt suggested a similar idea to Robert Aickman as an event for the IWA.

Aickman must have jumped at the proposal. The concept was just up his street. It was flamboyant enough to be exciting yet sound enough to be practical. He could see that an assembly of boats at some central location could be more than just a focus for members – it could also be a unique method of raising the public profile of the waterways. Aickman was years ahead of his time in recognising the value of publicity to a campaigning organisation and he would have known instinctively that if you could get boats travelling to a single point from all over the country, then it would be possible to tie local campaigns about the closure of individual canals into a national debate about the future of the whole waterways network. The plan for a rally was a perfect demonstration of how, when they worked together amicably, Rolt and Aickman were world-beaters.

And they did work together a lot. Founding a national campaigning organisation is not an easy task. It requires complete commitment and hard work, most of it unspectacular and mundane, and consisting for the most part of meeting after relentless meeting. There's a head office to be organised, there's a regional structure to be set up. There are members to be attracted, contacts to be made, policy to be formulated. Meetings here, meetings there, meetings everywhere. Those who have no experience of this sort of thing have no idea of the hours of tedious preparation which it takes just to achieve the simplest task. It's bad enough in a working environment, but at least there people get paid for their time. With a voluntary organisation you have to cajole your membership, you have to bribe it, you have to flatter it. You have to use every trick in the book to achieve your ends.

Rolt and Aickman couldn't have done this in the way they did unless they'd been able to rub along together for most of the time. It's just that rubbing together causes friction and at other times the two of them could burn themselves up with their squabbling. Even when they were thinking along the same lines they could actually be going up the track in opposite directions. They might be working towards the same end but they had an entirely different perspective on the world. Rolt was a diffident man, serious-minded and determined. He'd been drawn to the canals by the opportunities they offered to escape from contemporary life. Essentially he was a very private person. It wasn't in his nature to be gregarious and on those rare occasions where Aickman wanted to use him for campaigning or wanted to push *Cressy* into the limelight for publicity purposes, Rolt only agreed reluctantly, and often only after having his arm twisted.

Tom Rolt would have seen the rally as he had those early get-togethers of the Vintage Sports Car Club at Prescott: simply as an opportunity for a few like-minded people to socialise. As a way of demonstrating how people cared about the things they were interested in. Just a bit of fun really.

For Robert Aickman, it was an entirely different proposition: it offered a platform on which he could show off his organisational abilities and indulge his wider artistic and cultural obsessions – a stage on which he knew he could engineer events to finish up the leading actor.

He immediately hijacked the idea. The rally now became not just a boat festival but a Festival of Boats and Arts, growing in Aickman's grandiose imagination until the little town of Market Harborough in Leicestershire which had been chosen as the venue became in his mind a test bed for the Festival of Britain planned for London's South Bank the following year. Aickman was not strong on self-awareness; it's easy enough to laugh at his affectations. But there are a lot of people of his sort around – strong personalities so caught up in their own lives that they lose touch with reality and distort events in the process of persuading the rest of us of their vision.

So now there would be a waterways exhibition associated with the rally. There would be fireworks. There would be a fun fair. Boat trips. And there would be an art show too, with a display of paintings by Peter Scott, and a film festival, and – the *pièce de résistance* – a play produced specially for the occasion. You wonder who this was all for. Members of the IWA? The public who Aickman was confident would come flocking to the event?

Actually, you don't need to wonder – it was for Robert Aickman. And, of course, being the man he was, he didn't harbour the least doubt that he was doing the right thing.

Indeed, he was fiercely proud of the inspiration he'd brought to bear on the venture and many years afterwards he boasted with some justification that one of the reasons it developed in the way it did was because he personally 'wanted to run a Festival'.

Arrogant or what?

The relationship between Aickman and Rolt had altered fundamentally since Jane Howard's arrival on the scene, but their clash over Market Harborough represented a nadir between them. At the beginning, Rolt attempted to keep a level head about matters. He wasn't convinced that Aickman's plans for an arts element in the festival would achieve much for the waterways but he suggested reasonably enough that if they *had* to have a play as part of the programme, then maybe they ought to get some professional outfit like the Bristol Young Vic to produce it. The suggestion had the effect of sending Aickman scurrying away to cost the proposal and on discovering unsurprisingly that it was too expensive, suggesting that – well, who needs the Young Vic? – he'd do it himself.

It was the same when Rolt pointed out that the Market Harborough assembly rooms where the play was scheduled to be performed lacked a proscenium arch and wasn't really a suitable venue. Not a problem, said Aickman. There were two association members who would build a stage…

The whole thing became too much for Rolt. Working with someone so intractable was getting him down. More than this, his waterways interests were trespassing on the rest of his life. Rolt was a professional writer now and the IWA was taking up more and more of his energy, energy that he could have used more profitably on his own projects. He felt he wasn't his own man any more, that his time was being eaten up by a series of honorary positions which he somehow kept accumulating and which were curtailing the freedom he'd worked so hard to achieve.

It was bad enough that Aickman had drafted him onto the festival organising committee without consulting him, but the final straw was an officious letter summoning him at short notice from where he was moored on *Cressy* in Northamptonshire to a planning meeting on the other side of the country in Berkshire. At first he refused to go. It was his birthday. He'd arranged to take his mother to the theatre at Stratford. But Aickman, as was his way, insisted; and eventually Rolt succumbed to the pressure he brought to bear. It was the last time he ever would concede to Aickman though, and of all the rivers he negotiated in his life, crossing this Rubicon was probably the most significant.

Of course, there were weighty matters of IWA policy dividing the two. Should the organisation agitate for the restoration of all waterways or just a selected few? Should it prioritise the future of commercial traffic or should its first concern be the fabric of the waterways themselves? Should it campaign from within the establishment or confront the waterways authorities from the outside?

But people who are personally in tune with each other and who respect each other's integrity can usually find ways of resolving issues that divide them. Positions can be argued, opinions compromised. It's the trivial things that always prove the sticking point though, the host of small and insignificant irritants that when it comes down to it aren't small and insignificant at all because they betray what people really think about each other.

Like that mysterious 9/4d (48p) that Rolt owed or didn't owe Aickman, but which – incredibly – Aickman was still banging on about in his autobiography forty years later. Like the other argument between them that gets mentioned which seems to have arisen after Aickman, acting as Rolt's agent, sold a collection of ghost stories to the publishers Constables. Nothing more is mentioned about it – either cause or outcome. Which leads me to conjecture uncharitably that given Aickman's self-serving view of the world it was probably somehow tied up with his own as yet unfulfilled ambition to write himself. Perhaps the simple fact is he was jealous.

It couldn't go on like this. As Tom Rolt wrote, 'the brutal truth was now becoming only too clear, [the IWA] was becoming a band-wagon, as good causes, often started with the best of intentions, are apt to do… We, who had originally sought refuge on the canals to escape from all we disliked in the modern world, deeply resented what we felt to be our exploitation for such purposes by others.' In January 1950 – probably as a New Year's resolution – Rolt invited Aickman to visit him on *Cressy*. Aickman stayed the night and there, frozen in by ice so thick you could walk on it, Rolt told him he was going to resign as IWA secretary.

And at this point it would have been best for everyone if he'd been allowed to go cleanly, walking away from the organisation and severing his ties completely. But this wasn't Aickman's way. For Robert Aickman, Rolt's quitting represented a personal betrayal. And though he didn't want anyone around him capable of such disloyalty, he didn't want them to move outside of his sphere of influence either.

This left both of them in a bit of a Catch 22 situation.

It meant that things would get a good deal messier yet between them.

*

River towns, even London, are at their most inert from the water. Perhaps it's because towns change least in the aspect they present to the river. Coming into a new one on a boat it always seems as if they're locked into a different age. The exception to this is Tewkesbury. As soon as you catch sight of Tewkesbury from the Avon, you just know that this isn't a place that *seems* of a different century, this is a place that *is* of a different century.

What you see from the river is what you get. Walk up the main street, even on a Saturday afternoon when it's at its busiest, and you can squint your eyes and believe you're trapped in a time warp. Perhaps the place livens up in leap years. Or when there's an eclipse of the sun. On the other hand, like so many English towns, maybe its attraction is that it never does. To a visitor most people living in the place seem to be elderly. There are a lot of shopping trolleys in evidence. A lot of motorised wheelchairs zipping about the pavement.

As for Tewkesbury's younger elements… well, just outside town I'd seen a small cruiser moored on the river with the improbable name of – wait for it – *Flashes from the Archives of Oblivion*. As boat names go it's not one that trips off the tongue. But it gives you a good clue where the Tewkesbury under-25s are coming from.

This could be prejudice and maybe *Flashes etc* is owned by a middle-aged Church of England cleric with a soft spot for hippy rock and transcendentalism. After all, people are more complex than we give them credit for; they name their boats for a thousand different reasons. Often what they choose reflects their idealised view of the waterways and the role they expect their boat to play in their life, so that I've lost count of the number of *Narrow Escapes* and *Slow Motions* that I've seen over the years.

Sometimes names are twee like *Not for Sail* or – clever this for a small version of a narrowboat – *Along Shortly*. Other times people use them to make a joke, though like most jokes they pale with familiarity. Like the Grand Union boat *Union Bargee*. Or *Nervous Wreck*. Or the second boat owned by a family called the Nunns, *Second to Nunn*. One boat cruising the system has the beautiful Italian-sounding name *Tiami*, which you think must translate as a passionate declaration of love except that it's got more to do with the practicalities of marine finance. It's an acronym for 'This is a Major Investment'.

This sort of thing happens at higher levels too: one of the yachts in the Sydney–Hobart boat race a few years back was called *The Office*, which I suppose provided a ready-made excuse for those difficult telephone calls to which mobile phones have made us all susceptible.

'No, honestly, I'm at The Office. Would I lie to you?'

My favourite boat name however is *Sir Osis of the River*. I've never seen it on any river or canal anywhere and it's probably apocryphal. But who cares? A name like that you just want to be true.

★

Though quiet, Tewkesbury's rather a pleasant town in the summer when it's not raining and not cut off from the rest of the country by floods. There's a bank-holiday atmosphere about it which in part emanates from the colourful pennants the size of tablecloths which hang all over the place and give it a festive air. It makes the place feel like Siena before the *Palio* – the horse race which is held annually around the main piazza. The flags hanging there are those of the various neighbourhoods which compete against each other for prizes. In Tewkesbury, more darkly, they are the standards of the barons who fought each other to the death in 1471 at the Battle of Tewkesbury, the last Yorkist victory of the Wars of the Roses and the town's main claim to historical fame.

Not that everyone in Tewkesbury values this part of its past. A few years back the local council gave the go-ahead for a development on the battlefield site. It was to have been one of those awful postmodern executive housing estates I complain about, but the decision was overruled by Whitehall after an almighty row during which one councillor admitted he couldn't understand what all the fuss was about. The battle was just 'a couple of blokes having a slap', wasn't it?

I wandered around the town in the weak afternoon sunshine. It was a place I knew very little about except that the novelist Barbara Cartland had once lived here, and that it was where the comedian Eric Morecambe literally died on stage, keeling over one night with a heart attack. I finished up outside the John Moore Countryside Museum where in the front window was an engaging display of miniature models of Romany vardos – or caravans – which no doubt in some mythical time long since past used to travel the highways and byways of Merrie England. They were skillfully fashioned by a local craftsman, brightly painted and meticulously decorated. One I remember had a series of tiny copper cooking pots hanging from a rear door. On another was a diminutive cage filled with ferrets painted in such detail you could count the strands of their fur.

John Moore was a local writer, a man in the mould of Tom Rolt and Harold Massingham recording the disappearing cultural traditions of an older rural world. I reckon he must have been a fun sort of a guy too since the staff at his museum have obviously inherited his sense of humour. Well, I took it that they'd inherited his sense of humour since I can't believe that the timing of this exhibition was anything other than a droll joke, given the national obsession that summer with asylum seekers – many of them Romanies.

Earlier that week there'd been an incident in some one-horse town on the south coast where a couple of families from Slovakia who'd been persecuted at home had made a break for the bright lights of Albion – only to land up in a derelict flat on a run-down estate where as far as I could see the only bright light was the one remaining street lamp that hadn't yet been vandalised. Their appearance was the signal for a riot in which the locals complained of how foreigners were stealing their birthright and how – barring the erection of a twenty-feet-high barbed-wire fence around the entire coastline – the country was about to be overrun by swarthy hordes who would swamp their culture, being entirely untutored in Middle English and incapable of singing a madrigal.

Sad this, because in the past in this country anyone looking for shelter could have counted on our sympathy, if only because as a nation we have a naturally sardonic view of the world and know what a bastard life can sometimes be.

I stood entranced by the John Moore's vardos and before long a small but animated crowd gathered on the pavement with me, pressing their noses to the museum window. I'd bet not one of them made the connection between the models of the Romany caravans and the Romanies currently finding themselves hassled on the south coast. Any more than they'd make a connection between, say, contemporary Germans and our Royal Family descended from the Hanoverians. Contemporary Germans are too threatening. They are hell bent on world domination, and that failing they will take all the sunbeds round the pool. Royal Germans on the other hand – Germans from the past – are like traditional Romany gypsies. They have been historically appropriated and made safe, like torture implements of a bygone age which we hang on our walls as decoration.

This is typical of us English. We are frightened of the world, that's what it comes down to. It's the reason we sentimentalise it. Making miniatures is part of the process, we do it with everything. How else can you explain the plethora of advertisements in the tabloid magazines for tiny teapots or minuscule Toby jugs or Lilliputian reproductions of country cottages? It's extraordinary. I was in Bath recently and there is a shop totally dedicated to the stuff, filled with row upon row of figurines, none bigger than your thumbnail. Fairies, figures from the ancient world, historical characters. And teensy little gardens too, with teensy sets of garden furniture and teensy garden plants. And food as well, of all things. Dinky joints of ham, plates of bacon-and-egg breakfasts, platters of poached salmon.

Miniaturising like this is the only way we English can come to terms with the terrifying realities of a world the same size as us. Hitler missed a trick here in 1940. Instead of attacking us, he could have softened us up for invasion by flooding the country with diminutive SS Panzer divisions and dwarf wind-up gramophones playing *pianissimo* versions of 'Deutschland, Deutschland Über Alles'.

We'd have welcomed him with open arms then.

*

I left the crowd outside the museum stewing in its own paradoxes and walked round the corner to Tewkesbury Abbey, a great barn of a building which dates from the twelfth century. It has a cavernous nave with a vaulted ceiling supported by a couple of rows of huge Norman pillars so that just being in the place seems to generate an almost palpable sense of the past.

It would be wrong, however, to think the abbey's trapped in history, and walking around I came across more than one example of the contemporary pastoral work in which it was involved. There was a notice board I found particularly touching on which people had posted requests for prayers. One was from a woman who was in depression after having lost her husband not long after their golden wedding anniversary. Another was from a young couple whose 12-week-old baby had died suddenly. There was a barely legible appeal from an 8-year-old who was being bullied at school, and another from a man who admitted to writing the note in tears, frustrated at his much-loved teenage daughter with whom he felt he'd lost the ability to communicate.

Take it from me, reading this sort of stuff you begin to count your blessings.

There were other things about Tewkesbury Abbey that made me realise that recognising the importance of the past doesn't necessarily mean you have to be locked out of the present. There was a sculpture of an owl representing wisdom, for instance. It was fashioned out of domestic household items salvaged from a junkyard and it brought me up short when it struck me what the artist was saying about today's world. There was a modern-style altar too in one of the chapels, made out of what I took to be rosewood and carved in extraordinary lettering. Tewkesbury's regard for the craftsmanship of our modern age even extended to a functional but beautifully made set of storage cupboards tucked away in the back of church where if they'd have wanted they could have got away with stacking a pile of crates.

Except that doing that wouldn't have reflected the tenor of what this place was trying to do and how much people cared about it.

And people *do* care about places like this in contemporary England. Twenty years ago there was a bitter row in Tewkesbury about where to move the abbey organ – a dispute which eventually had to go to the church courts for resolution. And if you think that's archaic and not the sort of thing that could ever happen nowadays, let me tell you that that is precisely what *was* happening as I passed though Pershore where an equally bitter row had been rumbling on for years about the replacement of some pews removed from the church during building work. That too had to go to the church courts – except I don't think it was resolved. I doubt it ever will be.

For that's another thing about us English. Our concern about the detail of our lives can lead us, as it led Rolt and Aickman, to get worked up about the smallest things.

And God knows, we can bring a powerful stubbornness to bear on them once our blood's up.

TWENTY-ONE

A set of instructions from the authorities for navigating the Severn Estuary had arrived. They read like rules for rounding Cape Horn, filled with dire warnings about the dangers we faced doing the trip. Everything on a narrowboat, it seemed, was a hazard; everything so badly designed it was a risk. The main problem was that our hull was the wrong shape. It was flat-bottomed and too low in the water. The drainage holes on the deck which were designed to let water *out* on calm canals were too susceptible to letting it *in* on what was effectively a sea journey. And this was just the start of it. According to the authorities everything from our ventilators to our air intakes was too close to the water for a trip like this.

Even our diesel tank wasn't up to the job. Our diesel tank! I doubt I'd ever thought about the diesel tank on *Justice* once in the years we'd had her, except to notice when the diesel in it was running low. But no, apparently narrowboat diesel tanks were prone to fill with sludge which could get churned about in the swell and sucked into the engine where it would cause an immediate break down, leaving us drifting powerless as the ebbing tides flushed us into the Bristol Channel and certain death...

Well, something like that.

We were advised to 'purge' the tank. I had visions of feeding it a plateful of rhubarb and a cup of stewed senna pods. How else was I supposed to clean it? Open it up with a can-opener and give it a wipe down with Flash?

We were instructed to block up the drainage holes too. And sheet over the deck. We were recommended to do all manner of things except buy ourselves a new boat better equipped to do the trip – which was obviously what the authorities would have preferred us to do since every line of their advice carried the unstated subtext that we were lunatics even to think about doing this journey in a boat like ours.

Mind you, this was a view with which I was increasingly in sympathy. I was never *that* keen on doing the passage. It had been my brother's idea – well his, with Em's backing. I felt that I'd had my arm twisted into biting off more than I could chew, if you see what I'm getting at. What brought the enormity of it home to me was discovering that once on the estuary my 'movements' (the official word) were not now governed by the simple expedient of adjusting the tiller from one side to the other, but instead determined by the grandiose-sounding *International Regulations for Preventing Collisions at Sea*, a copy of which I was instructed must be an essential part of my equipment. This informed me that 'a vessel of less than 20 meters' (that is, me) should not impede the passage of 'a vessel which can only navigate within a narrow channel or fairway'.

Since, in effect, the whole of the Severn Estuary comes under the heading of 'a narrow channel or fairway', the message to a minnow of my sort was unmistakable: I was bottom of the food chain. Either I kept out of the way of the big stuff or I risked getting reduced to industrial scrap.

This was not reassuring.

Neither was the other equipment I was advised to carry with me, like life-buoys with smoke and light signals attached, and distress flares, two red and two orange – the colours no doubt carefully chosen so that as I was drowning I could coordinate to match my outfit. Other essentials I was instructed to take included tide timetables and Admiralty charts, both of which I dutifully obtained, only to discover that they were so incomprehensible, a book of Arabic grammar would have been more use to me. Tide tables? They reminded me of those books of logarithms we used at school. I couldn't make head or tail of them. It was the same with the charts. They looked like Ordnance Survey maps except that anything familiar which might have made them intelligible seemed to have been purposely omitted.

I was terrified about ringing the pilots to arrange the trip. I imagined them breaking down in hysterical laughter. 'Take you where? In *that* heap of junk? With *your* level of expertise? I think I'd rather not if it's all the same to you…'

In the event I needn't have worried. I spoke to a pilot who sounded about as excited at the job as waiting for a bus.

'I'll tape up all the doors and cover the deck with polythene,' I hastened to reassure him.

'Whatever. Anything you want…'

'I was planning on maybe blocking up the drainage holes too – cutting out wedges of wood and jamming them in…'

'Fine. If it makes you feel happier,' he said. 'When do you want to go anyhow? Next Wednesday evening OK? On the second tide?'

All this was a bit sudden. And a bit real as well. Until now this crazy idea of navigating the estuary had been a faraway fantasy. Now here was a pilot who seemed completely indifferent to committing himself and me to a boat that would almost certainly sink on us. One who was seriously asking me if I wanted to 'go' next Wednesday on the second tide. Go? Where? To hell? And on the second tide? Until he'd mentioned it, I hadn't even been aware there was a first one.

'Next Wednesday?' I repeated mechanically, feeling numb at the prospect. 'Next Wednesday,' I mumbled again.

And before I knew where I was, it was all sorted.

★

At least now there was a purpose to travelling. Before I hadn't even got a destination. Now I had a destination *and* a deadline. The following morning, I cast off from Tewkesbury passing through the lock and the small cutting that passes from the Avon and onto the River Severn for the 30-mile journey down to Sharpness and the sea. There was an unusual urgency to my movements.

Once on the Severn I was in a totally different environment, for if a canal differs in character from a river in the way it feels, then so too does a big river differ from a small one. The lower reaches of the Avon had been inhospitable enough – wider than I was used to, and blowing windier, and the water much choppier. But now, accelerating towards the sea at what seemed an alarming speed, I was having doubts about whether I should be boating at all on my own in these conditions. For a start, the river banks seemed not so much distant as attached to an entirely different waterway to the one on which I was travelling. Certainly too far away for me to swim to if ever – God forbid! – the need arose.

Additionally, what little of the water's edge I could make out in any detail as it rushed by seemed entirely unlike anything I was familiar with from the Avon. In the main it was composed of ugly hawthorn bushes not improved any by the host of plastic supermarket bags that were littering their branches as a result of past floods.

Of more immediate concern was finding myself in the eye of the second storm I'd faced inside a week. It blew up from nowhere without warning and it seemed to single me out for attention – or maybe it just felt that way since as far as I could make out I was the only boat foolish enough to be on the water. Wind came at me from two sides, hitting me on both my bow and stern, but in separate directions, so that *Justice* began to roll alarmingly. My stomach started to churn. It was all I could do to keep down breakfast.

The wind brought rain and this blew almost horizontally, pushing up some pretty impressive waves for a stretch of river which was, for all its tumult, nevertheless technically described as 'still' water. Soon it became a struggle just to keep on course for the boat began to pitch as well as roll, her bow towering up out of the water before plunging down again in a welter of crashing spray. All this was accompanied by some rather troublesome noises from below deck. From where I was standing – clinging on to the tiller for dear life – they sounded remarkably like plates and glasses smashing to the floor.

The dangers of the estuary were the last thing on my mind now. In truth I was wondering whether I'd get that far. If it had been possible I'd have moored as soon as I could and waited for conditions to improve, but what is true of the Avon is even more the case on the Severn. There simply aren't the places to stop and those few which were available I was passing at such a rate of knots that no sooner had I spotted one than it had flashed by, a quarter of a mile behind me and receding with every moment that went by.

The level of the river was rising – and rising at a spectacular rate. Although I didn't know it at the time, this was to be the pattern for the rest of the year. So much rain had already fallen on to the sodden countryside that it simply couldn't absorb any more. The fields were completely waterlogged and as quickly as it was falling, the rain was running off the land into streams and brooks – and finally into rivers like this which were already at the stage where they couldn't take more. Before the autumn not just the Severn, but the Trent, the Soar, the Ouse and a host of other rivers across the country would flood, causing widespread damage and distress to many thousands of people.

Near Apperley, where the B4123 crosses Haw Bridge, there are a couple of pubs and I was confident I'd somehow be able to manoeuvre myself into moorings there. But by the time I'd navigated the single arch of the bridge through which you're advised to pass, I'd been flushed so far downstream I doubted I'd have enough engine power to make it back against the current. Yet I knew that sooner or later this was exactly what I was going to have to do. You can't take a boat directly into a mooring when there's this much water running behind you. You'd be dashed against the bank. Instead you have to go past the spot you're aiming for and turn against the flow so that you can come in with at least a vestige of control.

Eventually I decided that I'd have to risk it regardless of the consequences and a mile or so further on, at the small hamlet of Ashleworth where I knew there was a landing stage, I turned against the full force of flow and revved the engine as high as it would go.

My heart was in my mouth.

Justice lurched uncharacteristically as the water hit her broadside, but I wrenched the tiller around and she straightened up against the current. There was a long, listless moment where she did no more than hold her own against the spate, hovering there surfing the flow. It was as if she was making up her mind whether she was capable of moving upstream against all this water. And then deciding whether she could be bothered… Eventually, after what seemed an eternity, she began to edge forward sluggishly. With some relief I found I could just about guide her to safety.

Tying up wasn't easy since the jetty was awash with water. Afterwards I glanced at my watch. I'd left Tewkesbury at about ten o'clock and travelled about eight miles, a journey I'd estimate might have taken me a couple of hours under normal conditions, perhaps a bit less.

I'd done it in half that time.

★

Ashleworth is a little gem of a place, like so many tucked away in the backwoods of rural England close to the waterways. Tom Rolt wrote about some of them in *Narrow Boat* and though the years have obliterated a few of those he identified which even then were remnants of another age, most still survive, surprisingly unspoilt. Many others which don't figure in the book – like Ashleworth – remain all but undiscovered even today, known only to locals or visitors from the river. The village is actually larger than it first seems because that bit of it closest to the water is separated by some distance from the rest and is really a separate hamlet. The Boat pub whose jetty I'd landed on lies at the end of a lane where there are about three or four other buildings.

One of them is a small fifteenth-century manor house standing adjacent to an unpretentious but exquisite parish church. Next to this is a farm and a massive barn which is the most interesting structure in the place. In the past it was used to store the produce from local farms paid over to the ecclesiastical authorities as tithes. It's still used as a barn today, though it's owned by the National Trust which presumably allows it to be occasionally used as a village hall too, since it was clear that it had only recently been the venue for a locally performed theatrical revue. Scripts of sketches lay scattered over the floor, and on bales of hay that had lately served as a stage were draped various costumes and props. There was a sweet smell of stage make-up in the air.

It was bizarre finding the place like this. On such a stormy day with the rain hammering down relentlessly, this part of Ashleworth felt totally uninhabited, the roads deserted, the manor house quiet and desolate. Despite it being lunchtime, even the pub was empty – though I'd have expected it to be packed to the rafters with trade from Gloucester which is only a short journey away by car. This all added to my strange sense that the village had somehow been abandoned, as if at the outbreak of a plague or the onslaught of some advancing army. The detritus littering the barn was eerie, as if people had been in the middle of clearing up but then had been abruptly interrupted in their work and had rushed away, leaving behind them a silent presence and the peculiar aura I could sense. It spoke not just of contemporary times but of worlds inhabited by countless generations before who had worked the land in these parts and used the barn for their own different purposes.

There were marks in the stonework that compounded this overwhelming impression I had of having stepped into another age. They were similar to ones I'd seen in Tewkesbury Abbey:

fastidiously fashioned initials in a scholarly classic style, every last serif etched with meticulous care. It was graffiti, but not graffiti as we know it today, produced instantly from a spray can by kids who have been made to feel so alienated from the culture in which they live that they don't feel they have a place in it any more. Kids who live in a world where change is fêted for its own sake so they don't expect permanence from anything.

These carvings were produced by people who were constrained by principles we'd frown on today to know their place in society, but who were at least secure in the knowledge that they *had* a place; so that what they were looking for wasn't to advertise themselves to their own age but ensure their place in posterity. Which I suppose they finally succeeded in doing.

I wandered into the church where work was underway. Activity here – like the barn – seemed to have halted abruptly too. There were dust sheets hanging from scaffolding, and bricks, and bags of cement stacked next to piles of hymnals and copies of the parish magazine, the *West of Severn News*. I took one back to the boat and later in the day I picked it up idly and began looking at it again. I found it compulsive. Eventually – sad or what? – I finished up reading it from cover to cover, even poring over the advertisements at the back.

It made me breathless, filled as it was with so many references to charity walks and jumble sales and bingo evenings and home furnishing classes and all the other thousand and one activities that engage a rural community. What I found fascinating was not how different to the urban world was the one it described, but how curiously alike they both were. I could have almost imagined myself back on the London local paper where I first started work as a journalist years ago.

There was a report of the parish council meeting which I found particularly interesting since, apart from the scale of it, it could have been an account of the proceedings of any London borough with exactly the same concerns for planning, road safety, crime and dog shit. Dog shit! Is there a community tucked away anywhere on this sceptered isle of ours that isn't obsessed with dog shit? Dog shit surely must have replaced royalty as our favourite national preoccupation.

Except that now we get just as worked up about the urban/country divide, one side blaming the other for the level of its subsidies, the other complaining about how its way of life is being destroyed. It's as if because we don't get so steamed up any more about our traditional class divisions we need to demarcate between us on new grounds. And for some reason we've polarised around how comfortable we feel about animals.

If we feel very comfortable about them – comfortable enough to start sticking our arms up their arses if they're ill – then we qualify as fully fledged country folk whose reward is to be able to dress up like a pillar box and kill foxes. On the other hand, if we don't feel at all comfortable, and certainty not comfortable enough to consider eating dead ones, then this marks us out as die-hard townies who shall be forever stigmatised by the mark of the green welly whenever we set foot outside the suburbs.

Until a few years back when the landing stage was built you couldn't moor at The Boat with anything like the ease you can today. If you weren't too deep in the water you could nudge the bow of your boat into the bank and moor to a tree; but if you weren't able to do that, you had to get as close in to the bank as possible, drop anchor and paddle the rest of the way. This was OK in the blazing heat of an August afternoon when the water was flowing clear and you were walking on clean and solid shingle; but it lost its attraction at other times of the year when the rain was running down your neck and the river bed had turned to quicksand. At times like this it was a temptation to give The Boat a miss and go to where there were other pubs which had less character but were more accessible.

So you can't blame the pub for installing a landing stage. All the same, it's sad when the unique is eradicated.

But isn't this the same across the whole country? Isn't too much of the uniqueness of England being eradicated and isn't our national soul being eradicated with it? And isn't this part of the reason that we're all at each other's throats so much? Aren't we all holding everyone else responsible for the loss of what we're all to blame for?

I'm as bad myself – worse, really – for didn't I bang on evangelically about how special the waterways were when everyone thought I was mad spending every spare moment God sent crawling through derelict bits of cities along rat-infested ditches? And didn't I get incensed, banging on the table and telling them that no, canals weren't like that at all, that mostly they were like quaint lanes winding through the fields, and anyhow the bits in towns could be a wonderful facility too if only people would think radically and wake up to their potential and spend some money on them?

Until one day they did and more and more people began to use the canals so that things began to change as a result. Not gradually, with the gentle passage of the seasons; but suddenly it seemed, time flying like an arrow, straight and abruptly, so that no sooner had I gone off to bed one night than I woke the next day to a new world in which everything I wanted to happen had come about, and in the way I had desired it.

Except that in the process of saving the canals the changes had destroyed so much of what made them special.

Can you blame me for belly aching?

*

I drank too much that night in The Boat which probably explains the way I felt. I got into conversation with an old guy who I chatted to most of the evening until it dawned on me that despite my first impressions, he was actually younger than me. A shock like that was what I needed to snap out of whatever mood it was that Ashleworth had put me in.

After all, I was going to Bristol. I'd got an estuary to deal with.

TWENTY-TWO

I set the alarm to wake early the next day with the intention of getting through Gloucester as quickly as I could. I know the place well and despite its cathedral and its impressive complex of docks, one of which houses the National Waterways Museum, I wasn't much attracted by the idea of a big city. Even though I'd been returning to London regularly throughout the summer to deal with the percolations plaguing the Crumbling Pile, the idea of staying somewhere large unnerved me after so long in the countryside. After all, Gloucester was the biggest place I'd passed through since Oxford.

But sometimes on a boat events conspire to thwart you. I struggled out of bed with a hangover, needing a hit of caffeine to jump-start me. In the state I was in, just finding the kettle was a struggle. Filling it was worse. I couldn't understand it. There didn't seem to be any water coming from the tap. In fact, there wasn't any water coming from it.

I was thrown completely.

It's bad enough any time of day when the material world fails to conform to predictable patterns. It's far worse after a night

on the tiles when you're not up to intellectual challenges like…
well, like thinking. I rubbed my eyes, fully expecting to find
myself still in bed and this some strange dream from which
I'd not yet woken. But no, for all intents and purposes a world
where water didn't come from taps appeared to be one I was
condemned to live in.

I checked the tap to reassure myself that it actually was the tap
and not the boat engine, the Forth Bridge or even the Cheddar
Gorge. Then I scrutinised it again. Finally, when I'd satisfied
myself that it was indeed what I believed it to be, I attempted
to turn it on once more since I couldn't be certain so early in
the day that I hadn't done something stupid turning it on the
first time. Like not turning it on at all. Like pulling it instead.
Or pushing it. Or even scratching my armpits because I'd been
asleep, and dreaming, and not anywhere near the tap at all.

Try as I might, no water came from it. This led me to one
inescapable conclusion. I had run out of water.

I paused for a moment or two considering the implications
of this discovery. Gradually it dawned on me that among the
various factors on a boat that govern the supply of water, one
is paramount. You can't connect to the mains. This means you
have to fill up your water tank regularly. I had some vague
recollection of doing something of this sort with a hose pipe
a while back in some village somewhere or another… but that
was a long time ago.. More recently, the only thing I could
remember filling up was me. With beer the previous night.

If this wasn't bad enough, when I attempted to fry an egg
in place of the boiled one I normally have in the mornings, I
discovered I'd run out of gas too. Not just my main bottle was
empty, but my reserve bottle as well. The one which I'd been
promising myself to replace for the last couple of weeks. There
was no cereal on the boat either. Or much else that was edible.

I was eventually reduced to having a glass of milk – and, to be honest, even that tasted a bit offish.

To cap it all, when I retired to the bathroom for my morning constitutional, I discovered that the lavatory was full and that what I was attempting to put in had an insistent tendency to want to come out.

There was nothing for it – regardless of whether I *wanted* to stop in Gloucester, I had no choice. I *had* to stop there. I needed to get my life in some sort of order.

★

Travelling on a boat, you know you're getting close to a town when the graffiti under railway bridges is less about the performance of local football teams and more about the performance of local girls. Don't ask me why this is. I put it down to the more advanced sexual maturity of your average urban oik. Despite all their braggadocio though, I don't think their know-how is backed by much in the way of hands-on experience, if I may be allowed to call it that. Or not at least judging by some of the depictions of the female form I saw as I got closer to Gloucester. These made it apparent the lads in these parts have got a thing or two yet to learn about female anatomy – though I don't suppose you can expect much better from a generation brought up on the pneumatic improbabilities of Jordan.

Later that morning I attempted to tie up next to the chichi bistros in Llanthony Basin which is close to the Waterways Museum and the most pleasant visitor mooring in the city. Of course – wouldn't you know it the day I was having? – every space was occupied and the only free place I could find was a floating pontoon beyond a swing bridge that crosses the water a little further on. This is opposite a derelict warehouse where, as if laid on for my delectation, a group of homeless punks covered in tattoos were sitting around a bonfire toasting sausages on sticks and listening to loud music through a ghetto-blaster. They could have been acting out a tableau entitled 'Urban Badlands'.

Now this sort of thing isn't unusual in towns in the Midlands or the North. In Gloucester though it's rare. This is not because there isn't as much poverty and privation in the city as other places, but because what there is of it is normally kept well concealed. As a visitor you can wander around for weeks thinking that Gloucester's just another English cathedral town frozen in the 1950s with very little function except as a location for classic TV whodunnits.

The derelict docks I was moored opposite were once the source of the city's wealth, and in the nineteenth century great ships of a thousand tons and more would sail up from the estuary laden with cargoes of timber and grain to feed the country and supply its industries. As that industry declined, so did Gloucester docks and Gloucester itself, leaving the place with a catalogue of the sort of problems that plague so many English cities today. Away from the small area of waterside redevelopment, and the cathedral precincts over the other side of town, there are some rough areas in Gloucester. There's a big drugs problem too. And a lot of raw violence seething under the surface.

As for the city as a setting for whodunnits – well, believe me, nothing could be further off the mark. I made a documentary about a real murder in Gloucester once. Take it from me, the police in that case acted nothing like Inspector Morse. Mind you, they didn't act much like the police either.

Working on that film I missed a much better story. We were looking for someone, and my researchers set off on house-to-house enquiries to get information. One of them knocked on a door in a place in Cromwell Street.

It was number 25, where the Wests lived.

★

At Gloucester the River Severn becomes tidal and so treacherous with sandbanks and rapids that it's unnavigable for shipping. In the late eighteenth century to ensure a more reliable route to the sea the Gloucester and Sharpness Canal was dug the remaining sixteen miles to the estuary.

Since I'd left Stratford and begun cruising on rivers I was travelling too far each day to worry about the Debsmobile and it had been left languishing, sadly if safely, at a farm belonging to some friends in Warwickshire. Now I was moving back onto a canal it became feasible to have it with me again to explore further afield, away from the waterways, where there was still a lot of English soul waiting to be explored. So that day, once I'd done everything I'd set myself to do, I hopped on a train to collect it. That afternoon I drove back to Gloucester by a route I'd devised to keep me away from main roads.

Unusual weather had been a characteristic of my whole journey and it was still odd and constantly unsettled. A period of violent storms and heavy rain would be followed by a day or so when the sky became a luminous blue and when it was suddenly so warm that you could almost believe you were in the Mediterranean. It was like this the afternoon I picked up the Debsmobile from outside Stratford. The sun was high in the sky and there was hardly a cloud on the horizon. It was uncomfortably hot but on occasions it was unusually fresh as well. Intimidating winds would blow up abruptly from nowhere, lapping around the treetops until they subsided apologetically, as if incapable of carrying out whatever it is they were threatening.

I folded back the roof of the car. Though I was open to the air I still couldn't get away from that delicious mustiness that characterises old vehicles. At the same time I was still acutely aware of the extravagant smells of the season that were assailing me from outside: the sweetness of hayfields or the occasional vehement blast of honeysuckle from a hedge. From time to time I would become aware of the cloying odour of warm tarmac, and occasionally as I passed under a dark canopy of trees I'd be almost overcome by the succulence of their cool leaves.

The Triumph Herald has a very low carriage so that you sit close to the ground which exaggerates its speed and makes you feel you're in physical contact with the road in a way modern cars rarely do. It makes driving feel more intimate and this sense of communion, man with machine, is intensified by its suspension which even on a straight, smooth road has a good deal of tremulous movement in it so that you feel like you're handling a nervous stallion.

If I love being on the tiller of a narrowboat because of its ponderous movement – the sense that you don't so much steer it as request it to make a movement with which it might consider complying – then I love being at the wheel of the Herald for exactly the opposite reason. It has an immediate hair-trigger responsiveness which keeps you on your toes and makes you think – not without cause – that if you let your concentration lapse momentarily you'll finish up in the nearest ditch.

Most people seem to know the Herald for its steering. Or at least they know it for its remarkable steering lock, which is tighter than a London taxi and means that you can swing the car around in a perfect circle, like a second hand on a clock sweeping around the dial. You have to have good clutch control to do it since you get 'scrub', which is the technical term for when your front wheels point in one direction so acutely that the rest of the car doesn't follow them and instead moves forward against the tread of the tyres. This manoeuvre has been known to strip the wheel of a Herald totally bare.

During the development of the car its road handling was a continuing problem, its tendency to be over-sensitive causing so much concern to Standard Triumph engineers during early tests that the suspension had to be damped down to make it safer. Much of the analysis which led to this and other modifications took place in road tests held, coincidentally, around the area through which I was driving. In these early days of motor manufacture, before there were the facilities to do everything in a workshop or on private tracks, the only way cars could be evaluated was by putting them through their paces on public roads under ordinary driving conditions.

One of the company's favoured routes for this was a 200-mile circuit from headquarters in Coventry and through the Cotswolds by way of Birdlip Hill, close to Gloucester. These excursions generally took place at night which you'd think was done out of concern for industrial espionage, except that so many Midlands' carmakers used Birdlip Hill for their 'secret' prototypes they were in danger of crashing into each other. The more prosaic reason for the night-time drives was so that the cars could be back at the factory the next morning in time for the engineers to spend the day working on modifications before sending them out again. Motor engineers were always running to a tight deadline and there was constant pressure to get mileage on the cars. Particularly with the Zobo on which so much was riding.

The second Michelotti prototype was delivered from Turin to Spain for more extensive tests in the spring of 1958. The car was given the registration number VRW 589 and there's a photograph of it on that trip filling up with petrol at one of those old-fashioned Iberian garages built like a hacienda, with great overhanging eaves and chunky biscuit-clay roof tiles. There's something about the picture that seems to epitomise Spain in those pre-EU years under General Franco when it seemed like a Third World country and not part of Europe at all. Perhaps it's the white brickwork of the building, a bare vine trained across the wall ready to burst into bud. Or maybe it's just that the weather's not really Spanish, for despite the sunshine casting sharp shadows across the scene it's chilly enough for everyone in the picture to be wearing a heavy topcoat.

Before it went on general sale the Herald was put through its greatest ordeal yet – a 10,000-mile drive the length of Africa, from Cape Town in the south to Morocco in the north designed to test its reliability. It was a journey that took the car to its extremes, pitting it against jungles and deserts, tropical rains and remorseless heat. Quite how such an ambitious itinerary came about in the first place is uncertain, except that whoever came up with the idea had so little grasp of what it actually involved that initially a journey twice as long was planned. It was a declaration of confidence, not just in the car, but in the fragile stability of this part of world which was in the death throes of colonisation, with the very names of the countries – the Belgian Congo, French West Africa and Rhodesia – a testament to the subservience of the continent to one European conqueror or another.

No company would consider such an odyssey today; the political situation would make it too risky. But in 1958, it was only in the final two weeks of the journey, three months after starting, that the Triumph team encountered any problems of this sort, having to call for military protection as they passed through Algeria where a civil war had just started, the beginning of the liberation movement which would eventually sweep the French from the country, the first of a series of such struggles which, fanned by the winds of change, would eventually spread across Africa like wildfire.

Mechanically, the Herald took the trek in its stride and apart from some problems with *that* suspension, the main difficulty facing the company as it prepared to unveil the car publicly to the world was what it was to be called. Until Africa, it had still been known to everyone on the project as the Zobo but in the summer before it went on sale Alick Dick called a board meeting at which the directors carefully considered a series of options before deciding in the absence of anything better that it should be christened the 'Triumph Torch'.

There wasn't a lot of enthusiasm for the name though, but because Dick had 'a relaxed and open management style', discussion on the subject continued beyond the point it probably should have ended. Eventually one board member suggested that what was needed was 'a name heralding Triumph's positive emergence from the greyness of motor vehicle similarity'.

'Heralds blew funny trumpets,' someone observed. 'We can't call the bloody thing a Triumph Trumpet.' But eventually they all bowed to the inevitable and went home happy. The wonder was not that they finally arrived at the name, but that it took them so long to choose it when it was staring them in the face.

The board meeting was held on a boat belonging to Alick Dick. It was called *The Herald*.

★

The car was launched to a fanfare of enthusiasm by the motoring press who welcomed it as 'Britain's outstanding new car', singling it out as 'one of the most exciting... for a long time'. It was put on the market at an unprecedented speed so that the entire project went from prototype to production in just 19 months, a rate we couldn't compete with today despite computer technology. The orders came in by the thousand and the car soon became the company's best seller.

The Herald somehow transcended the statistics of its own history and became something more, redefining what people thought cars were, and what they could be. It became a paradigm not just for the industry, but for its age. And in the process it touched people emotionally and won a place in their hearts.

Just as well it did really, because as a nation we weren't winning much else at the time. It was the period just after the Suez fiasco and though we didn't fully realise the implications of what was happening, we were losing our Empire.

It was an empire spawned by an industrial revolution fed by canals.

Funny how it should end in a wrangle over one.

★

I spent a disturbed night next to the punks in Gloucester, the only thing to be said for it being that I learnt everything there is to know about punk music. This can be summarised under three headings:

1. Take two dissonant chords.
2. Play them very loudly.
3. Play them again.

Erm... that's it.

The next morning I couldn't get away fast enough and I cruised the ten miles or so down to Frampton on Severn in exquisite silence, arriving in time for an early lunch of sausage and mash in a pub overlooking the huge village green there. This green is supposed to be the biggest in the country and I've no reason to believe otherwise. OK, it may not be as big as some of the gardens you get in stockbroker Surrey but it's certainly bigger than most French farms. If it were a French farm it would be big enough to qualify for an EU grant. Mind you, it probably does anyway, and thinking about it, most Surrey stockbrokers are probably claiming one too.

The pub specialises in sausages and is famous locally for the range it serves. I would have enjoyed lunch more except that it struck me soon after sitting down that there are as many ways to eat a sausage as there are types of sausages to eat. Not all of them are pleasant. I could just about bear the bloke at the next table slurping noisily over his Leek and Garlic, but the woman opposite who was eating with her boyfriend was an altogether more difficult prospect. Some of the things she was doing with her Traditional Pork and Sage verged on the obscene.

But it was the guy in the corner of the room I found worst. He was so into his Rough Chopped Spanish Chorizo that I swear you could have used him as a spirit level by putting him in the centre of the room and seeing which side he dribbled from most.

I didn't tarry long over coffee.

*

Like the Suez Canal, the canal between Gloucester and Sharpness was built for ocean-going ships and, unusually for ventures like this which were almost exclusively funded by private capital, it was financed by government money. It opened in 1827, ten years before Queen Victoria came to the throne and in the early years of the imperial period which it reflects in the confidence of its design. It's wide and straight and deep and has an indisputable grandeur which speaks of an age proud of its great civic projects. You see this most at the bridges which had to accommodate the towering superstructures of large commercial vessels and so were built as swing bridges, each operated by bridge-keepers who were once housed in cottages built alongside, though these have long since been sold into private hands.

These cottages have great style, for they were built to a classic design, each on its own pediment and each with a set of fluted Doric columns so that they look like little temples transported from the Peloponnese – a conceit with which some of the current occupants have conspired by putting bay trees in plant pots outside their front doors.

That afternoon I reached Saul Junction where the Stroudwater Canal cuts across the Gloucester and Sharpness in an unusual crossroads junction, more like a road than a canal. The Stroudwater is derelict now, though like most abandoned canals of any importance it's being restored. Once completed it will be a critical link in the waterways system, connecting to the River Thames at Lechlade above Oxford which is currently the limit of navigation.

The junction's one of those messy but intriguing spots which is a magnet to a canal enthusiast like me. Nestling among a group of higgledy-piggledy buildings is a lock cottage, a boatyard and a dry dock, and there are enough idiosyncratic boats and odd engines lying around to make you lose all sense of time as you wander about.

The shadows were already lengthening when I set off back to *Justice*. On the other side of the wide estuary, the sun had thrown the hills of the Forest of Dean into shadow so it looked like a great cloud on the horizon. Even so, the canal itself was illuminated like an airport runway, a dazzling mirror reflecting the flaming sun which became more burnished as it moved ever lower in the sky. On such a fine evening there were a lot of people fishing which normally wouldn't interest me very much. You know what they say about fishermen. Give a man a fish and you feed him for a day; teach him how to fish and you give him an excuse to sit around endlessly playing with maggots.

But this is zander territory, a fish that is supposed to be one of the tastiest and most delicate to be had in British waters – and one I'd never eaten. I was hoping that with a bit of luck and a smile, I might be able to blag one or two out of a keep net. They are foreign predators – Germans to boot – which doesn't exactly endear them to the country's coarse fishermen. Neither does it help that they prey on our indigenous fish and have been so successful in colonising us over the last few years that in some places they've taken over completely and fishermen are encouraged to kill them on sight to give the local species more of a chance of survival.

But fishermen are canny people. They spend a lot of time in their own company, pondering the nature of the universe and their place in it. None of them is a mug, especially not in this part of the world where they know the worth of a fish like a zander which can fetch £20–25 a portion in a London restaurant if you're lucky enough to find one which serves it.

I was put in mind of that story about the guy who was browsing in a second-hand bookshop in a back street in the middle of nowhere a few years back when he came across an original Gutenburg Bible. This is one of the most valuable books ever printed and he could scarcely contain his excitement. He nonchalantly sidled over to the owner of the shop.

'So how much do you want for that old Bible over there, then?' he asked.

'Oh, the Gutenburg? Give me a couple of million quid, and it's yours, mate.'

Not true of course – but it was like that with the fisherman on the Gloucester and Sharpness that night.

'So what are you going to do with those nasty beady-eyed bastards with teeth like razor blades?'

'Oh those zander? I sell them for twenty quid a piece. There's a bloke I know who'll take as many as I can catch.'

It's a shame fishermen don't catch more of them for they've become a big problem recently and a lot of money has been spent unsuccessfully trying to keep them under control. These 'freshwater sharks' as they've been christened were introduced into the country by the Duke of Bedford in 1878. He shipped 24 of them over from Schleswig-Holstein where they were classed as a game fish and much valued for their flavour which, like their appearance, is a cross between pike and perch. One of them proved too much of a temptation for His Grace and it immediately finished up on the dinner table at Woburn Abbey where at least it caused no damage to anything – with the possible exception of the Duke's aristocratic digestion.

The rest were released into the estate lakes where a century later, thanks to some inane bureaucrat at the Great Ouse River Authority, a few were set free into the Fens. This was done on the pretext of providing more interesting sport for fishermen and is akin to liberating a virulent virus in order to give doctors more interesting work.

Its success is mainly down to the unique quality of its eyes, which allow it to see in almost impenetrable gloom by reflecting light back onto its retina. This leaves it at an advantage over indigenous species like roach which need more than a trip to Vision Express to compete at this level. The rise and rise of the zander has been inexorable, and there are now great swathes of the country infested to such an extent that British Waterways have been reduced to culling them by (honestly!) mass programmes of electrocution. The trouble is, they don't work. And anyhow, why bother? Because along with their other questionable charms, zander are cannibals. Leave them alone long enough and they regulate themselves.

But like buses, you can never get a zander when you want one.

I went back to *Justice* empty-handed so that my recipe for zander poached in wheat beer, or baked with a mustard crust, will have to wait for another day. Instead, here's one for a more commonly available freshwater fish – trout. It's based on a Jane Grigson recipe from the north of France where, in season in places like the Val de Loire, there are so many of them waiting to be caught they've introduced a queuing system at the hooks.

We're not quite so lucky on English waterways, but these days you never seem to be far from a commercial trout lake where you can sometimes pick up a couple cheap if you've got the gall to ask. They can taste a bit muddy though, and they benefit from a night soaking in fresh water with a good squeeze of lemon juice to freshen them up.

The Final Recipe

This dish is very quick to prepare, so ensure that if you're going to eat it with potatoes that they are almost cooked before you start, and that your oven or back-cabin stove is up to heat. This way everything will be ready at the same time.

Finely chop a medium onion and a carrot, along with two or three of the pale green inside leaves of a stick of celery if you happen to have them to hand. Scatter them across the bottom of a generously buttered ovenproof dish with some parsley, a bay leaf, salt and a generous pinch of coarsely ground black pepper. Put the trout on the top and dribble some more melted butter over it. Then pop it in the top of the oven at about 200°C for about 15 minutes or until the skin begins to burn and you're getting the odd black spot appearing. Take it out very quickly and douse it with a glass of white wine. Then pour a small carton of double cream over it along with a good squeeze of lemon juice. Put it back in the oven for another couple of minutes until the cream has heated.

To serve, extract the fish carefully to avoid breaking it. Give what's left in the dish a good stir before arranging it tastefully around the edge. Don't under any circumstances be tempted to ladle the sauce over the top of the fish which is guaranteed to make the whole thing look a mess. If you have to put something on the top, make it a couple of lemon slices or a single sprig of fresh parsley.

This goes very well with a green salad served with a sharp dressing to counteract the cream.

TWENTY-THREE

You can never plan anything on the waterways; there's too much that can go wrong. The uncertainty is the only thing you can rely on.

We were hoping to make the estuary crossing on the Wednesday. Em had taken time off work for it and was getting excited at the prospect. Even I'd finally got my head around the idea that since I had to die sometime, I might as well make a bit of an event of it. I had visions of hitting an unexpectedly violent storm like the one I'd just been through on the river. I imagined *Justice* starting to take water until we had to abandon ship. I could picture myself kissing Em lightly on the cheek as we said our goodbyes, me tossing the hair from my eyes before peeling off my sweater to lay it across her shoulders comfortingly. Finally, I saw the two of us as if in a scene from *Titanic* stepping off the stern deck hand in hand as the boat succumbed to the battering waves, my last words to her a reassurance that we'd see each other in a better world…

But on the Friday night after I'd got back from Saul Junction it began raining. OK, I have to admit this wasn't exactly an unusual occurrence on this trip. What *was* unusual was its intensity. And the fact that it didn't stop. It was still raining on Saturday morning when I collected Em from the station. And still raining on Sunday too. In fact, it didn't let up for one moment the whole weekend, great raindrops the size of dinner plates battering down on the roof the whole time.

On Monday I rang up the pilot again as we'd arranged. 'Everything OK for later in the week?' I asked.

I could almost hear him sniggering. I could almost picture him covering the receiver with his hand, shouting to one of his mates: ''Ere – listen to this one Fred – there's a bloke here on a narrowboat thinks he going down the estuary Wednesday. After all this rain. What a wally, eh?'

Instead, he said: 'Well, it's up two feet already and there's a Force Nine coming over from the Azores and the current's running to fifteen with a twenty cross wind and several gumbos coming up from the rear and strawberries and cream expected in the next post…'

Or at least that's what it sounded like to me…

Anyway, I got the message clearly enough: we didn't stand a snowball in hell's chance of getting across the estuary on Wednesday. I should ring him the following week, maybe conditions might have improved. I should be prepared to be patient and wait.

*

There is a temptation with every narrative to want to make it seamless, as if life itself were seamless and moved smoothly from one event to the next towards its inexorable conclusion. But this isn't the way it happens. Most of life is disjointed, random, without any of the structure we later endow it with. The truth is very few things in this world run harmoniously.

Certainly the estuary crossing didn't.

With no immediate hope of making the trip, Em left later in the week. After she'd gone I moved a mile or so up the canal to Patch Bridge, close to Peter Scott's Slimbridge Wildlife and Wetlands Centre, where there was a boatyard and a waterside pub with a car park convenient for the Debsmobile. I only thought I'd be there for a couple of days – a week at most. As it turned out I was there so long I could probably have got on the electoral register if I'd filled in the right forms. I was there so long I became a local landmark and people taking their dogs for a walk would ask after my family.

The rain, you see, just wouldn't let up.

Days became weeks, and the weeks became a month, and still it continued to pour down incessantly. It rained every day without respite, every hour that God sent – day after relentless day, and night after remorseless night so that the towpath became a quagmire and the river and estuary a raging torrent so swollen that not only could I not get to Bristol, I couldn't even have got back to Gloucester. Like it or not, my only option was to sit it out and wait.

I spent a lot of time at the Slimbridge Centre. With the wetlands being wetter than usual and visitors being thin on the ground, the birds were having a fine old time of it and a sort of riotous party mood prevailed with much squawking and ruffling of feathers whenever I gatecrashed the fun. There was one goose which particularly fascinated me. It was called a *Cereopsis* and it lived alone in a wired compound down by one of the ponds, an unprepossessing creature to look at. But it was so pugnacious it would have had your hand off given half a chance. Curiosity got the better of me one day, and I risked getting close enough to its pen to read a sign about it. It said 'Beware – Aggressive Species'.

Every couple of days, by way of a distraction, I'd ring the pilot for a weather update and a chat. I reckon he used to look forward to my calls. He knew there was something special between us.

Or maybe not. Maybe I was just a pain in the neck.

Hassling him didn't help.

'You'll have to wait a little bit longer. It's really not safe at the moment,' he'd always say.

'But it's nearly the end of the summer,' I'd protest. 'If I don't get away soon I'll be stuck here until next year.'

'What am I supposed to do, let you drown? You'll just have to wait. Conditions just aren't safe at the moment.'

Eventually I was there so long I couldn't bear to be there any longer, so I left and drove back to London where in my absence the Crumbling Pile had developed two or three more inexplicable oozing ingresses somewhere skyside of the back bedroom window. This could have kept me happily playing around in damp proofing and wood shavings for weeks on end – except that during one of my forays up a ladder in the name of home maintenance my mobile rang.

I could see from the number that it was the pilot. He was ringing. Ringing me! I was in so much of a fluster I almost fell off with the excitement of it.

'It could happen this week,' he said conspiratorially, as if we were arranging the illicit exchange of some military secret.

'This week? But it's still raining here,' I said. 'I can testify to this. Indeed, even as I talk to you, evidence of it is running down my neck…'

'It's raining here too,' he said. 'But that's not the point. The point is that soon it will stop raining. And then the estuary will drain, and soon after that conditions will become…' – he lowered his voice – '… perfect.'

'Perfect?' I repeated.

'Perfect,' he said again, such an unmistakable note of confidence in his voice that I could almost picture him tapping his nose with his forefinger. 'I would advise you to be ready.'

★

The next day I went back to Patch Bridge and as always on the waterways, when you leave a place you've been for any length of time – even somewhere you've been compelled to stay – you become sentimental about your departure. That night as the rain finally began to abate, I took a walk up the towpath in the soft light of a moon which for the first time in ages wasn't obscured by clouds.

It was along this part of the towpath that Peter Scott walked with Elizabeth Jane Howard one summer night in July 1946 towards the end of their marriage. In a spirit of reconciliation afterwards he wrote her a love letter describing, not the cliché of the stars in the sky, but the ones twinkling in the grass. They were glow worms lit by their own halos. It's a beautiful and touching piece of writing, one that could only have been produced by a naturalist, and then only by one whose heart was fixated so resolutely on another. 'I am afraid it will not please you if I tell you how much I love you,' he wrote. '*Embarras de richesse* – everyone loves you and why wouldn't they – poor things.'

The letter, of course, was never sent.

It was along this part of the towpath too that Scott kept his narrowboat *Beatrice* which in the summer of 1950 he took to Market Harborough in Leicestershire to become the official headquarters of Aickman's Festival of Boats and Arts. By this time Scott and Howard had begun divorce proceedings and her affair with Robert Aickman was more or less out in the open. However, the process wasn't yet complete and they were still, strictly speaking, married. It could have made things awkward between Scott and Aickman except by now the two of them had become close friends.

Perhaps it's natural that men attracted to the same woman should find they have things in common that draw them together. But what Aickman and Scott felt seems to have been more than this. Perhaps it was something connected to the intensity of emotion that Jane Howard was capable of inflaming, the heat of which could weld people together.

Earlier in the year the two of them had taken *Beatrice* on a 450-mile trip around the waterways which Scott had used to promote the concept of his Slimbridge bird sanctuary through a series of public lectures. It may have been a *quid pro quo* that afterwards Scott reciprocated by throwing himself behind Aickman's ideas for the festival, especially the controversial play which Aickman was still stubbornly determined to mount. Instead of a single play, he had by now decided to mount two productions: Alfred Sutro's *A Marriage has been Arranged*, and Benn Levy's farce *Springtime for Henry*, both solid middlebrow works. Scott guaranteed to underwrite their costs. He even took a role in the Levy play himself, despite the fact that all the other actors were professionals and he'd never set foot on a stage before. In fact, with Aickman asking Jane to produce the Sutro play, the theatrical part of the festival was a nepotistic affair – which can't have done much to make Tom Rolt feel any better about the idea.

On the contrary, it seems to have exacerbated his antagonism to it and he remained implacably opposed. 'I felt it was their job to organise a rally rather than spend time on a venture which I thought was of no conceivable use or relevance as far as the waterways were concerned,' he said with an outspokenness that irritated Aickman, who didn't respond well to this sort of criticism. But Aickman wasn't a man who responded well to *any* sort of criticism. He was incapable of accepting that other people might have views at odds with his own; anyone disagreeing with him was attacking him and guilty of disloyalty.

Another man might have shrugged off opposition on such a relatively minor matter, but the plays were the climax of a series of disagreements with Rolt. They'd become the ground on which Aickman chose to fight. Why did he do it? Jealousy at Rolt's success as a writer? Envy at his ability to forge a lifestyle for himself that Aickman himself wanted? Or was it more, something vaguely sinister perhaps? The single-mindedness of an autocrat? Or something more fundamental? Something that Aickman saw as impugning his manhood, challenging his status as an alpha male?

Perhaps it was simply the petulance of a spoilt child who wasn't to be thwarted in anything.

Whatever it was, an angry Aickman, stung by Rolt's opposition, decided to confront him. He tabled a motion to the festival committee demanding that Rolt resign. Since Rolt hadn't exactly been overjoyed at being conscripted as a member in the first place, this can't have been an entirely unwelcome development. He was anyhow in the process of relinquishing his official waterways' responsibilities and had only just managed to offload his role as honorary secretary of the Inland Waterways Association. This seems to have goaded Aickman even further and in a move that smacks of vindictiveness he attempted to stop the Rolts going to the festival at all by banning them – a strategy which provoked an angry row among the organisers and a resignation from the committee.

Until they received the letter telling them of the decision, Tom and Angela were in two minds about going. Now they were both livid. And determined to attend.

'As the IWA has grown in both stature and prestige so you have grown equally arrogant and intolerant of the views of others when they failed to coincide with yours,' Rolt wrote to Aickman in a long and bitter three-page letter. 'That you should dare to request me not to come astonishes me, accustomed though I am by long experience to your ways.'

The situation wasn't helped by Rolt's latest book *Inland Waterways of England* being scheduled for publication in the same week as the festival. It could have been useful promoting the canals – which was, after all, the principal purpose of the event. But Rolt's publisher Philip Unwin had been specifically instructed not to use the rally to advertise it, a decision bearing Aickman's fingerprints. The threat this posed to his livelihood outraged Rolt and for a while he considered taking the matter to court.

Thankfully wiser counsel prevailed and he decided against it, but from then on it was – as he put it himself – 'hell or Market Harborough'. From Lechlade on the Thames, where he and Angela were moored, he immediately set off northwards in *Cressy*, pressing on at such a pace that unusually they didn't even stop to look up friends as they passed through Banbury.

★

Despite the unpleasantness that characterised it, the festival ultimately proved to be a huge success. Initially some twenty or thirty boats were expected to attend but eventually 120 turned up from all parts of the country, and the weather remained perfect for them throughout. An astonishing 50,000 people attended – a single crowd of 20,000 turning out just for the fireworks display on the penultimate night. This was one of a series of public attractions, many of them the sort of activities you'd have found at any country carnival at that time, and which in many ways seem typical of the era, encapsulating something of the quintessential nature of England in the hiatus of those grey but somehow reassuring years between the defeat of Hitler and the release of the Beatles' first LP.

Apart from the controversial arts events, there were dancing displays and a police band; there was model car racing and a fancy dress dance for children; the election of a Festival Queen and – inevitably – a cricket match. Every night there was alfresco dancing to the Rogues of Rhythm Dance Band. The Rogues of Rhythm? The name itself is redolent of a lost age before the Cavern Club and the Mersey Sound changed the world.

Even Tom Rolt had to admit that he enjoyed the occasion, though on a personal level the atmosphere was poisonous. The row between him and Aickman had so festered that now it divided the whole of the IWA and the two factions they represented could hardly bring themselves to speak to each other the whole week, despite a brave attempt at reconciliation by the IWA president, MP and novelist Sir Alan Herbert. The truth was that a climate of such suspicion and mistrust had grown up between the parties that even the most innocent fraternisation was liable to be seen as provocative.

So the two camps epitomised by *Cressy* and *Beatrice* stood eyeing each other suspiciously like the flagships of two indomitable fleets facing each at anchor.

This sort of unpleasantness wasn't what Rolt had come onto the canals for, this wasn't part of his 'design for living', and it signalled the end of his days on the canals. But this would have happened anyhow, even without Market Harborough. The relationship with Angela, never easy, had been deteriorating and *Cressy* itself – the physical manifestation of their marriage – had been diagnosed with terminal rot in her hull. The festival and the bitterness engendered by Aickman may not have been the cause of his leaving the waterways but it was the straw that broke the camel's back.

For Rolt the waterways had anyhow always been an untenable fantasy – a hopeless way of escaping that painful paradox in which he was trapped. The paradox of having to live in a modern world when he resented so much of what the modern world was. But that's the nature of paradox. Like life, it's irresolvable. Rolt's dream was essentially a delusion. Canals might be a respite from contemporary life but they're no escape from it. Narrowboats, after all, aren't time machines.

Eventually, even on the waterways, things change. It was another contradiction of Tom Rolt's life – one for which I and thousands of others continue to be grateful: for in struggling with such futile enthusiasm to retain the things of the past, he created the shape of the future. He and Angela became like the Adam and Eve of every pleasure boater on the canals today, and *Cressy* the model for every boat that's afloat. Oh, how he would have hated it. And hated us too, I suspect.

All he wanted was to preserve the canals as he knew them, but in doing that he had to change them. It ensured that as far as this part of his life was concerned he could only ever fail in what he did.

Funny that, really, isn't it? To see your goal so clearly, and to work for it with such resolution, only to have everything bent out of shape.

Banana-shaped, I suppose you could say.

★

My long wait at Patch Bridge ended a couple of days later when the pilot's predictions proved spot on and the weather changed completely. Some pressure centre somewhere had shifted and it suddenly became stiflingly hot without even a breath of air to cool things down. More importantly, the sky became a perfect unblemished blue with not so much as a wisp of cloud to threaten further rain. The idea now was to move off on the Friday evening tide once my crew (that is, Em) had managed to get up from London. To that end, and on the pilot's advice, I'd alerted the harbourmaster at Sharpness who was made aware that yet another crazy flat-bottomed bastard in the form of nb *Justice* was going to play at real boats by trying for a passage to Bristol. The harbourmaster in turn had alerted the local British Waterways office who manage the sea lock and the approach to it, where there's a low-level railway bridge that has to be swung to allow access.

Something was bound to go wrong, wasn't it? It's sod's law. Like I say – you can never plan anything on the waterways.

I slipped moorings late afternoon for what was intended to be a pleasant potter in the sunshine to Sharpness where I'd already earmarked one of the spectacular moorings adjacent to the estuary wall and looking out across the reedbeds and the sandbanks to the river and the sea. But no sooner had I turned the gentle bend which takes you out of sight of Patch Bridge than 27HP of pulsating engineering was brought to an abrupt and humiliating halt by what turned out to be a length of slimy, water-sodden, triple-plaited ship's rope twelve strands thick. It took me two hours fishing around in the water to get it off the propeller.

It blew the estuary schedule wide open.

By now the bloke who looks after the two swing bridges which remained to be navigated before I got to Sharpness had packed up and gone home for the day. Mind you, who'd blame him? It was the weekend, after all.

So a new communiqué had to go out to the pilot, the harbourmaster at Sharpness, and British Waterways – all of whom by now had gone home too, and all of whom no doubt eventually concluded when they received the message I left on their respective answerphones that the crazy flat-bottomed bastard had had an attack of common sense and decided to abort the whole lunatic plan. And I probably would have done if I'd have been aware of what other pitfalls lay in wait for me before I completed the trip.

Instead, I moored the boat, cycled back to the Debsmobile and took the more conventional road route to Bristol where I picked up Em from Temple Meads Station. She was incredulous.

'You mean, after more than a month hanging about waiting for the right moment, you've got the pilot, the harbourmaster and British Waterways all expecting us out on the midnight tide tonight?'

I nodded.

'Except that we're not going to be on the midnight tide tonight because the tide is on one side of the swing bridge and we are on the other?'

I nodded again, sheepishly this time. 'That's about the sum of it, yes. I've left them a message though,' I added brightly.

'That'll be useful when they get it. Probably on Monday morning, I'd guess.'

'Well, they'll definitely know we're not going tonight when we don't turn up.'

'And that'll be great for our reputation for reliability. Not to mention our bank balance, since I presume that if the pilot turns out at that time of night he's going to want paying, come what may.'

'Good point,' I said. 'I suppose I better get on the phone again.'

Eventually I did manage to track down everyone, and the crossing was aborted and rearranged for the following afternoon. Unfortunately since you can't make Bristol on a single tide, this meant that it would be dark by the time we arrived at the mouth of the River Avon and we'd have to moor the night among the six-storey high leviathans which ply the water there bringing in most of the country's car imports.

It was like taking a pedal car onto the M1 and it confirmed my gut feeling that we weren't going to get out of this alive.

Em though was more up-beat. 'Don't be such a wimp,' she said. 'Let's have a drink and you'll feel better. Your round, isn't it?'

TWENTY-FOUR

The next day dawned bright again and as soon as the bridge-keeper had arrived and let us through, we cruised the short distance to Sharpness, where I tucked *Justice* into one of those moorings I'd had in mind the previous day. Em and I sat outside on the towpath in the warm morning sunshine, munching on a mound of bacon sandwiches as we looked out towards the wide mouth of the river where it meets the estuary.

I was still apprehensive about the day but at least the food settled my fluttering stomach. Not that I had much to worry about – conditions couldn't have been better. It was perhaps chillier than was ideal, with summer all but over now and autumn in the air; but it was so completely still and windless that across the black reed-covered mudflats and the derelict sunken barges that lie there, you'd have thought the water was glass; except that from time to time you could just about make out a gentle shimmering on the surface which was the movement of the river sliding towards the sea. Away in the far distance where the land rises towards Wales someone had lit a fire in a lonely house on the hillside and a thin plume of smoke rose almost vertically to the sky. Above us a small flock of gulls glided in the placid air, occasionally breaking the silence with their shrill cries.

A month earlier, before finally committing myself to the trip, I'd cycled from Patch Bridge to Sharpness to reconnoitre the lock. Your worst fears are usually in your mind and more often than not they can be assuaged by confronting them. I thought it would help to see what I was letting myself in for.

It had been a filthy day, rain-lashed and gusty with the wind kicking up and the estuary showing white horses to the horizon. I made my way to the lock and tentatively walked across the top gates facing the sea where the force of it was so strong I had to lean into the gale to keep my balance. Frankly, if the idea of all this was to make me feel better about things, it was clear it wasn't working. This was Sharpness and the estuary at its very worst. Eventually I plucked up courage to peek over the edge where waves were crashing relentlessly a vertiginous distance below. The tides in these parts, remember, are some of the highest in the world and the gates have to be tall enough to resist them. They were certainly tall enough to turn my stomach.

I kept asking myself how I'd got into this position and why I was even considering making the trip. It's not as if I've any inclination towards narrowboat adventuring as some people have. I was just a guy who wanted to be in Bristol and who, if he could have clicked his fingers and magically been there, would have done it without hesitation.

But now as Em and I surveyed the very same scene it was completely different. It was as if it wasn't Sharpness at all but another place entirely. In its own way it was equally as impressive and equally dismaying, since for anyone used to the restrictive spaces of inland waterways, always bounded by banks and towpaths, there is something daunting about a flat expanse of water like the one we were gazing at, stretching out endlessly on all sides to the faraway skyline.

We were scheduled to go into the lock at 4.30 p.m. when the low-level railway bridge blocking our way was to be swung open to allow us access, so we spent the day pottering around in the sunshine taking it easy. In fact, we took it so easy that it was suddenly four o'clock and we were running late. Doesn't it always happen this way? Getting off on time now became a panic and I suppose I was rushing a bit when I finally engaged gear and cast off, swinging the tiller to pull us out into the centre of the canal.

Even so, this doesn't explain the peculiar thing that happened next. Without warning the tiller rose out of its housing an inch or so, leaking a couple of pints of water over the stern deck; then it dropped back in what seemed to be the same position – but clearly wasn't because when I pulled on it, it resolutely refused to move except by jolting abruptly, locking at another equally unmoveable angle. At the first sign of trouble I'd instinctively gone into neutral gear but this left me without control. With our initial impetus still driving us forward we powered straight across the canal and hit a wall on the other side with a sickening crunch of metal and a cloud of brick dust.

It was then I noticed two men in British Waterways uniforms. They were part of the team who'd come to open the bridge for us and they'd been watching all this attentively. One of them smiled in that quietly censorious way that BW men do when they've caught you making a balls-up. I smiled self-consciously. The fault wasn't mine, but who'd ever believe *that*?

Yanking the tiller back to something resembling a straight line, we limped into the lock where we had an hour's wait for our pilot to join us, and where serious amounts of tugging and jerking and hauling did nothing to solve the problem – though it almost succeeded in putting my arms out of joint.

I guessed that I'd moored above a dislodged coping stone or something of that sort, and that when I'd engaged gear and *Justice*'s stern had dropped in the water I'd trapped the bottom of her tiller, causing it to rise from its housing and dislodge itself when it fell back. But who knows for certain? Maybe it was something entirely different. Maybe the previous night's cussed ship rope had something to do with it.

The question now was simple enough though: were we going to abort the trip or continue with it? Eventually we decided the safest thing was to let the pilot make the decision. Except that by the time he arrived the harbour authorities were already emptying the lock and we were dropping fast to sea level and he was shouting to us from the top to meet him at the jetty on the other side where he jumped on board at the first opportunity. Suddenly there seemed to be rather too much of an expanse of water ahead of us to start carping about details like how we were going to make the boat go the way we wanted it to.

Besides, the estuary's a couple of miles wide at Sharpness, broadening to – what? – four miles at Avonmouth? Five? It doesn't exactly call for precision steering, does it? Just as well really, since in practice we didn't have any steering. Or at least not in the sense that you'd normally understand the concept. OK, so it was actually still possible to make the boat go roughly in the direction you wanted by treating the tiller much as you might do opening a jammed door or a recalcitrant garden gate. That is to say that if you used both hands, leant against it and pushed it with all your strength until your eyes popped. But that was about as far as it went, and our pilot Jim who took over steering duties the moment he was on board nearly ruptured himself as soon as he attempted it.

'Bloody hell! It's a bit stiff, isn't it?' he said. I think he was miffed that *Justice* had not taken him immediately to her heart.

I shrugged my shoulders noncommittally. Jim had told me he'd once been something in the Merchant Navy. In my view he should have been used to this sort of thing. Anyhow, I couldn't see the use of worrying him unduly – especially when it seemed to me that a tiller locked in a single direction could actually make his life a good deal easier. After all, he hardly seemed to need to steer the boat. From the moment we'd left the lock we'd been moving down the estuary on a course that was so straight it wouldn't have shamed a flying crow. It seemed to me at this rate we could have left the boat to its own devices and it would have got to Bristol by itself.

It was like this for about an hour until Jim mentioned in the sort of offhand way you might point out a plane in the sky that we were passing a couple of nuclear power stations – one of which he'd heard that morning on the news was on red alert and in danger of exploding.

At first I didn't register what he was saying.

'Red alert? Exploding? Are you serious?' I stuttered disbelievingly.

'Absolutely serious,' Jim said.

I felt my breath leave my body, and my legs went weak. I grabbed at the handrail of the boat.

Jim threw back his head in a throaty paroxysm of laughter. 'Only joking!' he screamed. 'Hold on tight!' He heaved on the tiller and *Justice* turned a sudden sharp right angle, swinging over the other side of the estuary to begin the long approach which leads under the older, more elegant, of the two motorway bridges which carry the M5 across the water.

I'll be frank, I didn't find this funny. In fact, I found it distinctly *un*funny. Crossing the estuary in a narrowboat was bad enough, but worse was crossing it in the company of a superannuated comic whose sense of humour had been honed in the company of similarly crusty matelots fighting Force 10 gales off Finisterre.

Unfortunately this wasn't to be the last example of Jim's droll wit. Not long afterwards, as we passed under the motorway, *Justice* suddenly and inexplicably began shuddering violently in a way that made me think she was in imminent danger of breaking apart. Jim gave me a look of such pure, unadulterated terror that I'd have had to be made of stone not to have reacted to it.

Before I could say anything I was treated to another of the strangled outbursts of choking which he called laughter. Eventually he explained that the shaking was being caused by the interaction of the current and the ebbing tide over the shallows below. It was perfectly normal and nothing to worry about at all.

'Just pulling your leg,' he said, as if I hadn't worked that one out for myself by then. Then he nudged me in the ribs so hard it was a wonder I didn't go flying over the side.

By now I'd had enough of him and went off to join Em who'd been sitting quietly in the bow of the boat keeping watch. For people like us used to the sense of enclosure of the canal system, cruising in these expansive waters was a strange and unsettling experience. Offshore – at the distance of a mile and more – even nuclear power stations have a certain mystical grandeur to them. On such a calm afternoon with nothing else on the move and a thin mist beginning to rise from the estuary, it was as if we were gliding through a fantasy world where you half expected unicorns to rise out of the vapour.

Gradually the afternoon became evening and soon darkness began to fall and the gloom of the far-off shores became speckled with a myriad of lights in orange, white, red and green. Some were static, some blinking nervously, others winking lethargically.

This was the point at which I appreciated Jim the most, despite his terrible line in comedy, for without his experience it would have been too easy to become hopelessly confused by these nautical Christmas lights. Conditions were completely unfamiliar to ditch crawlers like us. We were even moving in a different way than I'd ever experienced before, the shifting waters drawing us along with them, compelling us to follow. If you concentrated on the clear surface of the water at the point where the wash of our bow broke it into waves, you could see the murky flow of the tide sucking underneath. It was at its fastest now and we were at its mercy, being carried along at the sort of pace that left you breathless.

It was clear that this part of the trip was trickier than any other so far. When I glanced at Jim on the back of the boat he was locked in concentration, the veins beginning to stand out on his brow as he was increasingly called upon to wrestle with the malfunctioning tiller, sometimes effecting quite spectacular changes of direction which even in these apparently calm conditions sent *Justice* skewing about, bobbing up and down like a cork.

I'm addicted to night-time boating of any sort. In summer it's a particular delight since even when it's overcast the sky illuminates the water and you rarely need to use headlights to see ahead. In the dog days of July, or under a harvest moon, the canal becomes a floodlit trail to the stars; and when it's balmy and the scent of new-mown hay is thick in the air, it's as if you become part of the countryside, quietly slipping through the night like some strange creature of the dark. Mind you, we did have a shock some years back when something out of *The War of the Worlds* with two great headlamps for eyes started lurching down a meadow towards us at about two in the morning.

It turned out to be a local farmer with a combine harvester making the most of the good weather.

Winter, of course, is an entirely different matter and I don't think that anyone in their right mind actually plans to be slogging up the Grand Union late afternoon on a bleak December day when it's turned dark and the wind's so fierce it's throwing freezing spray across your bow deck. But if you cruise at all in winter when you've only a few hours of light a day, you're bound to experience this at some time, delayed by an obstinate lock gate, or pressing on that extra mile to get to a favourite pub where you know there'll be a fire blazing in the hearth.

At times like this it's best to accept that boating can occasionally be a tough business and just knuckle down to the job in hand. And even in these conditions England has the potential for beauty like no other country in the world. I remember one winter coming into Leighton Buzzard on a frosty night against one of the most vivid scarlet moons I'd ever seen. The countryside was spectacularly burnished and the icy black boughs of the trees reflecting the colour looked strangely like those diagrams of the blood system you see in children's books.

*

The lights of Avonmouth gradually began to appear out of the gloom, and I took Jim a cup of tea and a sandwich to celebrate our arrival. A sharp wind had blown up but we were basically on a straight course again. He stood eating, the engine on *Justice* throbbing away so softly that you could hear the water lapping against her hull. Eventually he finished his snack and brushed away the crumbs from his coat, reaching at length for a VHF receiver which he'd earlier tossed into the back cabin. There was a lot of crackling and a technical conversation I couldn't have understood even if I'd been able to make it out over the distortion.

Afterwards he said, 'We'll head for that light over there.' He pointed it out. 'We should arrive in about twenty minutes, perhaps a bit less. You can take over the tiller then and I'll tell you where to bring her in. You can leave me on the landing stage…'

I looked at him with a sort of resigned smile on my face, half expecting him to throw back his head in one of those cackling outbursts that accompanied his attempts to be funny. Because he was being funny, wasn't he? It was another of his jokes. Of course it was. It had to be. After all, we were going to Bristol, weren't we? This wasn't Bristol. This was Avonmouth, wasn't it? Or at least it *looked* like Avonmouth, judging by the shadowy outline of rows of massive oil containers and derricks which I could just about make out along the shoreline, not to mention the preponderance of enormous boats of one sort or another that were dotted about threateningly like ominous apparitions from hell.

Yes, I knew our departure time from Sharpness meant that we'd have to moor overnight until we could get to Bristol on a second tide. But I can't say I was entirely aware the pilot would be leaving us to do it alone.

'You don't have to stay here if you're not comfortable,' Jim said. 'You could always go up river and moor mid-stream until the water's high enough to get you into Bristol lock.

'Mind you, you'd still be on your own,' he added. 'But you do at least have a choice.'

Since this so-called 'choice' would have involved another couple of hours of night-time cruising, only this time unaccompanied; and since it would have meant navigating *Justice* around the lip of the estuary and up the mouth of a river neither of us knew; and since it would also have required us to drop anchor in the middle of nowhere and stay up half the night to ensure we didn't drift off, or something didn't hit us; then I don't think that strictly speaking the alternative he presented counted as a 'choice' at all. Or if it did, it was a 'choice' akin to being asked to select which of your two arms you'd prefer to have chopped off. Or which eye put out.

Reassured that the rest of the journey would be a doddle in daylight, we decided to stay put. So it wasn't until the morning that the full import of our predicament fully hit us. In the previous night's darkness Jim had guided us towards one light among a thousand speckled along the shoreline, and though I was vaguely aware that under his instruction we'd come into some haven and moored against another larger boat which was itself moored to a sort of jetty, I'd no real idea what sort of haven, or what sort of boat, or what sort of jetty.

Now it all became clear. I woke early, disturbed by the agonising sound of our mooring ropes groaning in the swell like a soul moaning in Hades. I slipped on a dressing gown and stuck my head out of the front door. Em was still asleep – but not for long.

'My God! This you have just got to see,' I said, shaking her. 'You have *got* to see this *now*.'

We were moored against a battered old dredger which was, I suppose, about five times our size. Yet this was nothing, for the dredger was itself moored to a block of flats. Or at least to something that looked like a block of flats. On closer inspection what it turned out to be was an immense wharf towering above us. It was constructed of steel and must have been a quarter of a mile long, curving around us like a protective arm.

Despite Jim's stricture that we weren't to get off the boat until high tide when we were scheduled to leave, we got dressed and took the opportunity of exploring. That's when we found out how high this colossal quay was because to get to the top of it we had to climb flight after flight of salt-rusted steps, like an endless fire escape to the sky. On the top the view was spectacular. It was another perfect day, the sun already brilliantly hot and the light so crystal clear that on one side in the far distance you could make out the two motorway bridges we'd come under the previous night, and on the other you could see the thin furrow of the faraway shoreline as it curved off towards Cardiff.

At first the panorama was empty of boats but for a yacht or two lazily tacking in the gentle breeze; however the closer we got to high tide at midday, the busier it became until it was positively hectic, swarming with vessels of different sorts including those vast vehicle transporters which ply this stretch of water and which seem less like boats than moving car parks. They'd been waiting for their moment, and as two or three of them began to lumber in towards land, the waters around became active with flotillas of tugs buzzing around like flies on cattle.

We decided to keep out of the way of them for the moment. We had no alternative. If we'd been foolish enough to get in the way of these leviathans, they'd have ploughed over us like a car flattening a Coke can. And worse, they wouldn't even have been aware that they'd done it. At length things began to calm down and finally we saw a gap in the traffic and made our move. In what was a manoeuvre of no more than twenty minutes, we rounded the low spit of a mudbank and darted into the sanctuary of the river where we were soon heading upstream towards Bristol in the wake of a couple of other boats, who'd seen the same opportunity and gone for it as apprehensively as us. God knows why they were worried though. One of them was an ocean-going yacht, the other a small ship. They could both move faster than us.

The tenor of the Avon changes almost as soon as you leave the estuary. No sooner are you clear of Avonmouth than the industry which is so predominant vanishes, and what one moment was a workplace becomes a park. At first the banks are like those of any other tidal river, lined with expanses of cracked grey mud; but they gradually get higher and higher until almost without you noticing they've mutated into a series of thickly wooded cliff faces with paths at the top and bottom. On the fine Sunday this had turned out to be, it felt like the whole city had decided to come here for a constitutional. There were families out strolling with the kids, groups on bikes, lovers sauntering hand in hand, and so many dogs being exercised I couldn't help but remember how the canine contribution to the state of the towpath in Oxford so many months before had prompted my decision to abandon going to Bristol at all and made me decide to head north, until I'd discovered I could get there by this roundabout route.

And now here I was coming into the place by the back door, a passage made by – what? – a dozen or so narrowboats a year out of the thirty thousand on the system. It was strange because even though I had the impression I was creeping into the city up some back alley, at the same time the streams of people along the banks – many of them waving as I passed – made it seem as if I'd come to the conclusion of an exhausting marathon and they were welcoming me home. The long shadow of Isambard Kingdom Brunel's famous suspension bridge at Clifton crossing the roof of *Justice* became a sort of finishing tape as I navigated under it.

Of course, my journey hadn't been a race, or anything like it – though it was difficult to see what it *had* been, especially since it started so negatively and with such apparent purposelessness. But I guess that's the way a lot of things in life are.

But the trip had developed its own justification, however haphazardly. Admittedly, I hadn't travelled far – the sort of distance you could probably cover in a couple of days in a modern car if you put your mind to it. With the Debsmobile I'd travelled along routes a vehicle like that would never normally take, and with *Justice* I'd followed an itinerary it never could. It had taken me through some of the most attractive parts of the country and led me to some of its most hidden places. The journey had given me the opportunity to cogitate a bit too. About myself. About England. About some of the people who'd contributed to the present in a tiny way – their achievements modest but, even so, greater than anything most of us will ever accomplish.

And if nothing else, I'd had the chance of cooking and eating some decent food, and drinking some good beer. And having a laugh from time to time.

Can you expect any more from any journey?

Even life itself?

Now it was time to get back to London, time to find *Justice* a mooring of longer duration for the winter that was fast approaching. The graceful suspension bridge receded behind us and we prepared ourselves for the last manoeuvre of the river, the passage through the lock into the safe waters of the Floating Harbour, that triumph of Victorian architecture which laid the foundation for Bristol as one of the greatest trading centres of its age.

A number of other boats were already in the lock when we got there, most of them expensive sailing vessels with vulnerable hulls made of fibreglass not much thicker than a yogurt carton. After the trip we'd just completed we felt fairly relaxed about the operation.

Too relaxed.

Coming across the estuary, the pilot had throttled up *Justice* to its maximum, winding up the speed wheel which controls the engine. I'd done the same thing as we'd come up the river that morning, pushing hard to get as much power as I could to punch the flow.

But in screwing up the wheel so tightly, I'd loosened the nuts that hold it in place. Coming into the lock, with the best part of a quarter of a million quid's worth of luxury ocean-going yacht directly ahead of me, it came off in my hand…

TWENTY-FIVE

At least with a journey, when it comes to an end it's over and that's that.

Stories are altogether more complicated. They don't exist in isolation, they're just part of other stories. They're like strands of a rope which are woven into other strands which themselves are woven into bigger strands until one fragment becomes so much a part of the whole that you can't say where it begins or ends.

Tom and Angela Rolt went back home to Banbury after the Market Harborough festival was over. It was a grim voyage for both of them. The end of a love affair is always painful and their marriage was on its last legs. Tom reflected later that the problems between them sprang from the psychological burden Angela had to carry after being cut off by her parents for marrying him – but that puts too much of the blame on her weakness for my liking. Angela herself probably got closer to the truth years later, not long before she died, when she hinted that a major reason for their break-up was the clash that ensued from her desire to travel and his deep commitment to England and the English way of life.

They'd already cruised the Irish waterways, providing Tom with material for a book *Green and Silver*. Now she wanted them to explore further afield. 'I said, "Why don't we buy another boat? Let's go and get a bigger one and go and explore the French canals." But this didn't appeal to him. You see he hadn't even enjoyed our cruise across Ireland... simply because it wasn't England. He refused to live anywhere else and during that winter he didn't seem to want to budge out of *Cressy*. He just sat there chain smoking at his little desk, deeply hurt by the unpleasantness at the IWA.'

'I didn't relish the... prospect of continental travel, even by canal,' he admitted later. 'With all their faults it was the British Isles that had prior claim on my affections.'

Tom would later describe this winter and the following spring as the most unhappy period of his life. The nadir was when Angela left him. She bought herself an old banger for £10 but being the woman she was, even that had a certain style about it and she chose a two-seater Morris Oxford coupé. Tom did it up for her. He watched her from the deck of *Cressy* as she drove over the wooden lift bridge at the end of Factory Street. Afterwards he went inside the boat which 'suddenly seemed to have become very silent'.

It was twenty years before they met again.

Angela joined Billy Smart's Circus where she took up with the ringmaster and sometime clown Joe Isaac, with whom she travelled for many years until she finally came into the family money and settled in the Dordogne, and lived there until her death.

Left on his own, Tom attempted to sell *Cressy* – but to no avail. With a mixture of wet and dry rot plaguing her hull, no one would buy her at any price. For a couple of years she lay at a boatyard in Staffordshire before she was eventually broken up and burnt. It was an ignominious end for a vessel which had become an icon of the waterways movement and yet, as one commentator observed, *Cressy*'s destruction by fire was 'in the best tradition of long and narrow boats through history'.

Tom used to dream about her for years afterwards. Generally there'd be some dire emergency threatening and he'd be drifting powerlessly towards a dangerous weir, or something similar. He explained it to himself as the price he had to pay for the hazards he'd managed to escape during his boating years, though I think a modern psychiatrist might view that interpretation with some scepticism. After all, he conceived an existence on the canals as a source of joy and hope but all it brought him was anguish and disappointment so that he ultimately lost control of his own happiness.

In his subconscious he must have realised this.

All this was far from being the end of his life however, or even the end of his connection with canals. In later years he was persuaded to sit on a government committee on the waterways, and despite his initial reluctance he finally did go cruising in France, which he made the subject of his last canal book. But after the separation from Angela and the destruction of *Cressy*, his priorities changed. He still wrote, of course – it was his job. He specialised in biographies of the great Victorian engineers and his books about Brunel and Telford are still in print today and as highly regarded as they ever were.

He still found time for campaigning too, spearheading the fight to save the famous Tallryn narrow-gauge railway in Wales which became the model for every railway preservation society that followed and the basis of the Ealing comedy film *The Titfield Thunderbolt*. But domestic life now became the main focus of his energies and he moved back to the family home, remarried and raised a family of two sons.

He was 64 when he died in 1974.

★

Robert Aickman resigned from the council of the Inland Waterways Association in 1964 after yet another explosive internal row of the sort he was so regularly involved in that if you didn't know it already, you'd suspect these arguments had more to do with the sort of man he was than any weighty issues of policy. In the remaining seventeen years of his life he set about building the literary career he'd always coveted. Originally he'd seen himself as a novelist but it was as a writer of idiosyncratic 'strange tales' (as he called them) that he finally made his mark, publishing seven books of them before 1981 as well as editing eight collections of ghost stories for Fontana. He also published the first part of his autobiography.

The second part, *The River Runs Uphill*, which covers the IWA years, was published posthumously in 1986 after his own publishers had turned down the book during his lifetime. It's not difficult to see why. It's written with all the flamboyance of a set of committee minutes and with a pomposity that is sometimes breathtaking in its conceit. Aickman put the cap on it at the last moment by censoring nearly anything of any personal note that might have made it interesting. So there's nothing about his wife Ray and their break-up, very little about his affair with Elizabeth Jane Howard and almost nothing to explain his differences with Tom Rolt.

Two chapters of the book – an eighth of it – are devoted to just five days of his life: the period of the Market Harborough festival, which he describes as his 'happiest week' and the 'climax of my life up to that point'.

After the first night of the plays he'd fought so bitterly to mount he recounts that one of the lead actresses came off the stage and 'fell' into his arms.

'I am not sure I can recall any single moment in my life that excels that one,' he writes with such naive, boyish enthusiasm that you can't help but conclude that there was something very shallow at the core of this man.

A shame really, for he achieved so much of genuine and solid worth that you'd think he might have valued it more himself and been content not to have gone raking over old enmities.

And yet the only point where the autobiography sparks into life is in its terse and somewhat bitter final chapter, the single purpose of which is to put on record the separate authorship of the stories he and Jane Howard had written in their co-authored book *We Are for the Dark*. Aickman attempts to mitigate his bitterness towards her by being insufferably patronising, writing of her 'beauty and persuasiveness' in a way which compounds his petty resentfulness. It's a strange way to end any autobiography and you wonder why Aickman felt the need to do it. Except, of course, that knowing the sort of person he was you could have predicted that sooner or later Jane Howard would fall foul of him – as Tom Rolt had done before her, and as anyone close to him always did whenever they were presumptuous enough to assert themselves against him.

His wife Ray, on whom he'd always been strangely dependent despite his unfaithfulness, eventually lost patience with him and walked out. She became an Anglican nun in a convent in Oxfordshire, taking the name Sister Benedicta. After she'd left, Aickman was furious and broke off all contact with her. 'She was the sort of person made to be devoted to someone,' Jane

Howard said of her, 'and it was bad luck that she was devoted to him because she deserved somebody who was more rewarding. In the end she wanted someone to be devoted to, and God seemed the best bet.'

Jane Howard's own estrangement from Aickman came after she gave up her work for the IWA. 'I became *persona non grata*,' she said. 'Robert decided I was out of the IWA altogether and he didn't want me to have any contact with any of his friends.' Actually, it was worse than this: he literally wouldn't have her name mentioned in his presence; though oddly, Jane struck up a clandestine relationship with Ray and seems to have known that she was leaving Aickman even before Aickman himself did.

The best that can be said for *The River Runs Uphill* is that it's written by someone who never learnt much in his life. Not about the things that really matter, anyhow. When it was published the IWA were so sensitive to the running sores that still existed in the organisation that they wouldn't accept an advertisement for it in their magazine without prior sight of the manuscript.

You'd wonder then how Aickman could be so successful creatively. He writes in a curiously stilted, formal style, heavy with commas, so that it gives his writing a distanced feel, as if he's stammering, and is just writing as he thinks, adding one idea onto the next, until he reaches some sort of halting conclusion that adds to his uncertain edginess. His stories are full of characters with unsettling, unreal names like Wedley Roper, Nera Condamine or Perry Jesperson; and they all take place in a world where ultimately the normal rules don't apply, a world where central relationships between men and women are characterised by a perverse and corrupted sexuality and where there's always a moral vacuum at the heart of things.

A very modern world, in fact.

'She realised that to display moral qualities demands practice, just as much as intellectual and manual qualities,' says one of his characters of another you almost feel could be Aickman himself. 'She had never really attended when, down the years, such truths had been hammered into her.'

Some of the stories have been adapted for radio and it was after I'd missed one and was trying to get a tape from the BBC that I got a telephone call from someone involved in the project, curious to learn who else in this world could be as fascinated with Robert Aickman as he was. It turned out to be Jeremy Dyson, one of the *League of Gentlemen* whose eccentric TV comedy show was at that time scooping just about every industry award there was to win. We met one night in a pub and I wasn't surprised to find that Aickman had been a major influence on his writing, for you can see Aickman's vision stamped all over the characters in Royston Vasey, the grotesque and freakish Pennine village which is the setting for the programme.

Robert Aickman saw himself as a highbrow and I don't know if he'd have been flattered to have been at the heart of popular culture in this way, though I know he would have relished the fame that's accrued to him over the years, a fame which he never enjoyed in his lifetime. For he's become a cult writer. Tap his name into an internet search engine and you'll get scores of references to him, many of them dedicated sites run by people who testify to the way he's changed their lives. Jeremy could hardly believe Aickman's popularity in cyberspace. He could hardly believe that Aickman was the sort of person he was either.

'I still think I'd have liked him though – despite everything,' he said at one stage after he'd listened to me banging on about Aickman's faults.

And I know what he means. Strangely, I feel the same way. I went to the Robert Aickman Lock near Stratford-upon-Avon to commemorate the twentieth anniversary of his death. It is his only memorial. There's a bronze relief of him in profile set into an adjoining wall commemorating his work for the waterways. I'd publicised the anniversary widely and the IWA certainly knew about it.

Even so, only two other people turned up with me.

*

Elizabeth Jane Howard became a writer too, of course – though many think she never fulfilled the promise she showed in her first book which won her the prestigious John Llewellyn Rhys Memorial Prize. It was dedicated to Robert Aickman. Later in life she married the novelist Kingsley Amis, and regrettably – for she's one of the most interesting women writers of her generation – she's become known since then more for her personal life, and a list of former lovers which includes Arthur Koestler, Laurie Lee, C. Day-Lewis, and God knows who else too.

In fact, as the *Daily Telegraph* once said of her, 'There was a time in London when it was fashionable for a man to say he had been to bed with Elizabeth Jane Howard.' Her erstwhile stepson Martin Amis put it more delicately. 'Jane has been around,' he wrote, '– and at a high level…'

As one of the very few people involved in this narrative who is still alive I naturally wrote to her hoping that she might meet me. She was kind enough to reply personally with a polite note. Polite, but very defensive. Mind you, you can understand it. Jane Howard's been exploited by a large number of men in her life and it's hardly surprising if she's cautious about new ones appearing out of the woodwork claiming to be writing a crazy book about the canals. Especially when it involves Robert Aickman about whom, she admits, she still feels uncomfortable. Out of fairness though, this isn't because she's antagonistic to Aickman. They were reconciled during the final illness which led to his death and she gave a reading at his memorial service.

'It's just that she's writing an autobiography and she's under contract not to talk about her life,' her agent explained, a little unconvincingly.

'Well, couldn't I just sort of… well, you know, just meet her then?' I said, 'As a… a fan?'

I was told that she hadn't got any time for that sort of nonsense though I noticed a few months afterwards when some of her novels were serialised on the BBC that she struck up a friendship with the executive producer Joanna Lumley with whom she seemed to be forever having cosy get-togethers.

Mind you, you can understand that too. Me? Joanna Lumley? No contest really, is there?

*

I managed to avoid a collision with the posh yacht in the lock coming into Bristol. I somehow succeeded in stretching forward far enough to catch the connecting rod to the engine throttle before it fell off completely so that at least I avoided a catastrophe.

I eventually succeeded in getting to the Dome too before it closed. I went on the day thieves attempted to steal one of the exhibits, a diamond valued at more than £1 million.

They advertised the Dome as 'one amazing day'. It certainly was that day.

But still not quite as amazing as canals, which still obsess me in the way they always have.

ACKNOWLEDGEMENTS

In writing those parts of this book concerned with the life of Tom Rolt I have relied extensively on the second part of his autobiography, *Landscape with Canals*. For details of the life and correspondence of Robert Aickman I am indebted to David Bolton's *Race Against Time*, which is a good read and an excellent work of scholarship.

I have also found Roger Squires' *Canals Revived* and Ian Mackersey's *Tom Rolt and the Cressy Years* helpful, especially the latter which I have drawn on heavily in my final chapters, in particular his quotation about the fate of *Cressy*. Elspeth Huxley's biography of Peter Scott has also been useful.

Elizabeth Jane Howard's autobiography *Slipstream* was published after this book was written, and although it told me very little I did not already know about her affair with Aickman – indeed, it is disappointingly sparse on the topic – I have nevertheless incorporated occasional facts and quotations where it has seemed appropriate to clarify events.

I'd also like to express my gratitude to Graham Robson whose *Triumph Herald and Vitesse: The Complete Story* is a mine of information for any enthusiast. Tony Beadle has also been most helpful in this context too; his knowledge of classic car history is unparalleled.

Finally, thanks to my old mucker Miles Hedley whose careful subbing of this edition of the text has been invaluable.

NARROWBOAT
 DREAMS

A Journey
North by
England's
Waterways

 STEVE
HAYWOOD

NARROWBOAT DREAMS

A Journey North by England's Waterways

Steve Haywood

ISBN: 978 1 84024 670 4   Paperback   £7.99

Steve Haywood has a problem. He doesn't know where he comes from. In the south, people think he's a northerner; in the north, they think he's from the south. Judged against global warming and the sad demise of *Celebrity Big Brother,* this hardly registers highly on the Richter scale of world disasters. But it's enough to worry Steve. And it's enough of an excuse for him to escape the routine of his life in London for a voyage of discovery along England's inland waterways.

Travelling by traditional narrowboat, he heads north from Banbury in deepest Oxfordshire, through the former industrial wastelands of the the now vibrantly modern Manchester, to the trendy affluence of Hebden Bridge at the centre of West Yorkshire's ciabatta belt. With irrepressible humour he describes the history of the canals, his encounters with characters along the way, and the magic that makes England's waterways so appealing.

'Haywood imprints his inimitable humour on his descriptions of the people and places he meets along the way' BBC COUNTRY FILE

'... an enjoyable, moreish read, and one of the better British canal travelogues of recent years'   WATERWAYS WORLD

The Best of British Festivals

Food · Music · Theatre · Comedy · Dance · Kayaking · Drumming ·
Carnival Workshops and much, much more...

Barney Jeffries

THE BEST OF BRITISH FESTIVALS

Barney Jeffries

ISBN: 978 1 84024 656 8   Paperback   £9.99

The Best of British Festivals is the ultimate fun-seeker's guide, giving the low-down on the best events taking place up and down the country in every month of the year.

- soak up some culture at the Edinburgh festivals, where you'll find theatre, comedy, music, books and ballet

- spend midsummer weekend at the 3 Wishes Faery Fest, featuring unicorn rides, wing-making workshops and a masquerade ball

- get all shook up with a multitude of Elvis impersonators from around the world in Porthcawl

- enjoy a weekend of hedonistic partying, listening to some of the biggest bands in the business at Glastonbury or Reading

With cocktail competitions and canal festivals, kite-flying and international carnivals, pancake races and lantern processions as well as every type of music and theatre imaginable, there's something for everyone in venues ranging from country pubs to twelfth-century ruins.

FROM THE MULL TO THE CAPE
TO THE CAPE

A GENTLE BIKE RIDE ON THE EDGE OF WILDERNESS

RICHARD GUISE

FROM THE MULL TO THE CAPE

A Gentle Bike Ride on the Edge of Wilderness

Richard Guise

ISBN: 978 1 84024 674 2   Paperback   £7.99

Richard Guise yearned to take on a physical challenge before he reached the age where walking across the kitchen would fall into that category. And so he donned a cagoule, packed his saddlebags and set off for an adventure on a bike named Tetley. This is the tale of his 586-mile, 16-day ride through the Highlands of Scotland, along the dramatically beautiful west coast from the Mull of Kintyre in the south to Cape Wrath in the north.

Freewheeling along isolated roads where traffic problems consist of the occasional retreating sheep and stopping for lunch on deserted beaches, he has time to ponder the Laws of Cycle Touring and take in spectacular sights, from craggy, cloud-shrouded mountain ranges to lochside forests.

'... *the perfect companion for the traveller to the west coast of Scotland*'
FLIGHT magazine

'... *just might make you stir your stumps and get on your own bike*'
UNITE magazine

THE
BIG WALKS
OF GREAT BRITAIN

including South Downs Way, Offa's Dyke Path, The Thames Path,
The Peddars Way and Norfolk Coast Path,
The Wolds Way, The Pembrokeshire Coast Path,
The West Highland Way, The Pennine Way

DAVID BATHURST

THE BIG WALKS OF GREAT BRITAIN

David Bathurst

ISBN: 978 1 84024 566 0   Paperback   £9.99

From the South West Coast Path to the Great Glen Way, from the Cotswold Way to Hadrian's Wall, and from the Yorkshire Wolds to Glyndwr's Way, there are big walks here to keep you rambling all year round. And what better way to discover the landscapes of Great Britain, from green and gentle dales to majestic mountains and rugged cliffs?

An indefatigable walker, David Bathurst has unlaced his boots to produce this invaluable companion to the 19 best-loved long-distance footpaths. His appreciation of the beauty and history of the British countryside and his light-hearted style will appeal to experienced and novice walkers alike.

- The definitive guide to the national trails of England and Wales and the Scottish National Long Distance Walking Routes

- Detailed descriptions of the trails and a wealth of practical information, including amenities available

- Recommends historic and geographic areas of interest on or near the paths, from ancient burial mounds to flora and fauna

'Meaty, practical guide jam packed with walks that promise to keep you rambling all year round'   SUNDAY EXPRESS

Have you enjoyed this book? If so, why not write a review on your favourite website?

Thanks very much for buying this Summersdale book.

www.summersdale.com